New Casebooks

POETRY

WILLIAM BLAKE Edited by David Punter
CHAUCER Edited by Valerie Allen and Aries Axiotis
COLERIDGE, KEATS AND SHELLEY Edited by Peter J. Kitson
JOHN DONNE Edited by Andrew Mousley
SEAMUS HEANEY Edited by Michael Allen
PHILIP LARKIN Edited by Stephen Regan
DYLAN THOMAS Edited by John Goodby and Chris Wigginton
VICTORIAN WOMEN POETS Edited by Joseph Bristow
WORDSWORTH Edited by John Williams
PARADISE LOST Edited by William Zunder

NOVELS AND PROSE

AUSTEN: *Emma* Edited by David Monaghan
AUSTEN: *Mansfield Park* and *Persuasion* Edited by Judy Simons
AUSTEN: *Sense and Sensibility* and *Pride and Prejudice* Edited by Robert Clark
CHARLOTTE BRONTË: *Jane Eyre* Edited by Heather Glen
CHARLOTTE BRONTË: *Villette* Edited by Pauline Nestor
EMILY BRONTË: *Wuthering Heights* Edited by Patsy Stoneman
ANGELA CARTER Edited by Alison Easton
WILKIE COLLINS Edited by Lyn Pykett
JOSEPH CONRAD Edited by Elaine Jordan
DICKENS: *Bleak House* Edited by Jeremy Tambling
DICKENS: *David Copperfield* and *Hard Times* Edited by John Peck
DICKENS: *Great Expectations* Edited by Roger Sell
ELIOT: *The Mill on the Floss* and *Silas Marner* Edited by Nahem Yousaf and Andrew Maunder
ELIOT: *Middlemarch* Edited by John Peck
E.M. FORSTER Edited by Jeremy Tambling
HARDY: *Jude the Obscure* Edited by Penny Boumelha
HARDY: *The Mayor of Casterbridge* Edited by Julian Wolfreys
HARDY: *Tess of the D'Urbervilles* Edited by Peter Widdowson
JAMES: *Turn of the Screw* and *What Maisie Knew* Edited by Neil Cornwell and
  Maggie Malone
LAWRENCE: *Sons and Lovers* Edited by Rick Rylance
TONI MORRISON Edited by Linden Peach
GEORGE ORWELL Edited by Byran Loughrey
SHELLEY: *Frankenstein* Edited by Fred Botti
STOKER: *Dracula* Edited by Glennis Byron
STERNE: *Tristram Shandy* Edited by Melvyr
WOOLF: *Mrs Dalloway* and *To the Lighthou*

(continued overleaf)

DRAMA

BECKETT: *Waiting for Godot* and *Endgame* Edited by Steven Connor
APHRA BEHN Edited by Janet Todd
REVENGE TRAGEDY Edited by Stevie Simkin
SHAKESPEARE: *Antony and Cleopatra* Edited by John Drakakis
SHAKESPEARE: *Hamlet* Edited by Martin Coyle
SHAKESPEARE: *Julius Caesar* Edited by Richard Wilson
SHAKESPEARE: *King Lear* Edited by Kiernan Ryan
SHAKESPEARE: *Macbeth* Edited by Alan Sinfield
SHAKESPEARE: *The Merchant of Venice* Edited by Martin Coyle
SHAKESPEARE: *A Midsummer Night's Dream* Edited by Richard Dutton
SHAKESPEARE: *Much Ado About Nothing* and *The Taming of the Shrew*
  Edited by Marion Wynne-Davies
SHAKESPEARE: *Romeo and Juliet* Edited by R. S. White
SHAKESPEARE: *The Tempest* Edited by R. S. White
SHAKESPEARE: *Twelfth Night* Edited by R. S. White
SHAKESPEARE ON FILM Edited by Robert Shaughnessy
SHAKESPEARE IN PERFORMANCE Edited by Robert Shaughnessy
SHAKESPEARE'S HISTORY PLAYS Edited by Graham Holderness
SHAKESPEARE'S TRAGEDIES Edited by Susan Zimmerman
JOHN WEBSTER: *The Duchess of Malfi* Edited by Dympna Callaghan

GENERAL THEMES

FEMINIST THEATRE AND THEORY Edited by Helene Keyssar
POST-COLONIAL LITERATURES Edited by Michael Parker and Roger Starkey

---

New Casebooks Series
Series Standing Order
ISBN 0–333–71702–3 hardcover
ISBN 0–333–69345–0 paperback
(outside North America only)

You can receive future titles in this series as they are published by placing a standing order. Please contact your bookseller or, in case of difficulty, write to us at the address below with your name and address, the title of the series and the ISBN quoted above.

Customer Services Department, Macmillan Distribution Ltd
Houndmills, Basingstoke, Hampshire RG21 6XS, England

New Casebooks

E. M. FORSTER

EDITED BY JEREMY TAMBLING

Published by
PALGRAVE
Houndmills, Basingstoke, Hampshire RG21 6XS and
175 Fifth Avenue, New York, N. Y. 10010
Companies and representatives throughout the world

PALGRAVE is the new global academic imprint of
St. Martin's Press LLC Scholarly and Reference Division and
Palgrave Publishers Ltd (formerly Macmillan Press Ltd).

ISBN 0–333–60129–7 hardcover
ISBN 0–333–60130–0 paperback

This book is printed on paper suitable for recycling and
made from fully managed and sustained forest sources.

A catalogue record for this book is available
from the British Library.

Transferred to digital printing 2002
Printed and bound in Great Britain by
Antony Rowe Ltd, Chippenham and Eastbourne

Contents

Preface   vii

Acknowledgements   viii

General Editors' Preface   xi

Introduction: JEREMY TAMBLING   1

1. Forster's Trespasses: Tourism and Cultural Politics   14
   JAMES BUZARD

2. 'Aphrodite with a Janus Face': Language, Desire, and
   History in *The Longest Journey*   30
   RAE H. STOLL

3. Absent Father: Passive Son: The Dilemma of Rickie
   Elliot in *The Longest Journey*   51
   CAROLA M. KAPLAN

4. 'Islands of Money': Rentier Culture in *Howards End*   67
   PAUL DELANY

5. Gesturing Towards an Open Space: Gender, Form and
   Language in *Howards End*   81
   ELIZABETH LANGLAND

6. Edward Carpenter and the Double Structure of
   Maurice   100
   ROBERT K. MARTIN

7. Forster's Friends   115
   RUSTOM BHARUCHA

8. The Politics of Representation in *A Passage to India*   133
   BENITA PARRY

9. Forster's Imperial Erotic   151
   SARA SULERI GOODYEAR

10. Periphrasis, Power and Rape in *A Passage to India*   171
    BRENDA R. SILVER

11. *A Passage to India*: A Passage to the Patria?   195
    PENELOPE PETHER

12. A Disconnected View: Forster, Modernity and Film   213
    PETER J. HUTCHINGS

Further reading   229

Notes on Contributors   231

Index   233

Preface

I would like to thank all those who have discussed E. M. Forster with me: Richard Allen, Roger Day, Nick Furbank, Douglas Kerr, John Marshall (over many years), Graham Martin. Others have helped me indirectly over post-colonial issues or have supplied references: Ackbar Abbas, Maryanne Dever, Jonathan Hall. Mao Sihui's comments on the film of *A Room with A View* when I showed this in China and lectured on it were useful. Lau Wai Wah helped infinitely with the preparation while Martin Coyle and John Peck as the series editors made life very smooth generally and were masters of tact. My wife Pauline's support has always been forthcoming and is much appreciated.

I would like to dedicate this book to my brother William, who read *A Passage to India* before I did.

Jeremy Tambling

Acknowledgements

The editor and publishers wish to thank the following for permission to use copyright material:

Rustom Bharucha, for 'Forster's Friends', *Raritan*, V. No. 4 (Spring 1986). Copyright © 1986 by *Raritan*, New Brunswick, by permission of *Raritan: a Quarterly Review*; James Michael Buzard, for 'Forster's Trespasses: Tourism and Cultural Politics', *Twentieth Century Literature*, 34, No. 2 (1988), 155–79, by permission of *Twentieth Century Literature*; Paul Delany, for '"Islands of Money": Rentier Culture in E. M. Forster's *Howards End*', *English Literature in Transition*, 31 (1988), 285–96, by permission of *English Literature in Transition*; Carola M. Kaplan, for 'Absent Father, Passive Son: the Dilemma of Rickie Elliot in *The Longest Journey*', *Twentieth Century Literature*, 33, No. 2 (1987), 196–210, by permission of *Twentieth Century Literature*; Elizabeth Langland, for 'Gesturing Towards an Open Space: Gender, Form and Language in *Howards End*' from *Out of Bounds: Male Writers and Gender(ed) Criticism*, ed. Laura Claridge and Elizabeth Langland (1990). Copyright © 1990 by The University of Massachusetts Press, by permission of The University of Massachusetts Press; Robert K. Martin, for 'Edward Carpenter and the Double Structure of *Maurice*', *Journal of Homosexuality*, 8, Nos 3/4 (1983), 35–46, by permission of Haworth Press, Inc.; Benita Parry, for 'The Politics of Representation in *A Passage to India*' from *A Passage to India: Essays in Interpretation*, ed. John Beer (1985), 27–43, by permission of Macmillian Ltd; Penelope Pether, for 'E. M. Forster's *A Passage to India*: A Passage to the Patria?', *Sydney Studies in English*, 17 (1991), 88–120, by permission of the author; Brenda Silver, for 'Periphrasis, Power and Rape in *A Passage to India*', *Novel*, 28

(1988), 86–105. Copyright © 1988 NOVEL Corp., by permission of NOVEL: A Forum on Fiction; Rae H. Stoll, for '"Aphrodite with a Janus Face": Language, Desire, and History in Forster's *The Longest Journey*', *Novel*, 20 (1987), 237–59. Copyright © 1987 NOVEL Corp., by permission of NOVEL: A Forum on Fiction; Sara Suleri, for 'Forster's Imperial Erotic' in *The Rhetoric of English India* (1992), by permission of The University of Chicago Press.

General Editor's Preface

The purpose of this series of New Casebooks is to reveal some of the ways in which contemporary criticism has changed our understanding of commonly studied texts and writers and, indeed, of the nature of criticism itself. Central to the series is a concern with modern critical theory and its effect on current approaches to the study of literature. Each New Casebook editor has been asked to select a sequence of essays which will introduce the reader to the new critical approaches to the text or texts being discussed in the volume and also illuminate the rich interchange between critical theory and critical practice that characterises so much current writing about literature.

In this focus on modern critical thinking New Casebooks aim not only to inform but also to stimulate, with volumes seeking to reflect both the controversy and the excitement of current criticism. Because much of this criticism is difficult and often employs an unfamiliar critical language, editors have been asked to give the reader as much help as they feel is appropriate, but without simplifying the essays or the issues they raise. Again, editors have been asked to supply a list of further reading which will enable readers to follow up issues raised by the essays in the volume.

The project of New Casebooks, then, is to bring together in an illuminating way those critics who best illustrate the ways in which contemporary criticism has established new methods of analysing texts and who have reinvigorated the important debate about how we 'read' literature. The hope is, of course, that New Casebooks will not only open up this debate to a wider audience, but will also encourage students to extend their own ideas, and think afresh about their responses to the texts they are studying.

John Peck and Martin Coyle
University of Wales, Cardiff

Introduction

JEREMY TAMBLING

E. M. Forster (1879–1970) has never lacked for readers, is widely studied, has had his novels turned into highly marketable films, and has encouraged criticism usually of a strongly liberal-humanist kind. Of this criticism, Lionel Trilling's book *E. M. Forster* was a pioneering prototype, and P. N. Furbank's excellent *E. M. Forster: A Life*, indispensable for any work on Forster, is a fine point to mark a limit.[1] The essays in this volume, while respecting this kind of criticism of his work, much of which is still written today, go in other directions. They were all written after 1979, and they refer to each of the novels, giving two to *The Longest Journey*, a text which earlier criticism tended to downplay, one to *Maurice*, which was published only in 1971, and so played no part in earlier assessments of his work, and they also include an original essay on the Merchant–Ivory, David Lean and Charles Sturridge films which have newly defined Forster for the 1980s and 1990s.

That said, Forster has generated only a limited amount of new critical writing: work informed by narrative theory, post-structuralism, psychoanalysis, feminist or gender-criticism or by Althusserian Marxism or Foucauldian approaches to discourse. I believe that some of the best of what there is has been included here, but it is worth asking why there has not been so much re-reading of Forster in the light of 'critical theory' as I expected to find when I began making this selection. The argument for leaving Forster alone cannot be simply that some of the early novels are lightweight: since they belong to the discourse of a particular period, they will show that up in terms of illuminating the dominant discourses, indicating even in the texts' very silences the gaps and absences which point to repressions and displacements in the culture itself. Even their 'slightness' – assuming the validity of this charge, which comes from an older critical perspective that discusses a text in terms of its completed achievement and ability to fulfil a consistent intention – would be a matter for discussion. For what reason is so much left out?

More has been got into the novels than is often assumed; but nonetheless in this introduction I want to raise some questions about Forster by suggesting three interrelated areas in which recent criticism, illuminated by critical theory, has fastened its attention on Forster, and show how these areas are reflected in the present selection of articles.

1 ENGLAND, 'ENGLISHNESS' AND MODERNISM

Forster wrote most of his short stories and four novels – *Where Angels Fear to Tread, A Room with a View, The Longest Journey* and *Howards End* – before 1910. But as Virginia Woolf expressed it famously, 'On or about December 1910, human nature changed.'[2] Literary 'modernism' was in the air: in the work of Eliot, Pound, Woolf, Joyce, or in European terms, Proust or Mann or Musil or Kafka. Forster never became a modernist: in fact he wrote only two further novels, *Maurice* (1914) which he kept private all his life, and which came out of his association with Edward Carpenter in 1913 (though he had known his work beforehand), an association that made him think of himself in positively homosexual terms, and *A Passage to India* (1924). Though *A Passage to India* is sometimes discussed as modernist, it is no more so than D. H. Lawrence's novels, which remain largely realist and antagonistic to modernism's experimentation and interest in language at the level of the signifier rather than at that of the signified. If forced to find analogies between Lawrence, who himself has very interesting points of comparison with Forster, and modernism, they might be located in a certain homoeroticism and a proto-fascism,[3] as well as in an attitude to character which sees it as something in process rather than fixed, but clearly Lawrence rejected most of the tenets of modernism and Forster did the same by his virtual silence as a novelist after *A Passage to India*.

An approach to this as a problem might begin by examining the marginal status of modernism itself in Britain, and its minor role in the national ideology,[4] and it would suggest that Forster's attachments are nostalgic, dwelling on a Britain which is agricultural, non-industrial, pre-motor car. (The Merchant–Ivory film of *A Room With A View* fetishises the use of the bicycle and its different pre-war varieties, just as the films generally offer a touristic sense of Edwardian England – of Cambridge, of London architecture, of

the discreet charm of the Home Counties.) The escape ending of
Maurice fits with this nostalgia: as Forster commented on it in
1960:

> it belongs to the last moment of the greenwood. *The Longest Journey*
> belongs there too, and has similarities of atmosphere. Our greenwood
> ended catastrophically and inevitably. Two great wars demanded and
> bequeathed regimentation which the public services adopted and
> extended, science lent her aid and the wildness of our island, never
> extensive, was stamped upon and built over and patrolled in no time.
> There is no forest or fell to escape to today ...[5]

Modernity may be defined in terms of the experience of the
urban.[6] The denial of the experience of the street and the crowd
(contrast *Ulysses* or *Mrs Dalloway*), the return to pastoral, which
Penelope Pether writes about in her essay on *A Passage to India*
(essay 11), marks the Forster text as in retreat from otherness and
clinging to an ideology of 'Englishness'. This clinging to the local,
which runs counter to the very internationalism of modernism, fitted
the projections of England that were necessary for it to maintain an
imperialist status, as at the centre of the empire, and helped to preserve an England which paradoxically Forster could never be happy
with – for example, for its intolerance towards homosexuality, and
for its imperialism; for its lack of liberalism, indeed. But this contradiction of attitudes to the dominant culture informs all Forster's
work. He is both in it and rejects it.

But it is possible to overestimate the adherence to 'Englishness' in
the novels. The use of Italy and of India in the novels is only in a
very complicated way a reassertion of England's values. The books
the very advanced Mr Emerson has on his shelves ('Twelfth Chapter'
of *A Room With A View*) are an interesting example of how far Forster was prepared to go beyond nineteenth-century realism – and
how far he was not. Mr Emerson has *A Shropshire Lad* (Housman's
poetry: homoerotic, pastoral, classicising), *The Way of All Flesh*
(Samuel Butler: a Bloomsbury novel which attacks Victorian religious hypocrisy and which was a powerful influence on Forster),
Gibbon (anti-modern, of course, but also anti-Christian), Schopenhauer (fashionable in the 1890s, with such novelists as Hardy and
Gissing, but German, and certainly the antithesis of anything
English), and Nietzsche, the philosopher who stands most firmly
against nationalism, and against fixed positions in terms of subjectivity, or gender, or commitment to positivistically established

truth. There are conservative elements here, in this choice of reading, but it is not simply parochial or anti-modern.

2 GENDER AND HOMOSEXUALITY

Recent critical theory has given a strong central attention to questions of gender and to feminism, and to the argument that the voice that speaks in the text is already constructed by a whole ideology which ascribes to men and women gender-specificity. Forster has been accused of misogyny (see Rae Stoll's essay, number 2), in which case he would be following one aspect of modernist discourse that I have commented on already, but Elizabeth Langland's essay (5) on *Howards End* examines the construction of gender in that novel to suggest that a femininity within the text attacks the patriarchy which is embodied by the Wilcoxes. Brenda Silver's essay (10) on *A Passage to India* similarly finds something positive in the attention given to Adela Quested as a marginalised subject within the patriarchy of Anglo-India.

But examination of gender must confront Forster's homosexuality. Recent gay and lesbian studies have gone in two different, if not irreconcilable ways. One has stressed the affirmatory nature of gayness, asserting its importance and transgressive value, as *Maurice* perhaps does, especially as Robert Martin reads it in essay 6 here. Modernism itself, after all, stresses the transgressive, which would often be evoked through homosexual themes: as in Wilde, who anticipates modernism, in Freud, Proust, Musil in *Young Torless*, Mann in *Death in Venice*, Woolf, Radclyffe Hall in her lesbian novel *The Well of Loneliness*, and even *The Waste Land*, or in Lawrence, as in the abandoned Prologue to *Women in Love* (reprinted in *Phoenix*), which made Birkin's relations to Gerald homosexual. Modernism cannot but be transgressive: 'the whole of modern thought is imbued with the necessity of thinking the unthought ... for modern thought, no morality is possible' writes Foucault.[7] Following this line, the argument for a transgressive writing would be that modernity is connected with the breakdown of the category of the single-subject, that is, the human thought of as delimited by constraints which may be known positivistically or empirically, under the surveillance of the eye of power. In so far as homosexual behaviour is a breakdown of established ways of coding the male and the female, it becomes essential that modernism should be thematised around it, that homosexuality should become a paradigmatic case of modernist transgression. Yet that said, few would find the leading monuments of British modernism obviously transgressive. *The Waste Land* is an example: a text which may be obsessed with the sexual, but which also contrives to be highly conservative in the authors and traditions it draws on, and to lend itself immediately to canonical status. A deep repression, which may also be a class-consciousness, prevents the emergence of the transgressive in the terms Foucault is discussing. Forster's work belongs with this modernism which unsays its transgressiveness as fast as it articulates it.

But theorisation of the subject of homosexuality also goes in another direction, as I suggest in my notes to Martin's essay. Homosexuality was made an issue of a person's subjectivity in the nineteenth century; it became a way of reading and defining character. Hence for the modernist to accept himself as homosexual means buying into the cultural/ideological assumptions associated with that, becoming minor, accepting a marginalised subject-status. Wilde was different in that he used his sexuality positively in a form of self-fashioning to critique the values of bourgeois, imperialist society.[8] It seems a pity that Forster simply internalised the negativity implicit in referring to the self as homosexual (though the carnivalesque bathing-party in the chapter in *A Room With A View*, significantly only called 'Twelfth Chapter', keeping it anonymous, suggests that there are positive aspects to Forster's sense of homoerotic and homosocial bondings as well). The negativity, even self-hatred, produces the bleakness which runs through *Maurice*:

> Clive sat in the theatre of Dionysus. The stage was empty, as it had been for many centuries, the auditorium empty; the sun had set though the Acropolis behind still radiated heat. He saw barren plains running down to the sea, Salamis, Aegina, mountains, all blended in a violet evening. Here dwelt his gods – Pallas Athene in the first place: he might if he chose imagine her shrine untouched, and her statue catching the last of the glow. She understood all men, though motherless and a virgin. He had been coming to thank her for years because she had lifted him out of the mire.
>
> But he saw only dying light and a dead land. He uttered no prayer, believed in no deity and knew that the past was devoid of meaning like the present, and a refuge for cowards.
>
> Well, he had written to Maurice at last. His letter was journeying down to the sea. Where one sterility touched another, it would embark and voyage past Sunium and Cythera, would land and

embark, would land again. Maurice would get it as he was starting for his work. 'Against my will I have become normal. I cannot help it.' The words had been written.

He descended the theatre wearily. Who could help anything? Not only in sex, but in all things men have moved blindly, have evolved out of slime to dissolve into it when this accident of consequences is over. μὴ φῦναι τὸν ἅπαντα νικᾷ λόγον, sighed the actors in this very place two thousand years before. Even that remark, though further from vanity than most, was vain.

(p. 103)[9]

This in its nihilism, which draws on Schopenhauer, especially in the reference to 'this accident of consequences', anticipates Mrs Moore's experience in the Marabar caves when the echo tells her that 'everything exists, nothing has value'.[10] Mrs Moore's loss of faith in 'value' means not only the collapse of her European sense of values and her British liberalism, it also has a sexual register. Both she and Clive fear a world of no difference, where difference is eliminated. In Lacanian psychoanalysis, sexual difference is the principle upon which meaning in language is established. The failure of sexual difference, which Clive seems to intuit, and which seems the point behind the emptiness of the caves, promises to render a world without difference. The failure of anything positive in the way sexuality is written about in Forster, the failure of the non-homogeneity of the sexual and of the plurality of modes of existence is the point. Difference threatens to be reduced simply to the male–female polarity through dominant ascriptions of gender. The essays on *The Longest Journey* (2 and 3), and that of Rustom Bharucha (7) included here deal with this topic. But in *Maurice* it is not clear that Clive's nihilism is really lifted by anything else in the text. The context is relevant: this is the Dionysiac world which Nietzsche evokes in *The Birth of Tragedy*, a philosophical text which celebrates the breakdown of tight (if not uptight) individuality in favour of emotion, enlarged experience and dangerous living. *The Birth of Tragedy* is a rejection of what it calls Schopenhauer's 'weak pessimism'. There is nothing Nietzschean or Dionysiac in this extract from *Maurice*, though there could have been since, as a god, Dionysos seems to be bisexual.[11]

The reference to the Mediterranean, which summons up not only Greece but Italy, that alien 'other' to England in *Where Angels Fear to Tread* and to 'Sawston' (perhaps Surbiton in Surrey) in *A Room with a View*, suggests the power of the classical world for Forster.

James Buzard brings this out in his book *The Beaten Track* of which part has been reproduced here (essay 1).[12] The inability to affirm differentiates Forster from Wilde. So does the inability to ironise experience, which distinguishes his text from *Death in Venice* (which, though it is not free from nostalgia and a feeling of hopelessness itself, by its irony allows no view of life to exist on its own terms – heterosexual or homosexual, Platonic or Nietzschean). These failures would belong to Forster's acceptance of the dominant interpretations of his time. It all suggests the absence of a powerful critique in the areas either of politics or sexuality in Britain during the Edwardian and Georgian period which could allow the writer to become transgressive.

3 ORIENTALISM, EMPIRE AND THE OTHER

The third area where Forster criticism has functioned is in his critique of empire. *Howards End* is now read as a reflection on imperialism, and *A Passage to India*, which played a significant part in the thirties and forties in changing public opinion towards Britain being in India at all, is now sometimes accused of being unconsciously racist towards India. The essays by Rustom Bharucha (7), Benita Parry (8), Sara Suleri Goodyear (9) and Penelope Pether (11) all directly or indirectly address this question. It arises as an issue from Edward Said's *Orientalism* (1978), a text itself inspired by Foucault's work on how knowledge of another is a form of power over that other. *Orientalism* discusses how the East – the Orient – is created through Western discursive practices (anthropology, tourism, fiction, to say nothing of imperialism), and constructed as an 'other' which can, however, be known by the dominant discourse of the West, and thus be assimilated into its practices and pronounced inferior in so far as it does not come up to these. (The creation of 'homosexuality' is an analogous case: the homosexual defines by his failure to be heterosexual what normal sexuality is like; 'normal sexuality' does not have to describe itself any more than the West has to examine its own cultural assumptions.) In the context of a discussion of T. E. Lawrence, Said quotes from the very last words of *A Passage to India*, 'where Aziz and Fielding attempt, and fail at reconciliation':

> 'Why can't we be friends now?' said the other, holding him affectionately. 'it's what I want. It's what you want.'

> But the horses didn't want it – they swerved apart; the earth didn't
> want it, sending up rocks through which riders must pass single file;
> the temples, the tank, the jail, the palace, the birds, the carrion, the
> Guest House that came into view as they issued from the gap and saw
> Mau beneath; they didn't want it, they said in their hundred voices,
> 'No, not yet', and the sky said, 'No, not there'.
>
> (p. 312)

Said comments on this ending that Asia 'is brought tantalisingly
close to the West, but only for a brief moment. We are left at the end
with a sense of the pathetic difference separating "us" from an
Orient destined to bear its foreignness as a mark of its permanent
estrangement from the West.'[13]

For Said, the distinction of the West is proclaimed here to be its
capacity for friendship, which must exist, though, on its terms: the
Western imagination thinks of its own standards of relationship as
unquestionably right. Said returns to the attack on bourgeois novelists
of the nineteenth and twentieth centuries in his recent book *Culture and
Imperialism* in which he faults radical criticism and Marxist writers
such as Raymond Williams for their inability to read the English cultural tradition for its overt imperialism. This blind spot of the British
about their empire might be crucial for understanding Forster's
modernism or lack of it, and is certainly relevant for a discussion of
Howards End. Is Forster's vision limited because he can only partly
recognise the enormity of imperialism – as in, for instance, the treatment and defence offered of the Wilcoxes? Said implies in discussing *A
Passage to India* that its most interesting feature is

> Forster's using India to represent material that according to the can-
> ons of the novel cannot in fact be represented – vastness, incompre-
> hensible creeds, secret motions, histories, and social forms. Mrs
> Moore especially and Fielding too are clearly meant to be understood
> as Europeans who go beyond the anthropomorphic norm in remain-
> ing in that (to them) terrifying new element.[14]

India becomes the unrepresentable, and the heroism that is celebrated
is that these Europeans live in it at all. The normal viewpoint is that
of the European – and what falls out of European representability
becomes, on that token, outside the norm.

Said's argument assumes that Forster's stated hostility to imperialism is not the point: unconsciously the text undoes that hostility by
reproducing a Eurocentric point of view. That there is a 'political
unconscious' to the text is reinforced by Rae Stoll's essay (2) on *The*

Longest Journey, and it informs each of the essays on *A Passage to India*. A political unconscious – the formulation comes from Fredric Jameson's book of that name – uses Freud and Marx to suggest that there is an agenda controlling the text which is outside the intention of the writer, and in fact not knowable or namable by him or her. It may also suggest, as Fredric Jameson discusses it (without reference to Forster), that the text is motivated by a desire that it cannot name.[15] It is this that Bharucha tries to explore, and which Sarah Suleri Goodyear analyses in terms of a repressed homoeroticism involved in the coloniser's relation to the colonised.

A doubling of unconscious drives subtends *A Passage to India* on this reading. The text is aware of a hegemonic powerful homoeroticism suffusing colonial relations, cutting out the women and reducing Adela Quested's desire – independent of this male drive – for the real India, as an 'addled quest' indeed. The homoeroticism is expressed mournfully in Fielding's plea at the end to Aziz for friendship. At the same time that the text anatomises this, it also wishes to endorse that homoeroticism, but not at the level of dominance and subjection. The endorsement is partially because of Forster's own homosexuality, but also expresses a liberalism: hoping for a relationship between men which is friendship-based, not competitive, certainly not based on the public-school games ethos that is savaged at the beginning of *The Longest Journey*. The text's unconscious is split: both negative and positive/utopian. India stands for the possibility of something that indeed cannot be represented: a place of homoerotic acceptance. Yet it could not be so represented anyway, simply because of the historical conditions in which India exists: as a dominated power, held by the imperialists.

So the impossibility of representation must last at least as long as England keeps up a position of being a colonial power. 'Not yet' and 'not there' remain decisive negatives for Forster, and they mark out, equally, the pessimism of *Maurice*. But the lack of affirmation, which inscribes the text with nostalgia, characterises the trap that Forster's work belongs to, like so much partially emergent modernism in English writing.

4 'HOW DO YOU KNOW I'M NOT DEAD?'

The words are Forster's, in 1915, in response to a challenge from D. H. Lawrence.[16] Forster seems to have accepted that in some sense he might be dead, like the Victorian liberalism he stood for, and criticism has systematically tended to downplay him, giving him the status of a 'minor classic', or being more dismissive, as in the devastating words of Katherine Mansfield, 'E. M. Forster never gets any further than warming the teapot'.[17] Returning with this in mind to the initial question I raised, why Forster criticism has produced only a limited amount of new critical writing, it may be said in reply that recent criticism has tended to find Virginia Woolf a more interesting modernist, while the reaction against Lawrence has not worked to instate Forster's importance. It may even be that criticism has to catch up with Forster. But the triangular relationship of Forster to modernism, homosexuality and empire is problematic, and I have tried to show that it is one central issue. His interest in 'friendship' – with its complex relationship to homosexuality – made him unable to move out of nostalgia, or sexual diffidence about himself and about gender-issues, or to become incisive about the enormity of British rule in India.

The subject of male 'friendship' as it exists within patriarchy is savaged by the feminist critic Eve Kosofsky Sedgwick who suggests that in patriarchy – which she defines following Heidi Hartmann as, 'relationships between men, which have a material base, and which, though hierarchical, establish or create interdependence and solidarity among men that enable them to dominate women'[18] – dominant relationships are male-based, perhaps covertly and systematically homoerotic, but expressed in terms of 'homosociality' where male friendship and comradeship (the very spirit that was marshalled so much in imperial conquest) excludes women. Sedgwick does not discuss Forster, though she refers to his 'objectification of proletarian men',[19] but the implications of this influential criticism are severe, especially if we consider Stoll's argument (essay 2) that Forster does not like women. One aspect of feminism (not Langland's, in essay 5), would read Forster as patriarchal, arguing that his actual homosexuality does not lead him to any revaluation of gender-relations. Here a variety of positions could all be argued for: (a) that Forster's conservatism and non-modernism, determined by his entrapment in 'Englishness', makes for a decisive limitation; (b) that Sedgwick's thesis downplays the specificity of homosexuality within sexual relations and tends to align homosexuality with the oppressiveness of patriarchy, which is, of course, homophobic; (c) that Forster's texts show a feminism that Langland and Silver (essay 10) respond to; (d) that Forster is alive to power relations and a critic of patriarchy.

The reader will make up his or her own mind on these matters. For me, English modernism itself failed to revalue gender issues and collapsed back into a conservatism that did not spur Forster to anything new after *A Passage to India*. Forster failed to make anything of his own homosexuality, which in some ways is understandable, given this English conservative agenda, and though he justified his failure to himself on the grounds that his novels were to speak for all, not merely for a homosexual grouping, his liberalism prevented the emergence of anything more interesting and transgressive, kept him from a socialist vision and kept him from seeing fully the structures of oppression – class, race and gender-based – that he was part of. Though his liberalism permitted him to see much of what was involved in imperialism, his homosociality made for a foreclosure on the implications of that, too. Yet criticism needs to engage with Forster, not just to pick up on the positive aspects of his work which are easily elided in discussion, but also to read that institutional dominant discourse which belonged to the national ideology, to understand which liberalism was so inadequate a paradigm (as well as complicit with it). It was this discourse which prevented the emergence of modernism and radical thinking. Looking back from the standpoint of the 1990s, with the Forster films in place, it might almost seem that nothing has altered since the failure of modernism to change anything in England in the first decades of the century, when Forster was writing.

NOTES

1. Lionel Trilling, *E. M. Forster* (Norfolk, Conn., 1943); P. N. Furbank, *E. M. Forster; A Life*, 2 vols (New York, 1977–8).

2. Virginia Woolf, quoted in *Modernism*, ed. James McFarlane and Malcolm Bradbury (Harmondsworth, 1976), p. 33.

3. For the argument that modernism has a gender-orientation which downplays femininity, see Andreas Huyssen, *After the Great Divide*, (London, 1986). On modernism in relation to fascism, see Fredric Jameson, *Fables of Aggression: Wyndham Lewis: The Modernist as Fascist* (Berkeley, Cal., 1979).

4. For the absence of modernism in English writers who were not 'exiles' or 'émigrés', see Terry Eagleton, *Exiles and Emigrés* (London, 1970; he discusses *Howards End* pp. 58–60). For much of his argument about what Britain repressed in its culture Eagleton depends on Perry

Anderson, 'Components of the National Culture', *New Left Review*, 50 (July–August 1968). The relationship of Lawrence to Forster is discussed in Furbank's *Life*, but see also Margaret Procter, 'Possibilities of Completion: The Endings of *A Passage to India* and *Women in Love*', *English Literature in Transition*, 34 (1991), 261–80. On Lawrence, see Paul Delany, *D. H. Lawrence's Nightmare* (Brighton, 1979).

5. *Maurice* (Harmondsworth, 1972) 'Terminal Note', p. 221. All other references are to this edition.

6. See Marshall Berman, *All that is Solid Melts into Air: The Experience of Modernity* (London, 1983). Also, see Raymond Williams, *The Country and the City* (London, 1973).

7. Michel Foucault, *The Order of Things* (1966: English translation, London, 1970), pp. 327, 328. See also Foucault's essay 'A Preface to Transgression', *Language, Counter-Memory, Practice* (Ithaca, NY, 1977).

8. See Jonathan Dollimore, *Sexual Dissidence: Augustine to Wilde, Freud to Foucault* (Oxford, 1991) for an excellent critical book that is gay-oriented; Dollimore does not deal with Forster specifically.

9. The Greek, from Sophocles's *Oedipus at Colonus* 1224–5, reads 'Not to be born is best'. See Sophocles, *The Three Theban Plays*, trans. Robert Fagles (Harmondsworth, 1984), p. 358.

10. *A Passage to India*, ed. Oliver Stallybrass (Harmondsworth, 1979), ch. 14, p. 160. All other references are to this edition.

11. See David Farrell Krell, *Postponements: Women, Sensuality and Death in Nietzsche* (Bloomington, Ind., 1986).

12. Elsewhere in this book Buzard discusses the relationship of Forster to Greece. For an interesting discussion of Forster's relationship to both Orientalism and Hellenism, see David Roessel, 'Live Orientals and Dead Greeks: Forster's response to the Chanak Crisis', *Twentieth Century Literature*, 36 (1990), 43–60. Discussion of Forster in relation to the Greeks is related to his interest in paganism: see, for example, J. H. Stape, 'Comparing Mythologies: Forster's *Maurice* and Pater's *Marius*', *English Literature in Transition*, 33 (1990), 141–53.

13. Edward Said, *Orientalism* (New York, 1978), p. 224. For the literature on Said and post-colonial criticism, see the Further Reading section, as well as the essays by Bharucha, Parry, Suleri Goodyear and my notes on these.

14. Edward Said, *Culture and Imperialism* (London, 1992), pp. 241–2.

15. Fredric Jameson, *The Political Unconscious* (London, 1981).

16. Quoted, P. N. Furbank, *E. M. Forster: A Life*, vol. 2, pp. 9–10.

17. Quoted, Philip Gardner, *E. M. Forster: The Critical Heritage* (London, 1973) p. 162. In this anthology of criticism, I find the comments on Forster by Virginia Woolf, pp. 319–28, 332–6 the most interesting. But it is also noticeable how unchanging over the years the critique of Forster is: the terms of a 'minor classic' remain unchanged.

18. Eve Kosofsky Sedgwick, *Between Men: English Literature and Male Homosocial Desire* (New York, 1985), p. 3.

19. Ibid., p. 174.

1

Forster's Trespasses: Tourism and Cultural Politics

JAMES BUZARD

Through tourism, Forster learned early and well that the approach to 'the real' in culture or history always proceeds through some 'prior textualisation', and that the urge for a new start, a reform that would sweep away all previous texts – an urge he felt quite acutely – finds utterance in only another text.[1] Perhaps this is why tourist/ guidebook satire plays only a relatively minor role in a body of work otherwise so often concerned with tourism. As he shaped *A Room with a View* into its final form, Forster cut the lengthy passage describing Lucy's observations in Santa Croce, and others like it, down to mere passing jokes; dispensing a few satirical doses, the story came to centre on Lucy's personal development, her *Bildung*. What tourism now afforded Forster was a frame of public situations and contexts in which the events marking that educative process took on a greater than personal significance – and in which quixotic efforts to tear down the discursive and material structures surrounding 'the real' appear wilfully self-deluded.

Forster's relationship to tourism was not, then, so simple as to thrive exclusively on the local skirmishes that satire could provide. Shifting attention from the outward fetish of tourist satire – the guidebook – to a view of tourism *from within*, Forster illuminates a disciplinary system of definitions, validations, and prohibitions. His art provides what Louis Althusser called 'an *internal distance* ...

from the very ideology from which [it] emerged'[2] – a view both implicated in the system of meaning and revealing of the conditions and strictures inside the system's ideological boundaries. The special project of Forster's early work (establishing patterns for the later writings) is to investigate existence within the discourse and the 'state' of tourism and the possibilities of circumventing or transcending the obstacles tourism places between 'travellers' and the understanding they seek, both of themselves and of the places they visit.

Forster the writer begins in tourism – or, at least, in ironic and uncomfortable relation to it. After going down from Cambridge in 1900, Forster was presented with the unexpected opportunity to re-enact a portion of the education-completing Grand Tour, in the form of a year's visit to Italy. Conscious of his homosexuality and afflicted by a wide range of self-doubts, he was continuing to cope with the dependence on maternal figures he had known since childhood. This latter problem the circumstances of his tour did nothing to alleviate, since the money that enabled him to travel was a legacy from his great-aunt, Marianne Thornton, and since Forster travelled with his mother, whose long widowhood had kept her unusually close to his life.[3] Forster's letters of the period attest to his frustration at having failed to break out of his accustomed domestic circle. Arrived in Italy and settling into the routine of the English *pensione*, Forster bristles at the shallowness of his exposure to the country; he complains to Goldsworthy Lowes Dickinson, 'I wish I didn't see everything with this horrible foreground of enthusiastic ladies, but it is impossible to get away from it.'[4] Standing between him and the features of Italian life he longs to contact, the ladies are the sentries of his dependence and immaturity. Even the proprietress of the *pensione*, who 'scatters her Hs like morsels', patronises him, calling him '"the young gentleman"'.[5]

Forster's experience of tourism in this stifling atmosphere dominated by middle-aged women, so disappointingly similar to all he had known before Cambridge, offered no chance for an encounter with bona fide otherness, but only the absurd repetitions and grotesque exaggerations of domestic pressures. The Italian trip provided the efficient cause that stirred Forster's frustrations into expression in 'The Story of a Panic', his first work of fiction, a fantasy of deliverance from the tourist world. The story reveals, however, that personal wish-fulfilment necessarily impinges on the broader dynamics of tourism, often with unforeseen consequences. A projection of individual liberation ultimately reflects the cultural conflict at the heart of tourism. [At this point Buzard gives an account of 'The Story of a Panic' (1902), where the boy Eustace on holiday in Italy is taken over by Pan and bonds in a homoerotic relationship with the hotel-waiter Gennaro, whose body asserts itself against the idealised and unreal life of Italy described in tourist guide-books. Ed.]

Many of Forster's subsequent plots are devoted to the staging of such sudden revelations as that which overtakes Eustace in 'The Story of a Panic'; often these changes of life result from a character's crossing or being pulled across the boundary encircling the tourist world. Yet the futility of personal exemption from tourism and its effects remains a debilitating factor in such projections, causing Forster's texts continually to split into opposing narratives of fantasy and materiality. *A Room with a View* translates the 'body politics' of the early story into a seemingly conventional marriage plot. Once again a powerless and sexually naïve protagonist – here, the *ingénue* Lucy Honeychurch – lurks behind the screen of custom, class, and sex that guards the tourist from contact with indigenous life. Forster again invests the notion of active participation in foreign life (or indeed in 'life' itself) with the promises and dangers of sexual passage. The boundary dividing that phoney culture which is tailored to tourists' needs from 'the authentic' is identified with the hymen locking Lucy in aloof virginity; she will descend into 'real living' only when the marriage plot has run its course.

But the marriage plot flirts with consummation. The scene that depicts Lucy's 'symbolic loss of virginity' is among the best known in Forster's work.[6] Defying the prudent counsel of the spinster, Miss Alan, Lucy has left the safety of the Pensione Bertolini to walk alone, at dusk, through the streets of Florence. She feels confined, as had Forster, by the tourist routine, but she lacks 'any system of revolt. Here and there a restriction annoyed her particularly, and she would transgress it, and perhaps be sorry that she had done so. This afternoon she was peculiarly restive. She would really like to do something of which her well-wishers disapproved.'[7] Going into a souvenir shop, she buys a number of 'inappropriate' postcards – Botticelli's *Birth of Venus* is mentioned – but 'though she spent nearly seven *lire*, the gates of liberty seemed still unopened' (p. 40). 'Nothing ever happens to me,' Lucy thinks as she enters the Piazza Signoria; the square, however, quickly becomes the site of a Forsterian vision of escape, a vision arising unexpectedly from a trivial quarrel between two locals. At the twilight 'hour of unreal-ity', the looming tower of the Palazzo Medici acquires lavishly phal-lic contours, appearing 'no longer a tower, no longer supported by earth, but some unattainable treasure throbbing in the tranquil sky'. The fight Lucy witnesses culminates in a direct and grotesque image suggesting 'lost virginity', with Forster's prose reflecting the blank puzzlement and horror which Lucy, who does not yet know what that event entails, might feel. 'They sparred at each other, and one of them was hit lightly upon the chest. He frowned; he bent towards Lucy with a look of interest, as though he had an important message for her. He opened his lips to deliver it, and a stream of red came out between them and trickled down his unshaven chin.' Lifting her eyes as she swoons, Lucy spies 'Mr George Emerson ... looking at her across the spot where the man had been' (pp. 40–1).

As in 'The Story of a Panic', Forster here enlists an image of viol-ent penetration to shatter the boundaries of touristic properties, and again, Forster's use of the Italian body sets up parallel but opposing readings for the scene. According to the ostensible fantasy plot, the relationship that began when Lucy, deprived of her Baedeker, wan-dered about in the Church of the Holy Cross – Forster's chapter title is 'In Santa Croce with No Baedeker' – is now continued by a chance encounter 'across' the site of an event symbolising what is to come. Lucy's first thought upon seeing George in the Piazza Signoria is 'How very odd! Across something' (p. 4). The novel plays here on the associations of 'cross' and 'crossing', ironically borrowing the theological notion of incarnation which reference to Santa Croce introduces: Lucy and George's prefigured union is a heavily mythol-ogised 'cross', a meeting of energies that is also a cross-over into a new domain of experience. What cannot yet happen for Lucy and George (indeed, the novel's deferring of their union is a condition of its continuance) can be symbolically enacted on the body of a ran-dom Italian and registered as foreshadowing: there is sexual fulfil-ment to come for Lucy, but we must all wait. The wish-fulfilment reading proposes an escape from alienation into spontaneous, instinctive participation in the elemental forces of life, which are embodied by the stereotypical image of the male Italian as a fount of uncontrollable passions. In this scheme, the tourist is the public image of the sexually uninitiated or even maladjusted individual, the virgin or voyeur, who has never learned to 'really live'. The associa-tion of sexual and cultural roles helps to sustain an extensive sym-bolic opposition between images reflecting deep involvement in the elemental and images reflecting the merely spectatorial relation of tourism and sightseeing. The Forsterian maiden aunts take up the tourist's protected viewpoint, remaining untainted by what they observe. Securely locked up in the *pensione*, old Miss Alan sighs 'in a voice of relief' at the end of a day that it is at last 'too late to go out ... All the galleries are shut'. But Lucy chafes at her confinement to the culture of galleries and Baedekers, longing to go 'round the town in the circular tram – on the platform by the driver' (p. 38). Taken late in the day and without an escort, her walk to the Piazza stretches tourist proprieties. The Forsterian vision attends only those who abandon the behavioural beaten track.

Now, we should note that the wish-fulfilment fantasy of 'escape' operates in some discord with the goal of licensed sexuality that constitutes closure for the socially conservative marriage plot. The dark and turbulent energies aroused by the foreshadowed union with George – the kind of event that is classically offered as the ritual celebration and guarantee of social stability – may be accounted for by the allowance that *A Room with A View* is a marriage plot written by a homosexual man seeking some sanctioned vehicle for his own desires. At any rate, the piazza scene is put forward as presenting a moment of recognition, quickly repressed, of life's 'undeniables': violence, death, and sexuality. Yet the particular use of the Italian male body should alert us to the scheme of displacement informing the action. Once again, the Italian plays a crucial role in an allegory of a tourist's sexual/social emancipation. In 'The Story of a Panic', however, Gennaro's body had at least temporarily provided an image of intransigent cultural authenticity; here, the nameless victim of *A Room with a View* finds himself pressed into service as the very site on which the displaced consummation is enacted. Possessing a name and a history, Gennaro had been a presence of some kind, if not a three-dimensional character. His counterpart in the novel vanishes almost magically the moment his function has been performed: 'That was all. A crowd rose out of the dusk. It hid this extraordinary man from her, and bore him away to the fountain' (p. 41).[8]

Meanwhile, what happens to Lucy in this pivotal scene? Reading the scene in terms of the symbolic opposition outlined above, we find that she merely shuttles from one touristic perspective to another. Her desires to break through the tourist's boundary manifest themselves in the purely visual terms of postcards and sightseeing. Lucy finds herself a passive witness – a sightseer – at the very event that, according to the fantasy reading of the scene, transforms her, or at least initiates her long process of transformation. Even the infliction of the wound, the obvious figure for her sexual initiation, comes across in Forster's prose only as it appears to Lucy herself: as a light tap on the chest, which elicits but a frown and a passing entreaty from its recipient. The victim's 'message' for Lucy never reaches her. In a further displacement, the postcards end up stained with a dead man's blood, and must be discarded by George in the Arno; but Lucy herself remains unstained, and retreats from her compromising position with George into her characteristic *hauteur*. The whole proceedings, ironically, *confirm* the very authorities – the maiden aunts and their guidebooks – that had hitherto been the target for satire. Lucy learns, in effect, that innocence really does have to be guarded, since it can be put in jeopardy by even the most trivial of rebellions.

Of course the union of Lucy and George will eventually come, and I am not rejecting the reading that regards this scene as another of the many Forsterian rites of passage. Lucy and George are brought into association for this first time by a distorted representation of their own future fulfilment. In the staining of Lucy's photographs we may even detect resonances of a subtle 'Birth of Venus' motif that would presage Lucy's emergence as a sexual being: the drops of the Italian's blood go, with the pictures, into the Arno, and may, like the foam from Uranus' severed genitals, cause a new goddess of love to arise from the waters. The contradictory nature of the scene, however, bespeaks Forster's 'internally distanced' view of tourism. As in 'The Story of a Panic', we encounter a passive protagonist and an actively fantasising author, and we must take both roles together. Unable to free himself from the tourist state, Forster can project an escape for his character, but only by representing her as unable to effect *her own* salvation. Though in one sense Lucy 'causes' the events in the Piazza by breaking the rules about venturing out alone (without which action the stabbing would not take place in Forster's novel), her little trespasses are dwarfed by the magnitude of the public act of violence, and she remains passive before the external forces that may 'free' her. What is more, the fantasy of fulfilment may stumble over the corpse of the victimised Italian: efficiently employing and briskly disposing of the body, Forster appears to participate in the same kind of exploitation of Italian life and culture he was elsewhere so concerned to criticise. Just at the moment when the exigencies of the narrative take over – when an Italian body is required to fall at the feet of the hero and heroine – Forster transforms his own symbol of authenticity, the Italian male body, into an instrument entirely subsumed in its function within an English plot.[9]

Thus even transgression constantly threatens to become, in Forster's touristic world, a support of the system one longs to transgress. But in spite of the self-contradictory implications of his fictional projections, Forster continued to seek out and stage moments of anti-touristic vision. [Buzard continues with an account of another Forster short story, 'The Road to Colonus' (1904), with the subject of a tourist's approach to the spirit of Greece as that which is other to him, and 'The Eternal Moment' (1904), which through its heroine Miss Raby discusses the destructive effect that the system of tourism has upon a remote spot in Italy. Ed.]

Miss Raby is a character of depth and imagination who nevertheless shares in the unimaginativeness of the system she has unwittingly promoted; in this she resembles Philip Herriton, the reluctant hero of Forster's first published novel, *Where Angels Fear to Tread*. Jamesian parallels continue: if 'The Eternal Moment' is Forster's 'The Beast in the Jungle', the novel is his *The Ambassadors*. Like Lambert Strether, Philip is dispatched to retrieve a tourist who has overstayed the itinerary; like Strether he comes prepared for and confident of easy victory but is undone by his own wavering sympathies, finally falling victim to the system whose agent he purports to be. As in the James novel, 'more than personalities [are] engaged' in the campaign to bring the tourist home: 'the struggle [is] national'.[10] In Forster's novel the struggle pits England against a real Italy at odds with the touristic version England understands. A seasoned visitor to Italy, Philip has his campaign planned out before leaving home, but finds conditions in real Italy so different from what he had anticipated or recalled – and so unexpectedly appealing – that his mission eludes him. Philip 'had invented a dozen imaginary conversations, in all of which his logic and eloquence procured him certain victory. But how to begin? He was in the enemy's country, and everything ... seemed hostile to the placid atmosphere ... in which his thoughts took birth' (p. 16).

The possibility of positive commerce between the two worlds is embodied, here as in 'The Eternal Moment', in a child, and the question of the child's future is the question of cultural legacy as well. The child's mother is Lilia, an unmanageable young widow whose in-laws in respectable upper-middle-class 'Sawston' have packed off on a protracted tour of Italy; the father is Gino, a dentist's son in a small Tuscan town whom Lilia has rashly married. All the trouble results from Lilia's having taken too literally Philip Herriton's anti-touristic advice:

> Remember ... that it is only by going off the track that you get to know the country. See the little towns ... And don't, let me beg you, go with that awful tourist idea that Italy's only a museum of antiquities and art. Love and understand the Italians, for the people are more marvellous than the land.
>
> (p. 1)

Yet Lilia, like the errant Chad Newsome of *The Ambassador*, seems uninclined to love, understand, and leave, as even Philip takes for granted she must do. She marries Gino and dies in childbirth. At their mother's instigation, Philip and his grim Low Church sister Harriet try to rescue the child for a proper English upbringing. When attempts at a straightforward purchase of the baby fail, Harriet resorts to kidnapping, but the Herritons are defeated by their own devices: their absconding carriage overturns, and the infant is killed.

Tourism appears to figure only marginally in the novel, since we see little of Lilia on her journeys, but tourist images and institutions play a vital role in the Herritons' thwarted mission of expropriation. Philip has founded much of his image of himself on his experience of Italy and on his imaginative superiority to the run-of-the-mill tourist; he is what another unfortunate Forster character calls himself, the 'Inglese Italianato' (*Room with a View*, p. 97). Yet his enthusiasm for the country is not proof against his revulsion when he learns that Gino is not, as Lilia had intimated, a member of the old Italian nobility, but merely the son of a dentist in a provincial town. 'A dentist at Monteriano', Philip wonders:

> A dentist in fairyland! False teeth and laughing-gas and the tilting chair at a place which knew the Etruscan League, and the Pax Romana, and Alaric himself, and the Countess Matilda, and the Middle Ages, all fighting and holiness, and the Renaissance, all fighting and beauty! He thought of Lilia no longer. He was anxious for himself: he feared that Romance might die
>
> (*Where Angels fear to Tread*, p. 26)

Philip runs hard up against the banal contemporary existence of Italy; he is after all 'in love with a Baedeker Italy'.[11] For all that he figures himself a 'traveller' in touch with the people, not just the tourist attractions, of his favoured land, Philip clings to a shop-worn set of stereotypes about the Italians, whom he prefers to imagine in romantic and picturesque postures rather than in prosaic modern circumstances. His own sentiments come back to him in the deeply condescending note of Lilia's first letter home from Monteriano: 'We love this place, and I do not know how I shall ever thank Philip for telling me it. It is not only so quaint, but one sees the Italians unspoiled in all their simplicity and charm here' (p. 8). The revelation of Gino's origins, which would occasion class-anxiety at home, troubles Philip on what asks to be called a more philosophical level: the presence of dentists means the absence of Romance; confronted with evidence discordant with the 'Italy' by means of which he understands *himself*, Philip is in peril of losing his epistemological footing.

For Forster, the 'Baedeker Italy' regulates contact between touristic and Italian life, the latter defined in terms either of local colour or of necessary services for visitors. We recall Baedeker's aim of rendering tourists 'as independent as possible of the services of guides and valets-de-place, [of] protect[ing them] against extortion'; the guidebook was intended to be 'a means of saving the [Northern] traveller many a trial of temper; for there are few countries where the patience is more severely taxed than in some parts of Italy'.[12] In a well-known passage of *Where Angels Fear to Tread*, Philip's mother, her patience already taxed by an Italy she has never encountered, combs the family library for information she can use in the campaign she prepares to mount against Monteriano. 'She look[s] up the place in "Childe Harold"', only to find that 'Byron had not been there. Nor did Mark Twain visit it in the "Tramp Abroad"' (p. 11). Then she remembers to check Philip's Baedeker, opening it 'for the first time in her life'. She comes upon Forster's celebrated mock-Baedeker description:

> *Monteriano* (pop. 4,800) Hotels: Stella d'Italia, moderate only; Globo, dirty. *Caffè Garibaldi. Post and Telegraph office in Corso Vittorio Emmanuele, next to Theatre. Photographs at Seghena's (cheaper in Florence). Diligence (1 lira) meets principal trains.
>
> *Chief attractions* (2–3 hours): Santa Deodata, Palazzo Pubblico, Sant' Agostino, Santa Caterina, Sant' Ambrogio, Palazzo Capocchi. Guide (2 lire) unnecessary. A walk round the walls should on no account be omitted. The view from the Rocca (small gratuity) is finest at sunset.

History: Monteriano, the Mons Rianus of Antiquity, whose Ghibel-
line tendencies are noted by Dante (Purg. xx.), definitely emancipated
itself from Poggibonsi in 1261. Hence the distich, '*Poggibonizzi, fatti
in là, che Monteriano si fa città!*' till recently inscribed over the Siena
gate. It remained independent till 1530, when it was sacked by the
Papal troops and became part of the Grand Duchy of Tuscany. It is
now of small importance, and seat of the district prisons. The inhabitants are still noted for their agreeable manners.

The traveller will proceed direct from the Siena gate to the Colle-
giate Church of Santa Deodata, and inspect (5th chapel on right) the
charming *Frescoes ...

                                                                    (p. 11–12)

The step-by-step instructions and advice are ways of ensuring that,
for the brief duration of the tourist's visit, the inhabitants of Monteriano will preserve their 'agreeable manners' in the minor roles
assigned them in the tourist world.

'Not one to detect the hidden charms of Baedeker', Mrs Herriton
casts the handbook down in frustration, finding nothing in it but
details that will not assist her present efforts. But Philip, Forster let
us know, 'could never read "The view from the Rocca (small gra-
tuity) is finest at sunset" without a catching at the heart' (p. 12).
Like Miss Raby, Philip does possess 'imagination', he is susceptible
to what Germaine de Staël called 'enthusiasm', but these traits
afford him no exemption from the 'unimaginative' system of relations instituted in tourism. In an environment poor in nourishment
for the spirit, Philip clings to his memories of Italy, breathing life
into Baedeker's dry accounts.[13] To express the difference between
son and mother, we may borrow the terms which James applied to
Maggie and Adam Verver in *The Golden Bowl*: the one bears the
relation to 'culture' and artefacts which is borne by 'an earnest
young [person] with a Baedeker'; the other is someone 'to whom
even Baedekers were unknown' – which is to say, someone utterly
without compass or rudder in her encounter with the foreign. *Both*
relations are 'touristic'. Philip appears at least capable of understanding that Sawston is not the world, that it has deficiences; but of
course it is heavily ironic that his imaginative capacities should be
summed up in his response to the Baedeker phrase about the view
from the Rocca, which interrupts itself to offer helpful financial
advice for procuring the view.[14] And while Philip believes himself
uniquely able to discover and cherish the true Italy hidden beneath
'the awful tourist idea', he likewise harbours the illusion that his

form of contact with the foreign will involve no coercive pressure and will leave his lovely Baedeker Italy intact. Like James's account of himself to Charles Eliot Norton – as positioned 'very much as a man placed astride of a locomotive' and desiring only 'to stick on, somehow, and even to enjoy the scenery as we pass' – Philip's self-image portrays him as but a keenly sensitive passenger through life. He thinks he is 'fated to pass through the world without colliding with it or moving it', one to whom life 'is just a spectacle' (p. 121). Like John Marcher in James's 'The Beast in the Jungle', Philip considers himself one 'to whom nothing on earth was to have happened'.[15] But his 'superficialist' ideal does not prevent him from becoming a useful instrument of the Sawston siege of Monteriano.

In 'The Eternal Moment', Miss Raby's 'ugly [and] withered' body expressed the corruption of the new Vorta that she had helped to create; in *Where Angels Fear to Tread* the bodies of the Sawston representatives also suffer for the sins committed against Monteriano. Forster makes the bigoted Harriet endure a variety of minor physical ailments throughout the novel – someone steps on her corns, she gets smuts in her eyes, and so forth. The characters with more initial promise, like Philip and Lilia's companion Caroline Abbott, bear greater physical burdens for their complicity in the Sawston onslaught. Philip suffers a broken arm in the carriage accident, followed by a dark parody of the anti-tourist's goal, 'true contact' with the alien – the grief-stricken Gino beats him nearly to death (pp. 133–9). Caroline saves his life, but at the end of the novel she brings on his final degradation as she confesses her own to him. Impressed by her independence, Philip has begun to romanticise her, imagining her as a goddess and working himself up to a keen pitch of admiration. Riding the train out of Italy with Caroline and Harriet, Philip feels that he has 'reached love by the spiritual [not the bodily] path', that Caroline's 'thoughts and her goodness and her nobility [have] moved him [to love her]' (p. 141). But just as he embarks on this reverie, Caroline reveals that she has all along been longing for Gino in a most unspiritual fashion – 'I mean it crudely,' she sobs, 'you know what I mean' (p. 145). Philip's initial response to this information is to cast it in terms of a classical myth that suggests the inherently contradictory attitude of the Northern tourists, who idealise the places and cultures they visit while despising their crude or 'bodily' materiality: 'He smiled bitterly at the thought of [Gino and Caroline] together. Here was the cruel antique malice of the gods, such as they once sent forth against Pasiphae. Centuries of aspiration and culture – and the world could not escape it' (p. 146). Pasiphae desired a creature that was both god and beast; Philip has worshipped a 'spiritual' and reviled a material Italy; Caroline, who had shared Harriet's evangelicalism, is oppressed by her own feelings of 'bestial' lust. She tells Philip, 'if [Gino] had asked me, I might have given myself body and soul. That would have been the end of my rescue-party. But all through he took me for a superior being – a goddess. I who was worshipping every inch of him, and every word he spoke. And that saved me' (p. 147).

Caroline considers her salvation to be in escaping Italy and the passions she has felt there; she announces that she will never return to Italy 'because I understand the place. There is no need' (p. 141). In the end Philip revises his impression of Caroline and her feelings; he grasps at a salvation of sorts when he stops thinking in terms of Pasiphae's cruel fate and turns to the myth of Endymion. Now he sees Caroline as 'a goddess to the end', a spiritual being whose love for the human and material – even if she now smothers that love – was fulfilling, not degrading. As Philip considers her now,

> for her no love could be degrading: she stood outside all degradation. This episode, which she thought so sordid, and which was so tragic for him, remained supremely beautiful. To such a height was he lifted, that without regret he could now have told her that he was her worshipper too. But what was the use of telling her? For all the wonderful things had happened.
>
> (pp. 147–8)

It is only upon leaving Italy thus disillusioned with the romantic or spiritual dreams he had once cherished that Philip attains an awareness of an undegrading total love which is useless amidst the Sawston proprieties to which Caroline is returning. The journey and its misadventures have convinced Philip he can no longer live in Sawston, and his mind is set on a future of 'London and work'.

What the dweller in Forster's tourist world cannot escape is the materiality of culture, the mundane and unaesthetic living body on which the touristic fantasy-versions of places are constructed. Forster urges a view of culture as including, on equal terms, dentists and frescoes, physical urges, material needs, and aesthetic pleasures: a view of culture as 'a whole way of life', not held in solution for visitors to admire and 'appropriate'. However anti-touristic their sympathies, the tourists of Forster's cultural allegories continually commit what another story calls 'the sin against the body',[16] condemning it to bear the burden for their unimaginative imaginary exploitation. From the initial projection of a utopian alien body in 'The Story of a Panic' to that projection's ultimate coming-home-to-roost in the fates of Miss Raby, Philip Herriton, and Caroline Abbott, Forster's characters repeatedly enact a failed encounter with the 'real' which they believe themselves to have met. To adapt a phrase of Jacques Lacan's, they constantly attend 'an appointment to which [they] are always called with the real that eludes [them]'.[17]

Forster resumed his fictional treatment of tourists' chimerical quest for that 'real' in *A Passage to India* (1924). Many of the patterns characteristic of the 'tourist state' resurface in the imperial setting of this work. Significant meetings and strange allegiances still result from minor acts of trespassing – such as Mrs Moore's encountering Dr Aziz, with whom she establishes an unusual bond, by straying, alone and at night, into a mosque. The beaten track is still there to be denied and the anticipated experience to be thwarted: as the narrator remarks, 'Life never gives us what we want at the moment we consider appropriate. Adventures do occur, but not punctually.'[18] And well-meaning visitors' bodies fall prey to the institutionalised violence of the system they inhabit, as Miss Raby, Philip Herriton, and Caroline Abbott had fallen prey to the sublimated violence of their own touristic attitudes. In *A Passage to India*, Mrs Moore and Adela Quested (whose past-participle surname hints that her quest is over before it commences) arrive in Bombay longing to see 'the real India', an aim we quickly regard as inviting havoc. The novel makes clear that the desire for the 'authentic' Indian experience is regularly met by standard tourist activities organised by the English Club. Returning from her luminous encounter with Aziz, Mrs Moore re-enters the Club, in time to participate in this conversation with Adela:

> she went into the billiard room, where she was greeted by 'I want to see the real India,' and her appropriate life came back with a flash. ...
> 'I want to see it too, and I only wish we could. Apparently the Turtons will arrange something for next Tuesday.'
> 'It'll end in an elephant ride, it always does.'
>
> (p. 19)

Like the tourists of Forster's earlier work, the imperialists of *A Passage to India* are playing with fire. The political forces clamped down under the civilised bureaucratic surface of the Raj are brought into parallel with Miss Quested's chaotic emergent sexuality, which transforms the inevitable elephant ride (to the Marabar Caves) into another confrontation in which 'more than personalities are engaged'. Adela's desire for 'the real India' connects her with Lucy Honeychurch in Florence and with E. M. Forster in Italy on that first frustratingly polite and constrained voyage. Again, the contact with the alien takes the form of a projected, liberating sexual act (which, like other Forster protagonists, Adela both fears and desires, and of which she falsely accuses Dr Aziz). Adela flees madly through some cactus – a detail that has immediate and familiar results, for it allows Forster to linger over the vision of her body as it lies tortured by a thousand penetrations.

> Adela lay for several days in the McBrydes' bungalow. She had been touched by the sun, also hundreds of cactus spines had to be picked out of her flesh. Hour after hour Miss Derek and Mrs McBryde examined her through magnifying glasses, always coming on fresh colonies, tiny hairs that might snap off and be drawn into the blood if they were neglected. She lay passive beneath their fingers, which developed the shock that had begun in the cave. ... Everything now was transferred to the surface of her body, which began to avenge itself...
>
> (p. 184)

To recapitulate: in Forster, the anti-touristic desire to discover the 'real' and to show oneself in the act of discovery leads to the unintended violation of a body which may represent both a culture's independent identity and the possibility of non-coercive interaction between tourist and host. We may wound the body of foreign culture even when we mean to admire or assist it; and in so far as our relations with the *authentic* are a measure of the condition of our being, such injuries as we do to the foreign will recoil upon ourselves.

From James Buzard, *The Beaten Track: European Tourism, Literature, and the Ways to Culture, 1800–1918* (Oxford, 1993), pp. 291–315.

NOTES

[Buzard's essay, which picks up on Forster's enthusiasm for Italy as the 'other' of England, looks at tourism as a *discourse* at work in the nineteenth and early-twentieth centuries, constructing ideas of 'culture' and also creating the 'otherness' of the places and people tourism describes (as in Baedeker's guide-books) in a kind of objectification of them. There is no access to the real, in fact, except through the descriptions tourism gives. The argument about a discourse controlling ways of seeing and thinking comes from the French philosopher Michel Foucault; the sense that tourism makes for the encoded nature of experience is post-modernist, suggesting Jean Baudrillard's position that we are totally in the world of reproduction culture – i.e. that all we know is the 'simulacrum': the reproduction of the reproduction. It is the more ironic that Forster films contribute to this 'tourist' sense, offering a tourist-guide to an imaginary England of the Edwardian era, a world as unreal as that depicted in Baedeker or Murray's nineteenth-century presentations of Italy. Ed.]

1. See Fredric Jameson, *The Political Unconscious: Narrative as a Socially Symbolic Act* (London, 1981), p. 35.

2. 'A Letter on Art', in *Lenin and Philosophy and Other Essays*, trans. Ben Brewster (London, 1971), pp. 222–3.

3. See P. N. Furbank, *E. M. Forster: A Life* (New York, 1978), I, 80–96.

4. See *Selected Letters of E. M. Forster*, ed. Mary Lago and P. N. Furbank (Cambridge, Mass., 1983), I, 52.

5. *Selected Letters*, I, 48.

6. See Barbara Rosecrance, *Forster's Narrative Vision* (Ithaca, NY, 1982), p. 92.

7. *A Room with a View* (1908; London, 1977), p. 40. Subsequent references are cited in the text.

8. In this detail, the Merchant–Ivory film version (1985) of *A Room with a View* diverges from the novel. While Forster's text dispatches at once with the Italian body, the film dwells upon the victim (recording his screams, following the procession that bears him away, and so on).

9. Or, as it turns out, within an Italianate plot for English consumption: Miss Lavish transforms the piazza scene into the result of a lover's triangle in her local-colour novel *Under a Loggia*. This is the book (published under pseudonym Joseph Emery Prank) that appears in the garden at Lucy's family home Windy Corner, spurring George and Lucy's courtship with its sensationalised account of their own previous encounters (*A Room With a View*, pp. 148–60).

10. *Where Angels Fear to Tread* (1905; London, 1975), p. 50. Subsequent references are cited in the text.

11. Wilfred Stone, *The Cave and the Mountain: A Study of E. M. Forster* (Stanford, Cal., 1966), p. 165.

12. *Northern Italy* (11th edn, Leipzig, 1899), p. v.

13. See David I. Joseph, *The Art of Rearrangement: E. M. Forster's* Abinger Harvest (New Haven, Conn., 1964), p. 42.

14. On the 'Baedeker parenthesis' see Edward Mendelson, 'Baedeker's Universe', *Yale Review* (1985), 397.

15. See Stone, *The Cave and the Mountain*, pp. 165n., 179n.

16. *The Eternal Moment and Other Stories* (New York, 1928), p. 36.

17. *The Four Fundamental Concepts of Psycho-Analysis*, trans. Alan Sheridan (New York, 1981), p. 53.

18. *A Passage to India* (1924; London, 1978), p. 20. Subsequent references are cited in the text.

2

'Aphrodite with a Janus Face': Language, Desire, and History in *The Longest Journey*

RAE H. STOLL

> I measure
> the world of fancies, seeking one like thee,
> And find–alas! mine own infirmity.
> (Shelley, *Epipsychidion*)

In June 1964, when he was eighty-five, E. M. Forster went to visit William Golding in Wiltshire. There they walked the chalky soil of a pagan entrenchment, the Figsbury Rings, and talked of the possible extinction of Chalk Blue butterflies by the use of pesticides in the area. Sixty years before, Forster's first encounter with the Rings had released and connected for him a number of deeply felt desires. They had also provided him with a symbolic centre around which to cluster these longings in the most autobiographical of his novels, and his favourite among them: *The Longest Journey* (1907). Despite the reminder the butterflies provided of the now commonplace destruction of the pastoral English world which Forster had celebrated in his novels, the Rings confirmed his belief that in creating the flawed character Stephen Wonham, he had nevertheless given to the world from which he had taken inspiration a fictional character whom he could think of as a living child.[1] After his day on the Rings with Golding, Forster wrote in his diary, recalling that at the end of *The Long-*

est Journey Stephen's young daughter sleeps with her father on a Wiltshire hillside in view of the Rings:

> I exclaimed several times that the area was marvellous, and large – larger than I recalled. I was filled with thankfulness and security and glad that I had given myself so much back. The butterfly was a moving glint, and I shall lie in Stephen's arms instead of his child.[2]

In hoping to insert himself into the space filled by the child of his own creation, Forster revives the central fantasy which motivated his book and is reflected in its character relationships as in an array of mirrors: the fantasy of reproduction achieved through the identification and completion of one's self in another. This fantasm or underlying master narrative, as Fredric Jameson calls it,[3] seeks, in the production of the text, a symbolic representation or realisation of desire. Rereading *The Longest Journey* with insights provided by Freud's speculation on the dynamics of homosexuality, Lacan's inquiry into the linguistic-social nature of the constitution of the subject, and Jameson's discussion of the political unconscious opens up this text as a psychologically and socially acute portrait of the artist.

Such a reading discloses secrets buried in the language of the text and helps to put into perspective the radical decentredness of its main character, Rickie Elliot, whose lack of a central unity and coherence has long been attributed to Forster's failure to maintain sufficient control over his materials. Following Lacan, I suggest that this complaint is based on a false assumption: that of the essential unity of the individual. What Forster presents in the character of Rickie is, in fact, much closer to Lacan's dispersed or disunified individual whose supposed identity is fraudulently constituted in the symbolic order. It is illusory to assume that a truly unified subject arises out of what is, in fact, a system of differences in which the identity of a member of one 'sex' derives from his arbitrary, symbolic (phallic) opposition to the Other, whose own identity is a product, first, of her phallic lack and, in consequence, of her exclusion from the forms of power, including discourse, assumed by the possessor of the phallus – the differentiating marker. The primary role of this possessor is father in the nuclear family – the social place (not, of course, necessarily the individual family) in which children are socialised and sexed – largely through being admitted to the symbology of language. Luce Irigaray explains the male 'identity-claiming assumption' as a statement that 'I am a unified, coherent being, and what is significant in the world reflects my male image'.[4]

In exploring Rickie's attempts and failures to locate what is frequently referred to in the novel as the 'real', and thus to gain a stable identity, the text itself implies the need for precisely this questioning of phallocentric discourse. I shall trace several ideological reasons provided in the text for why it cannot fully engage or resolve the questions it raises.

I

The Figsbury Rings, an Iron Age earthworks, are as Forster describes them in *The Longest Journey*, where they are renamed the Cadbury Rings: two concentric embankments of grass with crops growing in between and a small tree in the centre. Forster first visited the site in September 1904, when he met there a shepherd boy with a club foot. Like other features of this visit which are dispersed throughout the narrative of *The Longest Journey*, the club foot assumes a central, symbolic role in the novel. It is transferred to Rickie Elliot, in whom it figures as a genetic disqualification and as an emblem of his true homosexual nature. In contrast to the enclosed Madingley dell near Cambridge, where Rickie brings only the most intimate friends from his small circle at the university, the expansive Rings in the Wiltshire countryside are the resting place of common soldiers and farmers, who died in defending their homes. The desire Forster expressed to lie in Stephen's arms in the Rings, as in blissful, self-fulfilled death, recalls the story of these ancient men who are said in the novel to lie together in common burial. They are connected with Rickie's desire for democratic brotherhood, his need to unite his social self with what Stuart Hampshire calls the proletarian, sexual self of the unconscious. The Rings are at the heart of the novel, and at their heart a single small tree – alternately identified with Rickie's mother and his brother, Stephen – who represent the principles of generation and continuity, from which Rickie is excluded.

An early outline for *The Longest Journey*, dated 17 July 1904, suggests the effect Forster's first visit to the Rings had on the evolution of his novel.[5] The original plan was for a well-plotted novel which began in the highly recognisable world of Cambridge and then moved to the estate of an Englishman in Italy, where the young Cambridge graduate, Humphrey, would discover his 'natural' brother, Pasquale. Besides these somewhat improbably named brothers, the outline also projects disrupters in Humphrey's life: 'a "brainy, uncouth" friend who "ran" him at Cambridge and a pushy wife who would also try to run him'. The novel was to end in death by fire for both brothers – a scheme suggesting Forster's plans to borrow heavily from Wagner, as well as from Shelley, whose anti-monogamist lines in the *Epipsychidion* give the novel its title.[6]

[Stoll here refers to the Shelleyan influences on the early versions of *The Longest Journey*. Ed.]

The *Longest Journey* reworks fantasy in the direction of greater faithfulness to a complex and contradictory situation, at once social and psychological. The narrative connecting Rickie to Stephen is a complex exploration of the basis of Rickie's desire for such a brother, of his adoration, envy, and near-masochistic need to sacrifice himself for Stephen, and of the roots of these needs in Rickie's desire for social and sexual inclusion and in his complicated love for his mother, who is referred to in the novel only as Mrs Elliot.

While much of the original plan of the novel remains intact, the triangle of protagonist, mother, and natural brother becomes the emotional core of the novel. The major deviation from the original plan, the continuation of Stephen, involves a psychological transaction: the brother and friend Rickie desires becomes the *self* Rickie would have to be in order to possess the things he wants most: a place in the continuous stream of life, male camaraderie, and the instinctive impulse to social action.

Rickie, who believes 'that one can like many more people than one supposes' (p. 20), leans toward the position of his socialist uncle, Mr Failing, who 'believed that things could be kept together by accenting the similarities, not the differences of men' (p. 98). Opposing him in this desire for brotherhood is Stewart Ansell, the brainy friend, who defends his right to hate members of the 'beefy' set and who refuses even to admit the existence of someone as remote to his life and as threatening to his interests as is Agnes Pembroke. Ansell's denial of 'reality' to Agnes in the opening scene of the novel when he refuses to shake her hand or to acknowledge her claims on Rickie as his guest, or in any other capacity, reflects the social reality of Cambridge misogyny at the time in which the book is set. Ansell also does to Agnes what the world outside seemed to be doing to intellectual male Cambridge: denying it significance as a creative and influential force.[7] As a social outsider, but primarily as a sexual intruder, Agnes is denied both human form and potential human merit by Ansell. His attitude toward her resembles that of Clive and Maurice, the Cambridge friends and platonic lovers in the novel *Maurice* who regard the women in their families as members of a sub-species. Because Ansell re-enters Rickie's life as his liberator, urging him to recognise his brother and to dissolve his marriage to Agnes, while, in the words of Shelley's *Epipsychidion*, she becomes a 'jealous foe' (p. 158),[8] the motivating impulse toward social unity in the text becomes diffused.

In its animus toward Agnes, the text appears to advance both Ansell's misogyny and his contempt for Rickie's democratic feelings. The Agnes–Rickie–Ansell plot works against the values of union and inclusiveness associated with Rickie, his mother, and Stephen – values expressed by Mr Failing and Stephen's father, Robert, as opposed to Ansell. To a large extent, however, the masculine hauteur and the Shelleyan sentiments associated with Ansell are red herrings. Ansell is not simply an adherent of open and free relationships, as his opposition to Rickie's marriage seems intended to imply. He is also a 'jealous foe'. He, as well as Agnes, wishes to enter into an exclusive contract with Rickie, as does Rickie with him. Rickie's notion that their friendship, which the text compares to that of David and Jonathan, should be 'labelled', that their 'marriage of true minds' should be recorded in 'a kind of friendship office', draws approval from Ansell (p. 64). In fact, Rickie's desire for friendship with Ansell is voiced in the language of Shakespeare's Sonnet 116, which argues for constancy in love. Ansell's pseudo-Shavian claim that 'a man wants to love mankind; woman wants to love one man' (p. 272) is contradicted both by his own desire to be joined by contract to Rickie and by his confession that he is 'bored by the prospect of the brotherhood of man' (p. 207). Although Ansell's attitudes toward Agnes and marriage tend to obscure the connection, the 'Agnes' plot is linked to the 'Mrs Elliot' plot in ways that help to explain the antinomies of the text. These connections are involved in Rickie's constitution as a 'subject' – most especially in his symbiotic relationship to Stephen.

In the opening chapters of the novel, Rickie's beautiful mother, who died when he was fifteen, has been replaced by Cambridge. Since her death, Rickie has been bullied and frozen into an imitation schoolboy by a public school, but at Cambridge he regains a sense of his own reality: 'She had taken and soothed him, and warmed him, and had laughed at him a little, saying he must not be so tragic yet awhile, for his boyhood had been but a dusty corridor that led to the spacious

halls of youth' (pp. 5–6). In 'the spacious halls of youth' an extended
adolescence and, for some, a sexual quiescence are possible. There
young men, instead of maturing and marrying in order to reproduce
themselves, are simply replaced by other young men in most respects
duplicates of themselves. They are a somewhat larger version of the
boys under the supervision of Mr Read, Principal of Maurice's public
school, to whom 'they seemed ... a race small but complete, like the
New Guinea pygmies, "my boys". And they were even easier to
understand than pygmies, because they never married and seldom
died. Celibate and immortal, the long procession passed before him'.[9]
Celibate, or at least unmarried, and immortal: this, the Agnes–Ansell
plot of the novel suggests, would be the ideal state for Rickie.

For Rickie, Cambridge prolongs adolescence and fosters depend-
ency even as, to use Lacan's term, it provides him with a renewed
sense of himself in admitting him to the 'symbolic order' of masculine society. The 'imaginary' or mirror phase of Rickie's infancy
and young childhood, when his father was usually absent, retains an
exceptional hold on his emotions and his conscious memory. Bodied
forth from the mirror of his mother whose presence encircled him,
he experienced a completeness of identity; there was no gap between
himself as subject and the great world, such as opened up at public
school. At school, the naturalness and wholeness of a taken-for-
granted identity are dispersed by a system of fixed social and sexual
roles. To survive in this unreal world, he fabricates a persona
modelled on images he forms of the boys around him.

Ordinarily, the painful passage of the young boy from the
imaginary to the symbolic order is achieved by resolution of the
Oedipal complex. To have identity in this new order, he must accept
the absence of his mother's mirroring presence. Then the gap
between signifier and signified opens up for him, and he is cut off
from the 'real', which eludes any signifying system. Desire for the
real – that is, desire to recapture the object which bestows wholeness
and gives significance to all other objects – cannot be satisfied; nevertheless, it remains a driving force in individual life. As Eagleton
writes in an explanation of Lacan's theory that might well be a gloss
on this novel: 'an original lost object – the mother's body – ... drives
forward the narrative of our lives, impelling us to pursue substitutes
for this lost paradise in the endless metonymic movement of
desire'.[10]

In his rooms at Cambridge, which he loves 'better than any person', Rickie feels 'almost as safe as he felt once when his mother

killed a ghost in the passage by carrying him through it in her arms'
(pp. 58, 59). The ghost in the 'dark passage' (p. 23), suggesting
Ibsen's play, is Rickie's father, who is associated with Rickie's sexual
fears and with his sexual infirmity. Largely as a result of his father's
indifference, Rickie has failed to negotiate the Oedipal passage. His
identity is still tied to the body of his mother, in whose arms he finds
shelter from the threatening and divisive world of school and
society. After his return to Cambridge from a visit to Agnes
Pembroke and her brother, Herbert, at Sawston school, Rickie is
'like one who had escaped from danger' (p. 59). 'There was no ghost
now; he was frightened at reality; he was frightened at the splen-
dours and horrors of the world' (p. 59). His rooms are haven against
the love and death he has witnessed, just as his mother's arms were
security against his childhood ghosts. Back in his rooms, figuratively
back with his mother, he is safe again from the threat of sex. But,
because of his experience outside the university, he has learned to
define 'reality' differently from Ansell, who associates it with an
exclusivist 'salvation' of an elite group at the academy – in Plato's
words, 'the saving remnant'. In fact, back at Cambridge, Rickie
begins to worry that the university will itself come to seem to him
narrow and that Ansell is incapable of responding to the real 'splen-
dours and horrors' of the world: 'Ansell could discuss love and
death admirably, but somehow he would not understand lovers or a
dying man.... Would Cambridge understand them either?' (p. 57).
The movement of desire impels Rickie beyond Cambridge.

He had been initiated into other realities when he saw Agnes and
Gerald embracing and when, a few days later, Gerald was killed in a
football accident. Gerald, Rickie's old nemesis from public school to
whom he remains tied by ambivalent feelings of attraction and
repulsion, is the means by which Rickie is drawn to Agnes: he falls
in love with Gerald's love for her. Gerald, in fact, shows untypical
insight in recognising that Rickie's motivation for offering him and
Agnes money to marry on is somehow furtively bound up with
Rickie's desire to become part of their union: 'Marry us', Gerald
explodes to Agnes, 'he, you, and me – a hundred pounds down and
as much annual – he, of course, to pry into all we did, and we to
kowtow and eat dirt-pie to him' (p. 49).

Rickie's Cambridge-inspired Hellenism reinforces his attraction to
Gerald, whose 'figure' he regards as that 'of a Greek athlete' (p. 35).
The objective correlative of this attraction is the bust of Hermes of
Praxiteles, patron of athletes, which stands in the Pembrokes' hall

and which will re-enter the story when the dead Gerald reappears to
Agnes and Rickie in the form of another man. For now, the text
merely establishes a bond between the Greek-like bully, Gerald, and
his former victim, Rickie: 'Between Rickie and Gerald there lay a
shadow that darkens life more often than we suppose. The bully and
his victim never quite forget their first relations' (p. 38). For Rickie
this shadow is a kind of masochistic attraction to brutality and a
need for self-abnegation. The masochistic element in Rickie's love
for Gerald/Agnes is most evident at the moment Rickie and Agnes
agree to marry: 'Never forget that your greatest thing is over', he
reminds her. 'What he gave you then is greater than anything you
will get from me' (p. 74). Rickie marries Agnes as a poor substitute
for the man he insists on her thinking of as her real bridegroom, for
only with thought of Gerald's continuing presence in their marriage
can Rickie be a husband to Agnes. When Stephen breaks the bust of
Hermes which stands in the hall of Sawston school, he destroys this
relationship between Rickie, his wife, and her dead lover. At that
time, Stephen, whom Agnes momentarily confuses with Gerald,
replaces Gerald in Rickie's emotional life and destroys the marriage
between Rickie and Agnes. Gerald has prepared for Stephen in
another way, too: the self-loathing which characterises Rickie's
relationship with Gerald/Agnes anticipates his eventual mutilation
and self-sacrifice for Stephen's sake.

In the dell outside Madingley, Rickie's holy place at Cambridge,
he is totally safe. The dell is a magical circle which both contains
and enlarges; there Rickie re-enters the imaginary order in which
objects are seamlessly reflected in one another: 'The place looked as
big as Switzerland or Norway – as indeed for the moment it was –
and he came upon it at a time when his life too was beginning to
expand. Accordingly the dell became for him a kind of church – a
church where indeed you could do anything you liked, but where
anything you did would be transfigured' (p. 18). The transfiguring
effect of the dell is the result of Rickie's own creative imagination.
Its impression of size is merely one of reflection: the sky and the surrounding trees are mirrored, and thus multiplied, in the 'fiords and
lagoons of clearest water' (p. 18) left behind by the melted January
snows. This is a place of magnification and mirrors, of trans-
formations, which, during a January thaw, expands to the size of
Norway, replete with fiords. It is the true home of Rickie – and of
Forster, whose birth month was January. The winter child who
realises his desires only indirectly, through surrogates, especially

those of the imagination, creates for himself a version of the northern world to which 'the woman he loved' (p. 282), his mother, escaped with her lover. In the dell he dreams of what his brother – the child born in April, the child of Demeter – has so abundantly: the power through his own fecundity to make their mother live again. Stephen has the ability to realise the dreams which Rickie fulfils only in the imaginative act, in art. It is also in exclusive claim to this dell that an undergraduate aesthete remarks when he first enters it: '*Procul este, profani!*' (Unsanctified commoners, keep out!) (p. 18). The dell is both a social and a sexual retreat: it offers privileged protection to infantile desires and to a small coterie of friends. It is, at the same time, a powerfully evocative representation of the realm of the Imaginary itself.

The next passage Rickie attempts, his 'going down' from Cambridge into the venal world of Sawston is, on the one hand, a necessary step toward outgrowing his infantile attachment to his mother and alma mater. Rickie's marriage is a test of his adulthood and fitness to be a parent, on which account he is extremely anxious. On the other hand, it is a journey into a life of further division and unreality, in which differences – especially differences in sex and class – figure even more prominently. Sawston is the home of the refurbished, fake public school and training ground for the new class of technocrats and managers who are a threat to any kind of authenticity the text can imagine. Because his defection to Sawston (and Agnes) is also a betrayal of his mother, to whom the image-releasing dell is consecrated, Rickie's fall from sexual innocence cuts him off from the source of his creativity. His guilt-ridden attraction to Agnes, by whom he is finally 'entrapped' in the dell, dramatises Freud's theory that the homosexual man is attracted to women, but that he transfers the 'stimulus ... received from the woman to a male object ... [thus repeating] again and again the mechanism through which he acquired his homosexuality'.[11] 'By repressing the love for his mother', Freud explains, 'he conserves the same in his unconscious and henceforth remains faithful to her. When as a lover he seems to pursue boys, he really thus runs away from women who could cause him to become faithless to his mother.'[12] When Agnes calls to Rickie from within the dell, where he has declined to follow her, he drives his fingers into his ears, invoking the name of Gerald. Finally responding to her call, he enters but whispers to her: 'I prayed you might not be a woman' (p. 73). Rickie, in fact, alternately pursues male and female substitutes for the original object he wishes to repossess. In a series of abortive attempts to satisfy desire, he moves from his mother to Gerald to Cambridge and Ansell (the safe alter mater and platonic friend) to Agnes and, finally, to Stephen Wonham, who is so intimately linked with both Rickie's ideal self and his mother that the three are conflated at one point in a single Janus-faced image.[13]

In a fine example of intertextual play, Rickie, like Shelley's speaker, attempts to regain an ideal love, to find, in a series of replacements, the 'Being' whom the poet recalls from 'the clear golden prime of my youth's dawn' (pp. 190, 191). For the affective centre of *The Longest Journey*, however, Forster drew not only on Shelley's *Epipsychidion*, but, more profoundly, on the poems of another writer who shared his feelings about continuity and who took as seriously as he the Biblical injunction: 'Be fruitful and multiply'. The language in which Forster explores the nature of the relationship of Rickie, Stephen, and their mother – that is, the nature of Rickie's sexuality and of his constitution as a subject – is drawn not from the publicly acknowledged lines of Shelley which appear in the text, but from Shakespeare's Sonnets 1 to 17, the 'procreation sonnets'.[14] C. L. Barber calls attention to the resemblance of a pattern in the procreation sonnets to one which Freud found in his study of an infantile reminiscence of Leonardo da Vinci. This pattern is also clearly present in *The Longest Journey*. In each case – of the artist and subject of psychoanalytical speculation, of the poet-speaker of the sonnets, and of the hero of the novel – the central character in the drama preserves 'his relationship to a maternal presence by internalising her cherishing of him, becoming like her in narcissistically cherishing [a] young man'.[15] In a description that anticipates Lacan's placing of Desire at the heart of the constitution of the subject, Freud writes that

> the boy represses the love for the mother by putting himself in her place, by identifying himself with her, and by taking his own person as a model through the similarity of which he is guided in the selection of his love object. He thus becomes homosexual; as a matter of fact he returns to the stage of autoeroticism, for the boys whom the growing adult now loves are only substitute persons or revivals of his own childish person, whom he loves in the same way his mother loved him.[16]

The brothers Rickie and Stephen, each of whom fills the role of cherishing parent for the other, are particularly suited to dramatise

the way in which the lover narcissistically re-enacts the role of the
mother in his attachment to his beloved. As Jane Pinchin has per-
ceptively observed of Forster's fiction: 'Images of comrades and
siblings gave him the necessary fictive mask through which he could
deal with homosexuality, and often allowed him to dig to the roots
of sexuality in familial and friendship relationships'.[17]

In Rickie's love for Stephen, as in Shakespeare's love for the fair
young man, the idea of generation and continuation is twined with
the idea of reciprocal nurturing between lovers and of the reflection
of one in the other, just as child and parent are reflected in one
another. The child experiences itself through discovering itself
reflected in the parent; so, too, the lovers.

[Stoll here quotes Shakespeare's Sonnets 1 and 3. Ed.]

After the death of his child, whose deformity is worse than his own,
Rickie turns obsessively to Stephen, whom he had rejected just before
his marriage to Agnes. Before his reunion with his brother, however,
Rickie has a vision of their dead mother crying in his room: 'He whis-
pered, "Never mind, my darling, never mind", and a voice echoed
"Never mind – come away – let them die out – let them die out"'
(p. 193). Rickie comes to love Stephen as the means through which
'she whom he loved had risen from the dead' (pp. 250–1). The
Elliot line will end with the death of Rickie who already thinks of himself as 'dead' because he cannot 'contribute to the stream' (p. 192).
Rickie shares, but cannot realise, the desire of Gino Carella in *Where
Angels Fear to Tread* to 'have sons like him, to people the earth'. 'The
strongest desire that can come to a man', Forster writes in this earlier
novel, is 'that physical and spiritual life may stream out of him for
ever.'[18]

II

In contrast to Rickie, Stephen, fair child of the spring, is identified with
renewal and resurrection: 'Thou art thy mother's glass, and she in
thee / Calls back the lovely April of her prime.'[19] Stephen is born in
April, a birth-month to which the text calls specific attention. During his parents' scant two weeks together in July, Stephen is conceived. 'I am twenty-two in April', he writes to a child at Sawston
(p. 187). Through Stephen and his progeny, 'beauty's rose', the

youthful perfection of the mother of Rickie's infancy, will never die. Stephen becomes for Rickie what the young man is to Shakespeare: 'the world's fresh ornament / And only herald to the gaudy spring.' In the case of Stephen, however, the young man is herald not only to a single season or generation, but to a new race, a new social order. Stephen – who is born of a misalliance between a gentlewoman and an educated farmer and whose most distinguishing mark is his classlessness – survives as a prophetic harbinger of a new order of men who will 'inherit' England. Such men, it is vaguely implied, will heal social divisions and realise the lively promise of an older, pastoral England, turning out the grey technocrats, managers, and monopolists – the new controlling class whose disruption of the national life Rickie experiences as a member of the disappearing rentier class. the sexual component of this desire for social restoration and reunion, both inseparable from and homologous to it, is the relationship between Rickie and Stephen and their mother.

At the Cambridge dell and in his college rooms, Rickie's mother is his alone; he speaks of her to his friends, but withholds his most intimate and painful memories of her. Her role expands in the countryside of Wiltshire on the Rings – or the 'mystic circles' (p. 255), as the narrator calls them, thus connecting them with the 'mystic rose' (p. 278) which represents her as the mother of Stephen. As the mother of both Rickie and Stephen, she is the past, the earth, and Demeter, who is connected with death as well as with fertility. Through Stephen, her natural child and Rickie's fantasy brother, she reclaims Rickie from Agnes. As Stephen calls Rickie away from Sawston, he uses words similar to their mother's, speaking in her voice: 'Come, I do mean it. Come; I will take care of you, I can manage you' (p. 257).

It was through the birth of the fair Stephen that she learned to love Rickie, the child his aunt called 'the ugly little boy' (p. 242). With Stephen's birth, 'a curious thing happened. Her second child drew her towards her first. She began to love Rickie also' (p. 239). Stephen possesses those qualities required to make *Rickie* lovable. He is not only Rickie's anti-self, differing from him in 'disposition' and in fairness of form, but Rickie's completed self. Wilfred Stone's remarks about a narcissistic pattern in Forster's short story 'Dr Woolacott' are pertinent here: 'narcissism is not really love of the *self*, but love of one's *self-image*, a quite different thing. Clesant's desire to feel "attractive" led him to project a self-image and a lover of that image which were nothing but the measure of his self-contempt. Love of one's image is a way of keeping the self at a distance, as something alien, even as something odious.'[20] Like the ghost of a farm worker whose deathly embrace 'rescues' the invalid Clesant in the short story, Stephen is a splitting off of a self-image from Rickie, whose repeated failures to gain a stable masculine identity thwart his desire to be what his mother desires. That, the text makes clear, is the robust and inarticulate self-image, Stephen, not the clever weak boy, Rickie.

In the early thirties Forster gave a paper on memory to the Bloomsbury Memoir Club which related how the owners had turned his mother and himself out of 'Rooksnest', their beloved home in Herfordshire and the model for 'Howards End', where he lived until he was fourteen. He concluded his recollection with a remarkable statement: 'If I had been allowed to stop on there I should have become a different person, married, and fought in the war'.[21] To whatever extent Forster believed his sexual temperament and his pacific nature would have been altered by continuing to live in the English countryside, where traditional life strongly favoured marriage and continuity, he associated being cut off from the land with being deprived of home and of heirs. There is regret over both of these deprivations in all of his novels. Through Rickie, Forster appears to extend the internalised love of his mother to an idealised adult version of the undeveloped, cut-off child in himself, the one who, under other circumstances, would have grown up 'whole' in Wiltshire, or at Rooksnest: Stephen.

[A passage omitted here examines the novel's imagery, drawn from Shakespeare's Sonnets, to show the shift in values taking place in Rickie as he moves away from Cambridge to a more inclusive identity. Stoll sees Rickie's idealised love for Stephen as a reflection of his almost mystical love of his mother. In this homoerotic bonding, there is a further absence – Stephen's wife hardly appears. Ed.]

'He bent down reverently and saluted the child; to whom he had given the name of their mother' (p. 289): this, the last sentence in the novel, casts Stephen and his daughter in the role of the Holy Family, with Stephen serving as both madonna and donor.[22] In this capacity, Stephen is not the voice, but the silencer, of his wife and of Rickie's mother, neither of whom has a given name in the text. His mother's name, which the text does not speak, *he* gives to his daughter, who thereby becomes equally nameless. As Mary Dally has argued, the power to name is the power to exist humanly – in one's own right, rather than as a guarantor of another's truth, or reality (p. 8). In this respect, Rickie is quite right in blaming himself for loving Stephen only because their mother lived again in him, for loving him not openly as a man, but as a fantasy supplanter of a woman, whose Otherness, as Lacan shows, serves to secure for a man his own self-knowledge.[23] The subterfuge involved in this symbolic mediation, and the uneasiness it causes, explains the unreality of Stephen as an independent character and the punishment which is meted out to Rickie; it also points to the ambivalent attitude toward the Other of the familial protonarrative which is split between the idealisation of Rickie's mother and the misogyny directed at Agnes – the two Mrs Elliots.

In his raids on the sonnets, Forster takes possession of a symbolic language to probe the nature of a sexual psychology which, though shaped by the expectations and prohibitions of a particular familial-social-political situation, has roots in the source of all human sexuality. Like the poet's love for the fair young man, Forster's for Stephen involves an almost mystical recollection of infantile joy which remains in the adult as a substratum of emotional satisfaction and ego development. In an act that might have pleased Roland Barthes, who finds a similar *jouissance* in the pleasure the text takes in itself, Forster buries one more allusion to the sonnets in his text – this time playfully and irreverently. One of the most prominent candidates for 'Mr W. H.', to whom the sonnets are dedicated, was William Herbert, Earl of Pembroke. In *The Longest Journey* the character who is brother to Agnes and 'intimately connected' with Rickie's 'fortunes' (p. 144) is a pedantic house master at Sawston, Herbert Pembroke.

III

As part of an extended flashback revealing how Stephen came to be born, Stephen's father admits his love for Mrs Elliot to her brother-in-law, the socialist writer Tony Failing:

> 'Have I quite followed you, sir, in that business of the brotherhood of man?'
> 'How do you mean?'
> 'I thought love was to bring it about.'
> 'Love of another man's wife? Sensual love? You have understood nothing – nothing.' Then he was ashamed, and cried, 'I understand nothing myself.' For he remembered that sensual and spiritual are not easy words to use; that there are, perhaps, not two Aphrodites, but one Aphrodite with a Janus face.
>
> (p. 233)

The one Aphrodite of this novel is Mrs Elliot, whose Janus faces are the twin faces of her sons – one representing the spiritual side of love, the other its sensual side. On another level, they stand, like Janus, for an ending and a new beginning, for death and continuation. The further implication of the exchange between Robert and Mr Failing – that sensual love is a means of achieving social comradeship and democratic brotherhood – occurs frequently in Forster's fiction.

The desire for sexual and social union imaged in *The Longest Journey* in the Janus-faced figure of Aphrodite is an expression of deeply felt historical and personal divisions. Heirs to the liberal tradition at Cambridge at the turn of the century were confronted with a conflict between humanistic principle and class privilege, between the generalising sense of one's relation to a whole society and the intense parochialism involved in the formation of an intellectual elite. That such a conflict existed could not be ignored by Forster's generation as easily as it had been by previous generations of Cambridgians, for although Rickie and Ansell do not specify the reasons why the newspapers are complaining, as Rickie puts it, that 'Cambridge has lost touch with the times' (p. 62), these reasons were insistent and, despite Ansell's cavalier dismissal, compelling. Forster's undergraduate years at Cambridge were a period when its legitimacy as an all-male and class-restricted school was being seriously challenged by women from Girton and Newnham and by graduates of the grammar schools, on whose behalf there were numerous attempts to strike down the compulsory entrance exam in Greek, which closed Cambridge to almost all applicants other than graduates of the classical public schools. Even before the first world war, Forster's class was threatened – above all, by the new industrial classes – with the same impotence as a social force that he feared sexually. His psychosexual dilemma coalesced with a continuing crisis in the social world.

This dilemma is discernible only in its effects; it is to be understood, in relation to the symbolic text, as an absent cause, expressed in the text in oppositions *between* competing desires, as well as in the opposition to basic desires which the text realistically puts forward but can find no way of surmounting. Rickie is caught in a logical double bind by his desire for *union* – between individuals in marriage or within a small coterie or a university – and his impulse toward *inclusion*, which, paradoxically, results for him in isolation and separation . His longed-for acceptance into a select circle within

Cambridge competes with his nonetheless strong desire to break down sexual taboos and class barriers which Cambridge helps to reinforce. Both the social conscience and sexual fantasies of Forster's ego character impel him to desire inclusion, but such an impulse is regarded as impractical and idealistic not only by the aggressively bourgeois world of Sawston, but by Rickie's Cambridge friends, whose own identity is threatened by the new claimants to power in England, especially women and men of a lower class. In reality, the university had taken on the landed gentry and the industrial bour- geoisie, but it lacked the creative energy to take on the labouring class. It lacked even historical memory of the actual poor scholars for whom it was originally intended. It is precisely Rickie's desire for an inclusive life (uniting mind and body, marriage and friendship, upper and lower class) that, given his own sexual nature and his moment in history, defeats and isolates him just as it did Tony Failing.

[An omitted passage here discusses the pattern of exclusion and union in the text in terms of A. J. Greimas's structuralist approach to semiotics. Ed.]

Wholeness is a possibility for Forster as an attribute of a classless society and an unconventional family. The Janus-faced image of Aphrodite, the union of mother–brother–self (or mother–child–self), implies Forster' ideal solution to an historical and sexual impasse. Union may be achieved without exclusion only in a classless society, whose counterpart is an unconventional family unmarked by the phallic intrusion of the law of sexual division. The heavy reliance on visual imagery and the anti-intellectualism which often appear in For- ster's novels, the mistrust of articulated statement, may be a rejection of this law of the Father, which, as Lacan theorises, situates and separates the subject in the symbolic order of discourse. As Jacqueline Rose writes, '[for Lacan] refusal of the phallic term brings with it an attempt to reconstitute a form of subjectivity free of division, and hence a refusal of the notion of symbolisation [language] itself'.[24]

It must be remembered that, in considering the attainment of adult male identity to be the result of successful negotiation of the Oedipal passage, we arrive at an idea about what constitutes matur- ity, as opposed to weakness and inadequacy, in a circular fashion. We believe that passing through the Oedipal stage, and accepting the Law of the Father, is realistic and mature; but we believe this because we have already defined reality and maturity as the ability to pass successfully through this stage. It is impossible to see that socialisation and the law enforcing socialisation are identical; therefore, it is impossible to see how arbitrary the Law is – and how arbitrary our definition, and valuation, of social 'maturity' is – deriving as it does from our acceptance of the status of the phallus, which is, in fact, a fraud.

Rickie tries to achieve a more inclusive reality than is permitted in the pre-given structure of social and sexual roles in the symbolic order, but he, too, is inhibited by his socialisation so that he experiences sexual regret and social revulsion. Despite the attraction to Stephen that Forster himself expressed at various times in his life, Rickie's disapproval of Stephen, especially of his drinking and vulgarity, follows a pattern of attraction–repulsion on the part of an upper middle-class character to a lower class character which, as Stone's essay on Forster and class demonstrates, occurs repeatedly in Forster's work. The misogyny of this novel, which is more overtly displayed in the posthumously published homosexual fiction, is another expression of a disabling sexual socialisation. Despite its implicit questioning of phallocentric discourse, its struggle to achieve sexual and social inclusiveness, this text ultimately confronts an impasse which it cannot effectively resolve. That Forster should have shared with Shakespeare the conviction that failure to father children is a 'famine' (Sonnet 1), a 'murderous shame' committed against the self (Sonnet 9), a self-killing (Sonnet 6) is painful to realise. But it is this realisation that explains Rickie's relapse into anomie and the violence of his death which seems almost the punitive act of author against character. The judgement of Rickie is the same as that Shakespeare pronounces in Sonnet 11: 'Let those whom Nature hath not made for store, / Harsh, featureless, and rude, barrenly perish.' By condemning his own 'infirmity', by annihilating himself as a subject so that he may be replaced by another, Rickie engages in self-loathing and in mystification of the Other, rather than in genuine attempts to transcend the disfigurement of phallic discourse which has crippled him. As Lacan writes, 'After all in being Other there is no need to know that one is'.[25] Instead of accepting himself, Rickie invests in an 'ideal' self whom the text empowers with all the privileges of the resented Father – most specifically, with the power of naming.

There is no resolution to Rickie's dilemma within the conceptual-emotional schema of *The Longest Journey*. Rickie's consciousness remains disunified – torn within the system of differences in which he must live but to which he cannot 'adapt'. He is pulled between valuing the life of culture and the small coterie and desiring the vitality of the body and democratic brotherhood; between resentment and love of a woman; between the poles of a complex sexual and social psychology which, although it drives him to pursue his own self-knowledge in a series of Others, finally leads him back to his own infirmity: his sense of incompleteness and his need to seek completion in impossible fantasy rather than in self-acceptance.

From *Novel*, 20 (1986–7), 237–59.

NOTES

[This and the next essay make out a case for *The Longest Journey*, the novel of Forster's which has not been regarded as successful and which does not seem to possess a unity of its own. Perhaps significantly, it has not yet been filmed. Both essays find that a symptomatic reading of it – i.e. one that looks at its unconscious, and what is not fully articulated in it, what it cannot say but can only imply or point to as an absence – is more rewarding, however, than regarding it as a novel with an appearance of completeness. Stoll sees earlier criticism of *The Longest Journey* (which tended to dismiss the novel) as disabled since it made an assumption about the proper and essential unity of the individual as a centred subject. Following the French psychoanalyst Jacques Lacan, Stoll argues the text undermines this sense of the unified subject. Stoll uses Fredric Jameson to argue that every text works with an unconscious which *displaces* its subject-matter, and uses Lacan to argue that the subject has no essential being but is brought into focus ('constituted') through the ideological power of language, so that naming the subject mis-names it, mis-describes it, by assigning it a centre (e.g. as heterosexual or as homosexual). Stoll argues rather for de-centredness, and sees Rickie as mis-named by the educative and normalising pressures put on him. The text does not attend to homosexuality specifically; it is rather displaced into other love relationships and problems which are discussed, but in moving towards it, Forster is developing a perception of character as decentred, its energies not necessarily specifically directed. But at the same time, Stoll argues against the text's misogyny as raising questions about the price at which Rickie – or Forster – asserts a new kind of being. References are to the Abinger edition of *The Longest Journey* (New York, 1984). Ed.]

1. In a note partly reproduced in his Introduction to the World's Classics edition of *The Longest Journey*, Forster wrote: 'Although so vague and stagey, [Stephen] is the only character who exists for me outside his book... I received, I created, I restored' (quoted, P. N. Furbank, *E. M. Forster: A Life*, 2 vols (New York, 1977), I, 149.

2. P. N. Furbank II, 319.

3. Fredric Jameson, *The Political Unconscious: Narrative as a Socially Symbolic Act* (London, 1981), p. 180.

4. Ann Rosalind Jones, 'Writing the Body: Toward an Understanding of *l'Ecriture feminine'*, *The New Feminist Criticism: Essays on Women, Literature, and Theory*, ed. Elaine Showalter (New York, 1985), pp. 361–77, p. 364.

5. Forster's plot outline is reproduced in Furbank, I, 118.

6. The lines Rickie reads from Shelley, rejecting the notion that he should 'With one sad friend, perhaps a jealous foe. / The drearest and the longest journey go', appear on pp. 126–7 of the Abinger edition. For discussions of the uses of Wagner in Forster's text, see Tony Brown and Elizabeth Heine, Editor's Introduction to the Abinger edition of *The Longest Journey*, pp. x–xv.

7. See Rita McWilliams-Tullberg on the indictment of Cambridge by the press at the turn of the century, when its refusal to admit women as university degree candidates opened it to charges of ingrownness and social isolation. A typical criticism, in the *Lincolnshire Echo*, remarked on 'the species of a powerful University forgetting its logic in a fit of prejudice, selfishness and timidity' (Rita McWilliams-Tullberg, *Women at Cambridge: A Men's University – Though of Mixed Type* [London, 1975], p. 132).

8. 'Epipsychidion', *Selected Poetry*, ed. Neville Rogers (Boston, 1968), p. 246.

9. E. M. Forster, *Maurice* (Harmondsworth, 1971), p. 10.

10. Terry Eagleton, *Literary Theory: An Introduction* (Minneapolis, 1983), p. 183.

11. The novel does not, of course, 'endorse' Freud's theories concerning the origins of homosexuality. In fact, it leans towards the theory Havelock Ellis set forth in *Sexual Inversion* (1897) that homosexuality may be inborn and inherited. What the text offers is a psychosexual (and sociosexual) dynamics compatible with that explored by Freud and present as well in the procreation sonnets. Elizabeth Heine considers when and what Forster knew about actual Freudian theory regarding homosexuality (Editors' Introduction to the Abinger *The Longest Journey*, pp. xviii–xxvi). I would add to her remarks that awareness of Freudian theory was a possibility for him – via Ellis and G. L. Dickinson – before 1910, and I would certainly agree with her that Forster, like Freud, was enough of a symbolist consciously, as well as unconsciously, to have 'intended' what we would call the Freudian implications of many of his symbols and of the traits and relationships of his characters.

12. Sigmund Freud, *Leonardo da Vinci: A Psychosexual Study of an Infantile Remembrance*, trans. A. A. Brill (New York, 1916), p. 66.

13. In this respect the anagrammatic suggestiveness of Stephen's surname is striking; 'Wonham' yields the word 'woman', and it is phonetically close to 'womb'. The connections are consistent with other, recurrent impulses in Forster's fiction. Repeatedly in the fiction a central figure who is him (or her) self 'sterile' becomes a parent through a surrogate self, and the union that actually produces the child often violates sociosexual taboos which are considered in the world Forster writes about to be essential to the natural order of things. The great desire for progeny and the simultaneous identification with and resentment of women which these unorthodox unions and births reflect become disturbingly explicit in 'Little Imber', the last short story Forster wrote – in 1961, less than three years before he returned to the Rings, when he was almost eighty-three. The two central characters – the elderly, cultivated Warham (a reworking of Wonham, and an indication of the interchangeability of Forster's alter ego?), and a rough, virile, young man named Imber – meet during their missionary travels for a country in which the male birthrate has been drastically declining. Instead of impregnating the women of the colony they visit, as intended, they join their seed and produce not one child, but the beginning of a whole race of 'Romuloids and Remoids', each of whom desires his 'own younger brother' (E. M. Forster, 'Little Imber', *Arctic Summer and Other Fiction*, ed. Elizabeth Heine [Abinger edition, New York, 1981], p. 235). When finally the male and female birthrate figures are reversed, there is rejoicing because, in the last words of the story, 'Male had won' (p. 235).

14. In the diary entry which contains Foster's retrospective on 1907, the year *The Longest Journey* was completed, he includes a reading list largely composed of writers on homoerotic subjects. Among them were Whitman, Pater, Symonds, Housman, Edward Carpenter, Samuel Butler, Edward Fitzgerald, and Shakespeare (Furbank, I, 59n).

15. C. L. Barber, 'Full to Overflowing', *New York Review of Books*, 25:5 (6 April 1978), 35.

16. Freud, *Leonardo da Vinci*, p. 65.

17. Jane Pinchin, *Alexandria Still: Forster, Durrell and Cavafy* (Princeton, NJ, 1977), p. 95.

18. *Where Angels Fear to Tread*, ed. Oliver Stallybrass (Abinger edition, New York, 1975), p. 109.

19. Shakespeare, Sonnet 3. Cf. the lines from the *Epipsychidion* which use a similar set of associations to recall the poet's progenitor and ideal self:

> A Metaphor of Spring and Youth and Morning;
> A Vision like incarnate April, warning,

With smiles and tears, Frost the Anatomy
Into his grave.

(pp. 120–3)

That much of Shelley's and Forster's language may have shared a common source (an intertextual fact in which Forster, who loved to keep secrets from his readers, would have delighted) is tantalisingly suggested by a rejected passage from the manuscript of *Epipsychidion*, in which Shelley wrote:

> If any should be curious to discover
> Whether to you I am a friend or lover,
> Let them read Shakespeare's taking thence
> A whetstone for their dull intelligence.

(Selected Poetry, ed. Neville Rogers (Boston, 1968), pp. 34–7, 257)

20. Wilfred Stone, 'Overleaping Class: Forster's Problem in Connection', *Modern Language Quarterly,* 39 (1976), 401–2.

21. John Colmer, *E. M. Forster. The Personal Voice* (London, 1975), p. 3.

22. Comparable scenes occur in *Where Angels Fear to Tread*, with Caroline Abbott, Gino Carella, and his infant son – posed before an Italian landscape – explicitly described as 'Virgin and Child, with Donor' (p. 11) and at the conclusion of *Howards End*, where Margaret and Helen Schlegel are seated in the middle of a hay-making field with Helen's son. In each scene, one of the child's natural parents is missing, and in the cases just cited he or she is replaced by a 'truer' parent.

23. See 'A Love Letter' in Jacques Lacan, *Feminine Sexuality*, trans. Jacqueline Rose and Juliet Mitchell (London, 1983), pp. 149–61, especially p. 156.

24. *Feminine Sexuality,* p. 56.

25. *Feminine Sexuality*, p. 156. See also Lacan's discussion of the mirror stage in *Ecrits: a Selection*, trans. Alan Sheridan (London, 1977), pp. 1–7. For an elaboration of his concept of desire, see 'The Meaning of the Phallus' in *Feminine Sexuality*, pp. 74–85.

3

Absent Father, Passive Son: The Dilemma of Rickie Elliot in *The Longest Journey*

CAROLA M. KAPLAN

The fundamental task of every son, as the neo-Freudian Jacques Lacan has pointed out, is to come to terms with his father. In order to do so, he must abandon the imaginary state of non-differentiation or fusion with the mother to assume his symbolic place within the family triad. Not only the child's predecessor within the family, but the symbolic embodiment of law and language, the father is the transcendent signifier whose legacy is orderly progression both in life and in narrative. Since language expresses desire, which originates in absence, the child's acknowledgement of the father is accompanied by a permanent sense of loss. Accordingly, the child's accommodation is always problematical and imperfect. The imperfect outcome of this universal struggle gets expressed in the nature of narrative itself: although primarily linear and orderly, all narrative collapses at times into disorder – into digression, evasion, omission, ambiguity, and contradiction. Some narratives irretrievably founder on the way, either broken on the hard rock of Scylla, the father, or swallowed by the chaos and absorption of the mother, Charybdis.[1] *The Longest Journey* is such a narrative. While its unfolding appears to be linear, it is actually circular and repetitious. Finally it collapses upon itself.

The most unconscious and personal of Forster's published novels, *The Longest Journey* was, in Forster's words, the one he was 'most glad to have written'.[2] He nevertheless was regretfully aware that it was seriously flawed. Critics have generally agreed. Indeed, the book suffers from a number of problems, among them the author's ambivalence toward his protagonist, the contrivance of the plot, the heavy-handed symbolism, and the gratuitous 'sacrificial' death of the main character. Yet the book is fascinating, vivid, and strange: it has far greater vitality and psychological depth than Forster's more apparently finished novels of this early period, *Where Angels Fear to Tread* and *A Room with a View*. I would argue that the book's narrative problems, as well as its unique intensity, stem from the pervasiveness of the oedipal conflicts which it presents in disguised forms but fails to resolve within the text.

These conflicts centre in Forster's protagonist, Rickie Elliot. Having been abandoned in childhood by his father, first through neglect and then through death, Rickie as a young adult is confused and irresolute, fixed in the constellation of his childhood feelings – hatred of his father and idealisation of his mother. The novel stages a series of successive unsatisfactory solutions to Rickie's dilemma. While apparently charting a progression or movement in Rickie's life, the novel actually demonstrates Rickie's paralysis. In apparently different forms, the novel presents but fails to resolve the same psychological and sexual problems. The treatment of these episodes is marked by disguise and evasion, both socially necessary for the author and psychologically imposed upon the character, which result in the collapse of both the protagonist and the narrative.

The title of the novel, *The Longest Journey*, signals the central problem of the text. Drawn from a passage in Shelley's 'Epipsychidion',[3] the words in their original context are part of an extended declamation against the folly of loving one person to the exclusion of all others. In general, the title has been interpreted as Forster's criticism of marriage, in particular of the marriage of his semi-autobiographical protagonist, Rickie Elliot. Because this marriage denies and betrays his fundamental homosexuality, Rickie Elliot appears to be a martyr on the altar of conventionality. For this reason, the novel seems to be Forster's exploration of a 'There but for the grace of God go I' theme. In actuality, however, the exclusive and suffocating relationship which the novel inveighs against is Rickie's continued attachment to his dead mother, which makes both independent action and other relationships impossible for him.

On the surface, the novel asserts the value of Rickie's continued devotion to his mother. In fact, it offers as the only consolation for Rickie's death at the end the fact that, by sacrificing his own life to save that of his half-brother, Stephen, Rickie ensures that his mother's line will continue. Indeed, the novel's last words offer the comfort that Stephen has a daughter to whom he has given 'the name of their mother'.[4] On the other hand, the subtext of the novel makes clear that Rickie's regressive efforts to bring his mother back to life undermine him and that he thereby avoids the more difficult task, essential to his own salvation, of claiming his dead father both as genitor and as point of origin (what Lacan refers to as the Name-of-the-Father).[5] Only by fulfilling this task can Rickie assume his symbolic position as the third point in the family and social triad, permanently distinct from both mother and father, freed from the danger of reabsorption and death.

Because Rickie's loving but remote mother died when he was only fifteen, Rickie still longs for her and wishes to bring her back to life. Indeed, the novel offers Rickie two opportunities symbolically to do so. He finds these opportunities so irresistible that he succumbs to the second, while suffering from the disastrous results of the first.

The first opportunity offers itself to him in the figure of Agnes, who misleadingly reminds him of his dead mother. The second opportunity presents itself more ambiguously in the form of his half-brother, Stephen. Rickie's seductive opportunity to bring his mother back to life, his ability to get 'to a place where only one thing matters – that the Beloved should rise from the dead' (p. 249), proves to be a poisonous magic apple, luscious on the surface, lethal at the core. The subtext makes clear that the only way that the son can claim his own self is to leave the mother behind. In order to do so, he must undertake a quest for the absent father, an ordeal akin to the journeying of traditional heroes, including Oedipus and Parsifal, to whom Rickie is compared in the text. By finding, identifying with, repudiating, and finally transcending the father, Rickie can claim and name himself, freed from passivity to independent action. But, although offered many opportunities, Rickie is repeatedly unable to do so. Accordingly, his return to the mother proves to be 'the dreariest and the longest journey', indeed, one which offers no possibility other than death.

The novel opens on Rickie in a dormant state, a seed embedded in the fertile soil of Cambridge, ready to germinate. The opening scene, set in Rickie's room, emphasises his passivity and receptiveness:

while his friends argue both sides of the old subject–object opposition, questioning whether 'the cow is there' (p. 3), Rickie absorbs pleasant sensory impressions, savours the company of his friends, and observes of the two opposed arguments, 'Either way it was attractive' (p. 4). Although Rickie disparages himself for lack of ability at debate, the narrative supports him in his unwillingness to take an either or position and gently undercuts the narrowness of those who do. The imagery surrounding Rickie's philosopher friends – their shadows reflected on the walls of Rickie's firelit room – recalls Plato's Allegory of the Cave (the allusion to Plato is reinforced by the narrative reference to the group as a 'symposium' [p. 6]). Their limitations are further underscored when Rickie later acknowledges that Ansell cannot 'understand lovers or a dying man' and that Cambridge dons 'dealt with so much and they had experienced so little. Was it possible he would ever come to think Cambridge narrow?' (p. 57).

Yet, as Ansell observes, although Cambridge is a limited world, it is a good one, because it does not pretend to be the great world. The particular poignancy the Cambridge world holds for Rickie is its transitoriness: it is merely 'the perishable home that was his for a couple of years' (p. 59). While Cambridge has cared for him like a loving mother ('Cambridge ... had taken and soothed him, and warmed him, and had laughed at him a little, saying that he must not be so tragic yet awhile' [p. 5]), she will expel him into larger experiences, for which he feels unprepared. His experience at Cambridge is, moreover, the most satisfactory period of his life. Indeed, the disproportionately long 'Cambridge' section of the narrative prepares the reader for the fact that Rickie will never again enjoy so authentic an experience. As he points out to Ansell, 'There'll never again be a home for me like Cambridge. I shall only look at the outside of homes' (p. 63). The narrative demonstrates that Rickie's anxiety is justified, for he is doomed.

While Rickie is at Cambridge, Ansell attempts to save him from his doom. Ansell, whose strength of character derives largely from his balanced relationship with his father and clear distinction from him, raises for Rickie the central question of the book. After Rickie has asserted 'I hate no one', Ansell asks, 'Not even your father?' (p. 20). Answering this question is crucial for Rickie, and is fundamentally connected with his development. Rickie has not yet attained the inclusive outlook he admires and which the book on the whole advocates, an outlook which would synthesise intellect, imagination, and intuition, the book's three points of value. What appears to be inclusiveness at this stage in Rickie's life is actually indeterminacy and lack of definition. In order for Rickie to achieve his own integrated view of the world, he must learn who he is, a task he can accomplish only through knowing his origin. Yet Rickie never answers Ansell's leading question, choosing instead to elicit sympathy by telling his life story to his friends rather than take a position which might alienate some of them.

Because Rickie has failed to seize the opportunity that Ansell offered him, he goes on to make one of the crucial errors of his life. This mistake follows from an apparently innocuous incident. Rickie stumbles upon the lovers Agnes and Gerald, locked in each other's arms. This incident re-evokes for him what Freud terms the primal scene of early childhood,[6] the young child's inadvertent observation of his parents making love. That Gerald and Agnes are psychologically and symbolically equated with his parents in Rickie's mind is clear from the language of the text. Prior to this scene, Rickie has misinterpreted Agnes' breeziness and Gerald's brusqueness to mean that they do not love each other. His false misgivings derive from his connecting them in his mind with his parents: 'It was dreadful: they did not love each other. More dreadful even than the case of his father and mother, for they, until they married, had got on pretty well' (p. 39). As the scene proceeds, it appears to be a reworking in a more satisfactory way of a scene between his parents that Rickie had witnessed. Rickie had heard his mother crying, running from the bedroom, after his father had slapped her (p. 25). In the scene between Gerald and Agnes, Agnes complains that the rough Gerald is hurting her, until he kisses her, whereupon she appears transformed: 'Her face had no expression.... Then her lover kissed it, and immediately it shone with mysterious beauty, like some star' (p. 39). Rickie's response to this scene is clearly not that of a peer but of a child stumbling upon adults: 'It was the merest accident that Rickie had not been disgusted. But this he could not know' (p. 40).

Witnessing this primal scene between Gerald and Agnes reawakens Rickie's libidinous longings for his mother – longings which are intensified by Rickie's earlier refusal to acknowledge his father and his father's relationship with his mother. At first, Rickie's response is to idealise the lovers. But when Gerald dies, Rickie re-engages in the fantasy of possessing the forbidden mother. Again, the descriptions of Agnes and of Rickie's feelings about her point out the fact that Agnes is a stand-in for Mrs Elliot. When Rickie first brings Agnes to meet his Aunt Emily, she equates Rickie with his father and Agnes with his mother, pointing out that Agnes has uttered the 'exact words' his mother did on that occasion (p. 93). Finally, Rickie notes that Agnes is similar to Mrs Elliot in her reticence and emotional distance: 'She was not cold; she would willingly embrace him. But she hated being upset, and would laugh or thrust him off when his voice grew serious. In this she reminded him of his mother' (p. 168). Because his love for Agnes is but his love for his dead mother in disguise, Rickie feels extremely guilty. The language describing these feelings makes clear that it is not merely that Rickie feels unworthy of love and hates himself, but that he sees Agnes in particular as a forbidden love object because he sees her as belonging permanently to Gerald, who in his cruel treatment of Rickie, reminded him of his father:

> It was hard on Rickie thus to meet the devil. He did not deserve it, for he was comparatively civilised, and knew there was nothing shameful in love. But to love this woman! If only it had been anyone else! Love in return – that he could expect from no one, being too ugly and unattractive. But the love he offered would not then have been vile. The insult to Miss Pembroke, who was consecrated, and whom he had consecrated, who could still see Gerald, and always would see him, shining on his everlasting throne – this was the crime from the devil, the crime that no penance would ever purge. She knew nothing. She never would know. But the crime was registered in heaven.
>
> (p. 66)

In addition, Rickie's view of himself as an inadequate son, unable to take his dead father's place in his mother's life, taints the marriage from the start. Rickie feels so guilty that he needs to foredoom his efforts to possess the mother. Accordingly, he insists to Agnes, 'Never forget that your greatest thing is over.... What he [Gerald] gave you then is greater than anything you will get from me' (p. 74).

Although Rickie's marriage to Agnes is a serious error, it need not be a fatal one, for he is offered a second opportunity to claim his authentic self, through the appearance in his life of his half-brother, Stephen. From the first, Rickie recognises Stephen's importance for him. Even before he knows that Stephen is his brother, he has a vision, while out horseback-riding with him. In this vision, he sees himself and Agnes approach the Throne of God, as if to receive a judgement (p. 110). The imagery of this vision, which recalls the imagery of godhead surrounding Gerald in Rickie's mind, clearly links Stephen with Gerald. More importantly, this vision urges Rickie to a confrontation with the father in the image of deity, a confrontation he rejects, along with Stephen, when he abruptly decides to return to Agnes. Rickie later looks back on that scene with Stephen on Salisbury Plain as a supreme lost opportunity.

Later, after fainting at learning that Stephen is his brother, Rickie hears Stephen call his name. Hearing it, Rickie not only wakes up but 'For one short moment he understood' (p. 130) and is ready to accept Stephen as his brother. Not only does this scene signify some of the magical quality that resides in a name,[7] but it recalls the fact that it is the father who is the giver of the name. In this instance, Stephen calls him by his rightful surname 'Elliot', not Rickie, meaning rickety, the name his father had given him out of cruelty. In response, Rickie calls 'Stephen', before Agnes runs to restore him to the world of convention, calling 'Rickie! Rickie!' (p. 130).

Then Rickie makes one last effort to acknowledge Stephen. He says to Agnes:

> 'It seems to me that here and there in life we meet with a person or incident that is symbolical. It's nothing in itself, yet for the moment it stands for some eternal principle. We accept it, at whatever cost, and we have accepted life. But if we are frightened and reject it, the moment, so to speak, passes; the symbol is never offered again.'
>
> (p. 36)

Linking this moment in his mind with the moment in which he beheld Agnes and Gerald, Rickie knows that he must acknowledge his connection with Stephen by telling him they are brothers. Yet he is persuaded by Agnes not to do so. His denial of Stephen is connected with his denial of his father, for, so far as Rickie can know at this point in the narrative, Stephen must be his father's son. As such, Rickie reasons that Stephen must be bad: 'There will be no reward ... from such a man – the son of such a man. But I want to do what is right' (p. 137). Even when offered evidence of Stephen's goodness, as when a woman comes to thank Stephen for rescuing her child from the railroad crossing – Rickie denies it. Paradoxically, by his denial of the father, Rickie ascribes to him greater power than he could ever ordinarily have. He assumes that the father has absolute power to determine the nature of his offspring. Of course, by this reasoning, Rickie himself must also be bad, a conclusion which he simultaneously accepts (as evidenced by his self-hatred) and rejects (by identifying himself only with his mother). Thus, while maintaining that it is 'our duty to acknowledge each man accurately, however vile he is' (p. 137), by failing to apply this principle to Stephen and to his father, Rickie descends into unreality.

Rickie's repeated failures to acknowledge the father are in actuality a rejection in response to rejection. Not only has Rickie's own father been disappointing, but all father figures in the novel prove disappointing, including the ineffectual Tony Failing and the ghost-like Robert. In a sense, the figure of the father seems to split, like figures in dream and folktale, into good father and bad father. But even the good fathers, Tony Failing and Robert, are inaccessible. Good fathers, as well as bad fathers, are conspicuously absent: all are guilty of the ultimate abandonment through death of their natural and spiritual children (Rickie, we are told, is Tony Failing's 'spiritual heir' [p. 195]).

The narrative makes clear that Rickie cannot accept Stephen until he is ready to do so. By the time that Stephen reappears in his life, Rickie has been prepared to acknowledge him by the failure of his marriage, by the death of his child (which he sees as a proof of the error of his marriage), and by Stephen's vulnerable position (Stephen has been turned out of his aunt's house without any inheritance), for which Rickie is largely responsible. But Rickie wants to accept Stephen on his own terms: he wants Stephen to live in his house and function in his life as a re-embodiment of their mother, as Agnes was to have been. Clearly, the model for Rickie's treatment of Stephen is his mother's childhood treatment of him. Just as he had urged his mother to mould him to her own specifications, saying, 'I shall be as wax in your hands' (p. 27), Rickie proposes to mould Stephen by finding him a job, by ensuring his sobriety, and by keeping a watchful eye on him.

But Stephen sees through this offer and refuses it. 'I see your game. You don't care about me drinking, or to shake my hand. It's someone else you want to cure – as it were that old photograph [of their mother]' (p. 255). Rickie grants the accuracy of this accusation. 'The man was right. He did not love him, even as he had never hated him. In either passion he had degraded him to be a symbol for the vanished past' (p. 255). Stephen then proposes as an alternative that he and Rickie go off together, as men first, brothers second. 'Come with me as a man....Not as a brother; who cares what people did years back? We're alive together, and the rest is cant' (p. 257). The relationship that Stephen proposes would be very different from the one Rickie originally envisioned. This friendship would be based upon love, not nostalgia, and upon the acceptance of Stephen as a real person, flaws and all, rather than as a idealisation of a dead person.

Rickie tries to enter into a relationship with Stephen on these terms, but he is unequal to it. To do so would mean simultaneously to accept and to move beyond the symbolic figure of the father. It would also mean acknowledging the mother as a real woman, with her own sexual life, as well as symbolically, as the father's sexual partner (whether that of the good father or of the bad father does not matter). Finally, in order to forge this new relationship with Stephen, Rickie would have to give up the incestuous fantasy that Stephen is his own child, the product of his union with his dead mother, a being whom Rickie as the father can mould as he wishes.

Of course, Rickie, who has not consciously acknowledged any of these impulses, has great difficulty in this undertaking. In addition, the narrator, by idealising the description of Rickie's mother and of her lover, Robert, and by desexualising the narrative of their affair makes it appear not merely difficult but impossible for Rickie to do so. Robert is described in idealised terms, an improbable mixture of farmer and gentleman, who lives so short a time in the narrative and in Mrs Elliot's life that he need never be socially 'placed'. Even more tellingly, the narrative avoids looking straight at the sexual relationship of these lovers, as evidenced by the peculiar statement, 'They had...given him [Stephen] a cloudless spirit – the spirit of the seventeen days in which he was created'. To state that a child has been 'created' over seventeen days is to deny that he is the product of any single sexual act.

Because Rickie cannot give up the fantasy of possessing the dead mother or the attendant fantasy of returning to her bosom with Stephen as a twin brother, he has no way of claiming his own life, and his muddled journey ends in death. Similarly, because the narrative is undermined by a subtext that parallels Rickie's self-destructive course, it too is doomed to failure. But in its failure as a linear narrative, in its unwillingness to recognise the law of the father as the author of discourse, it raises interesting questions about the nature of narrative itself.

In Forster's introduction, written in 1960 for the Oxford World's Classics edition of *The Longest Journey*, he notes that, in the writing of the novel, 'sometimes I went wrong deliberately, as if the spirit of anti-literature had jogged my elbow'.[8] This spirit of anti-literature surfaces most particularly in Forster's overt essay-like criticisms of modern-day culture, whose spiritual centre is God the Father, whose social centre is marriage, and whose self-justification is the idea of progress.

Forster seeks to dethrone the patriarchal deity of Christianity and to reinstate in His place the nature of deities of earlier religions – Demeter, Artemis, and Pan. Forster's primary objection to Christianity is that the law of the Father imposes a strict moral dualism which is too narrow and coercive a guideline for human behaviour. Limited by this framework, even the benevolent Mr Failing condemns the humanly justified and psychologically fulfilling liaison of Mrs Elliot and her lover. That fixed ideas of good and evil are inadequate as criteria for human behaviour is reinforced by the narrator's comment on Rickie: 'Rickie suffered from the Primal Curse, which is not – as the Authorised Version suggests – the knowledge of good and evil but of good-and-evil' (p. 171).

Yet Forster felt great uneasiness and uncertainty in urging the return of the ancient gods, as his many revisions of the novel point out. While earlier drafts include extensive reference to these deities, including an entire chapter which allies Stephen with the god Pan and which shows his illumined outlook on life to result from a panic (from a direct encounter with the nature deity), Forster deleted these passages from later versions of the novel.[9] In the long run, he rejected so overt an effort to integrate mythic materials into the text. From early on, Forster felt ambivalence about attempting to write what he called 'prophetic fiction'. On the one hand, he criticised fiction that lacks a sense of mystery.[10] On the other hand, he retained a certain mistrust of fiction that attempts to integrate in a single work actions on different planes. He later expressed this uneasiness in *Aspects of the Novel*, noting the wrecked appearance of even the greatest prophetic novels, including those of Dostoyevski and Lawrence: 'The novel through which bardic influence has passed often has a wrecked air, like a drawing-room after an earthquake or a children's party.'[11]

These doubts surface repeatedly in *The Longest Journey*. They are expressed in Rickie's dismissal of his own short story of the supernatural: 'But what nonsense! When real things are so wonderful, what is the point of pretending?' (p. 60). They are voiced in Agnes' ironic description of Rickie's literary efforts: 'He muddles all day with poetry and old dead people, and then tries to bring it into life. It's too funny for words' (p. 50). They are reflected in Stephen's perplexed amusement at his story about a dryad: 'What a production!

Who was this girl?.... The girl was a tree!' (p. 119). Finally, Forster seems to express his own misgivings through the editor who tells Rickie, 'Your story does not convince' (p. 143).

Certainly, Forster's diary entry of 23 March 1906, after he had written most of the novel, expresses grave reservations: 'Doubt whether novel's any good: all ingenious symbols: little flesh and blood.'[12] Despite his longing to revive the old religious symbolism, Forster seems to have anticipated the criticism Lawrence later levelled at him: 'Your Pan is a stooping back to the well head, a perverse pushing back the waters to their source, and saying the source is everything. Which is stupid and an annihilation.'[13] At any rate, in a letter of 1907, Forster notes that although he thought the panic chapter 'rather jolly', he 'soon cut it out'.[14] That Forster's misgivings triumphed in his successive revisions suggests that his attitude toward Pan and other ancient deities was one of nostalgic longing rather than of conviction.

Forster experienced an equally serious dilemma in his desire to centre his novel on friendship rather than on the traditional subject of marriage. As he stated in a letter of this time, Forster was experiencing increasing difficulty in centring his fiction on the relations between men and women.[15] In *The Longest Journey*, Rickie expresses a similar regret: 'he wished there was a society, a kind of friendship office, where the marriage of true minds could be registered' (p. 64). Yet the text reluctantly acknowledges that this wish is confounded by reality: 'Abram and Sarai were sorrowful, yet their seed became as sand of the sea, and distracts the politics of Europe at this moment. But a few verses of poetry is all that survives of David and Jonathan' (p. 64). No doubt, Forster abandoned his original plan to have Stephen and Rickie go off together, because he realised that Stephen would have to produce offspring if he was to fulfil the social role the narrative prophesies for him: to guide the future course of England. As Stephen sees his role: 'He believed that he guided the future of our race, and that, century after century, his thoughts and his passions would triumph in England' (p. 289).

Surely, this peculiar and unsupported prophecy invites scrutiny. What specifically is to be Stephen's role in guiding England's future? How are he and his heirs to remedy the ills of modern society, so plentifully noted in the text? At first glance, Stephen's role seems to be a return to the land as an individual protest against the dehumanising movement from countryside to city that the narrative deplores. As the text notes, this movement cityward in search of work and in hope of economic gain has resulted in a loss of connection between people and land, of satisfying labour, and of the sense of community. Stephen's repudiation of this trend seems therefore a worthy rejection of the alienation and triviality of modern life. However, Stephen's return to the land is an option available only to a very few (surely it cannot be what Stephen alludes to as 'the future of our race'). This recourse suggests moreover flight and escape rather than moral leadership.

If, contrary to appearances, Stephen's role is not to escape into the idyllic past by living the life of an honest yeoman, perhaps it lies rather in making improvements to alleviate the worst abuses he sees around him. Indeed, the book applauds Stephen's small ameliorations: he has fired a bullying overseer, built cottages for workers and their families, and built a bridge over a dangerous railroad crossing. Yet these seem mere band-aids on the wounds of modern life.

The subtext of the novel seems to point in another direction. While deploring the abuses of capitalism (overdevelopment, pollution, crowding), it is concerned throughout with the right use of money – with rightful and wrongful inheritances and with the soul's currency ('Will it really profit us so much if we save our souls and lose the whole world?' [p. 227]). Fittingly, then, the novel concludes with Stephen making a good business deal for the posthumous publication of Rickie's stories. Thus, the narrative suggests that England's salvation lies in the hands of honest and right-minded businessmen such as Mr Ansell, whose money supports his son, and Stephen, or at least the person he eventually becomes. In other words, Forster seems to place his greatest hopes in men who use their business acumen to support and protect art and intellect. In fact, the narrative seems to indicate that without the support of the shrewd and hardheaded, these enterprises might not survive at all.

In short, Forster's narrative is ambivalent and vacillating in three of its primary concerns. The text seeks to dethrone God the Father and to return to ancient and more inclusive conceptions of deity, yet it lacks commitment to this vision. Secondly, it proposes to place friendship rather than marriage at the centre of the narrative; yet the friendship it labours to develop ends in a violent, apparently gratuitous death, which serves to pave the way for a fruitful marriage, whose progeny contain England's future. Finally, it criticises modern industrial development but applauds the business acumen that has produced it and the worthier products of that money-making talent:

the breakdown of class barriers, social amelioration, and the patronage of art and intellect.

The subtext makes equally subversive statements about narrative form as about narrative content. It demonstrates not only a distaste for linear narrative, but a mistrust of literature and of language as well. First, there is a strange indeterminacy about Rickie's fate and course of actions. Rickie suffers a strange series of collapses within the narrative, as if not only does he lose confidence in himself but the author loses confidence in him. Accordingly, right after he fails for the first time to tell Stephen about his parentage, we are told: 'The rest of the year was spent by Rickie partly in bed – he had a curious breakdown' (p. 140). After the death of his child: 'Henceforward he deteriorates. Let those who censure him suggest what he should do' (p. 193). Later, when Stephen seeks him out, he at first rejects him, but over ten days he experiences a spiritual regeneration – he moves 'from disgust to penitence, from penitence to longing, from a life of horror to a new life' (p. 249). He determines to invite Stephen to live with him but, when Stephen refuses and accuses Rickie merely of using him to reincarnate their dead mother, he collapses once again, 'heroic no longer' (p. 255). Once more, he bucks up, accepting Stephen's offer to take care of him, as they go off together, only to suffer a final collapse. Rickie is like a motor that keeps losing its generator. It is as if Forster is not only indecisive about Rickie's fate but unsure of how much autonomy to give him. Accordingly the action of the narrative veers between being mechanically foreordained and being subject at any moment to reversal of direction.

Second, the most important actions and insights are offered not in the form of event and action but in visions, dreams, and symbolic moments. That is, the novel progresses not by linear narration but by pauses or breaks in the narrative. The most important developments in the novel all take place in this way: Rickie's vision of the lovers Gerald and Agnes; Rickie's incomplete vision while horseback riding with Gerald; Rickie's lucid moment of claiming his brother before he fully returns to consciousness after fainting; Rickie's dream of his dead mother reassuring him after the death of his child; and, most importantly, Rickie and Stephen seeing their friendship affirmed in the arch of the flame boats on the water.

Finally, the narrative shows a profound distrust of books and a strong preference for gesture over language. All three characters who author books are unsuccessful in their lifetimes: Ansell's dissertation is twice rejected at Cambridge; Mr Failing's socialist experiments are unsuccessful during his lifetime and his book is published only posthumously, through his wife's efforts, accompanied by her introduction; and Rickie's stories are rejected during his lifetime and achieve success only after posthumous publication. In general, the novel argues for the supremacy of life over art. Rickie's dryad story is left to weather outdoors as Stephen falls into a delicious nap in the sun; and Mr Failing's book is battered when it is used as the weapon in a playful fight between Ansell and Stephen.[16]

In sum, much of the fascination of *The Longest Journey* lies in the ways it undermines its own narrative statements and structures. It criticises the traditional concerns of the novel – its emphasis on realistic social situations in a post-industrial society; its central treatment of marriage; and its code of values, based on patriarchal moral and religious assumptions. The circular structure and symbolism of the novel are therefore most appropriate. The circle signifies both implosion and expansion. In a sense the novel implodes. The protagonist, permanently paralysed and muddled, moves in circles, repeating his own history until his death. Recording his fate, the narrative collapses upon itself. Although critical of both the conventional concerns and forms of narrative, the novel fails in its efforts to establish new ones. But, by raising fundamental questions about the nature and limitations of fiction, the novel, like many of its symbols, opens out in ever widening circles of concentric meaning.

From *Twentieth Century Literature*, 33:2 (1987), 196–210.

NOTES

[Like Stoll's essay, Carola Kaplan reads Forster's text for a tendential modernism, and uses psychoanalytic theory, but links it to narrative theory (e.g. in Peter Brooks's *Reading for the Plot* [Oxford, 1984]) to suggest that a successful linear plot which moves towards a conclusion is one where an Oedipal struggle has been resolved. Failure to do this entails a narrative that repeats itself, that moves in circles. That this novel fails to establish itself as a linear plot suggests Forster's own failure to deal with the 'Father' – which in this case is Literature, 'normal' heterosexuality and marriage, and middle-class conceptions of progress. The novel's modernism, which would imply its radicalism, is its struggle to be 'anti-literature', but Kaplan points to areas of contradiction in Forster in the way he sets up his opposition, or fails to do so, finally compromising with the 'Father'. These failures, culminating in a compromise towards industry and business, anticipate the ground of

Howards End, but also point to Forster as compromising in the area of friendship and sexuality. Unlike Stoll, who reads *The Longest Journey* for its unconscious, displaced material, Kaplan reads for Forster's own failure in relation to the whole discourse of 'Literature' with its normalising demands. Ed.]

1. These ideas, fully presented in Jacques Lacan's *Ecrits* (Paris, 1966), are neatly summarised in Robert Con Davis, 'Critical Introduction: The Discourse of the Father', in *The Fictional Father*, ed. Robert Con Davis (Amherst, Mass., 1981), pp. 21–3.

2. E. M. Forster, 'Author's Introduction', *The Longest Journey*, ed. Elizabeth Heine, Abinger edition (London, 1984), p. lxvi. Subsequent references are to this edition, with page numbers cited parenthetically in the text.

3. The entire passage reads:

   > I never was attached to that great sect
   > Whose doctrine is, that each one should select
   > Out of the crowd a mistress or a friend,
   > And all the rest, though fair and wise, commend
   > To cold oblivion, though it is in the code
   > Of modern morals, and the beaten road
   > Which those poor slaves with weary footsteps tread,
   > Who travel to their home among the dead
   > By the broad highway of the world, and so
   > With one chained friend, perhaps a jealous foe,
   > The dreariest and the longest journey go.

   Percy Bysshe Shelley, 'Epipsychidion', *Selected Poetry*, ed. Neville Rogers (Boston, Mass., 1968), p. 246.

4. E. M. Forster, *The Longest Journey*, ed. Elizabeth Heine, Abinger edition (London, 1984), p. 289.

5. Jacques Lacan, *Speech and Language in Psychoanalysis*, trans. Anthony Wilden (Baltimore, Md., 1968), pp. 41, 127.

6. Sigmund Freud, 'A Case of Hysteria', in *The Complete Psychological Works of Sigmund Freud*, ed. James Strachey, 7 (London, 1964), pp. 79–80. See also 'Three Essays on Sexuality', pp. 196, 226.

7. In a note on the text, the editor, Elizabeth Heine, comments: 'Forster implies the almost magical power of personal names when Harold remembers his own at the sight of the Rings (p. 336) and when Agnes calls Rickie's name from the dell (p. 73) and in the Rings, when he is about to acknowledge Stephen as his brother' (p. 130). The mother's lack of a Christian name links her more directly to the ancient powers of the earth (*The Longest Journey*, p. 134).

8. Forster, 'Author's Introduction', p. lxvi.

9. 'Appendix C', in *The Longest Journey*, Abinger Edition, pp. 331–8.

10. Forster remained remarkably consistent in his literary opinions, as evidenced by a comparison of the views he expressed in his tripos essay, written in 1899, and those in the Clark lectures which he delivered in 1927, later published as *Aspects of the Novel*. A pertinent passage from the tripos essay occurs in his discussion of Fielding as a novelist: 'he wrote great books – but not the greatest books; he was too cosy and comfortable in his wayside parlours and stage coaches to wander out into the unknown country.' Autograph manuscript of English essay, 'The Novelists of the Eighteenth Century and Their Influence on Those of the Nineteenth'. E. M. Forster Papers, King's College, Cambridge. Permission to cite this unpublished material was granted by the Society of Authors on behalf of King's College, Cambridge.

11. E. M. Forster, *Aspects of the Novel* (New York, 1955), p. 125.

12. Heine, 'Editor's Introduction', *The Longest Journey*, p. xiv.

13. D. H. Lawrence to E. M. Forster, 3 Feb. 1915, Forster Papers, King's College, Cambridge. Permission to cite this unpublished material was granted by Lawrence Pollinger Ltd, the estate of Mrs Frieda Lawrence Ravagli, and Cambridge University Press.

14. Forster quoted in Heine. 'Editor's Introduction', *The Longest Journey*, p. li.

15. In his 16 June 1911, diary entry, Forster states that he feels 'weariness of the only subject that I both can and may treat – the love of men for women & vice versa'. Quoted by P. N. Furbank, *E. M. Forster: A Life* (New York, 1978), I, 199.

16. As a reviewer of this article pointed out, these episodes are prefigured in an occurrence in 'Ansell', one of Forster's early stories, published posthumously in *The Life to Come*. In 'Ansell', a bookish, frail university student re-encountered, on vacation at his cousin's estate, his childhood friend, Ansell, a sturdy, uneducated youth, now a gardener and gamekeeper. Inadvertently, Ansell drops the scholar's books into a ravine. Their loss proves to be the student's salvation: unable to complete his dissertation and to return to his dry university existence, he abandons himself to the physical pleasures of the outdoor life in the company of his robust friend. See *The Life to Come* (London, 1972), pp. 1–9.

4

'Islands of Money': Rentier Culture in *Howards End*

PAUL DELANY

I

When he was eight years old E. M. Forster inherited eight thousand pounds from his great-aunt Marianne Thornton, who came from a well-to-do family of Victorian bankers. His widowed mother had about the same amount of capital, ensuring him a comfortable home, and a Public School and Cambridge education. *The Longest Journey* deals with the emotional consequences of this secure and sheltered upbringing; *Howards End*, though not directly auto-biographical, examines Forster's *economic* origins. The novel's motto, 'Only connect ...' is usually read as a plea for emotional openness; but Forster is equally concerned with the subtle connec-tions between a class's mentality and how it gets its means of life. I want to show that Forster had a lifelong preoccupation with the morality of living on unearned income; and that in *Howards End* his aim was to move from his own experience of privilege to a com-prehensive judgement on the kind of country Edwardian Britain was, and should be.

Like Marx and Freud before him, Forster is possessed by the idea of *unmasking*; he wants to lay bare the tangled economic roots of com-placent liberalism. As wealth piled up in nineteenth-century Britain, the rentier class – those who lived mainly on investment income – had increased steadily in numbers and social influence (the Victorian cen-sus even had a special category for the 'Independent Classes'). This class produced generous supporters of the arts, philanthropy, and such good causes as the abolition of slavery; at the same time, it could be seen as compromised by its fundamentally parasitic status. 'The education I received in those far-off and fantastic days made me soft', Forster wrote in 1946, 'and I am very glad it did, for I have seen plenty of hardness since, and I know it does not even pay.... But though the education was humane it was imperfect, inasmuch as we none of us realised our economic position. In came the nice fat dividends, up rose the lofty thoughts, and we did not realise that all the time we were exploiting the poor of our own country and the backward races abroad, and getting bigger profits from our investments than we should. We refused to face this unpalatable truth.'[1]

What could be the worth or the use, Forster asked himself, of an entire class of people who lived on the labour of others? His part-time teaching at the Working Men's College, from 1902 onwards, helped sharpen his awareness of the gulf between his own comfortable existence and that of his hard-pressed students. In his darker moods he condemned himself as a milksop who lived with his mother, who was sexually backward, and who had been absolved by his inherited wealth from the need to seek a useful career.

Howards End starts from the principle stated by its heroine, Margaret Schlegel: 'independent thoughts are in nine cases out of ten the result of independent means.'[2] But if this proposition is accepted, it contains an uncomfortable lesson for people in Forster's position. It suggests that independence of mind is not entirely virtuous, because it is one of the privileges that accrue to the owners of capital. Or, to look at it another way: if independent thoughts are the result of something else, then they aren't really independent. Money talks, and money thinks; this is Margaret's claim when she goes on to tell her ladies' discussion group 'that the very soul of the world is economic':

> 'That's more like socialism', said Mrs Munt suspiciously.
> 'Call it what you like. I call it going through life with one's hand spread open on the table. I'm tired of these rich people who pretend to be poor, and think it shows a nice mind to ignore the piles of money that keep their feet above the waves. I stand each year upon six hundred pounds, and Helen upon the same, and Tibby will stand upon eight, and as fast as our pounds crumble away into the sea they are renewed – from the sea, yes, from the sea. And all our thoughts are the thoughts of six-hundred-pounders, and all our speeches; and because we don't want to steal umbrellas ourselves we forget that below the sea people do want to steal them, and do steal them sometimes, and that what's a joke up here is down there reality –.'[3]

Margaret's position is indeed 'like socialism' in saying that consciousness is determined by its economic base; but neither she nor her creator are ready to jump from this premise to revolutionary conclusions. All they feel obliged to do is to make the connection between the Schlegels' class and those, with very different outlooks, that are on each side of it. Below the Schlegels are the Basts, representing the half-submerged yet aspiring lower middle class; above them are the richer Wilcoxes, go-ahead business people 'whose hands are on all the ropes' and who stand for 'the robust ideal' (pp. 112, 38). The older sister, Margaret, concentrates on trying to understand the class above her; the younger, Helen, on understanding the class below. Each takes her sympathy to the point of sexual connection – Margaret's willed and reasoned, Helen's impulsive.

In defending to Helen her decision to marry Henry Wilcox, Margaret intellectualises her motives. 'If Wilcoxes hadn't worked and died in England for thousands of years', she bursts out, 'you and I couldn't sit here without having our throats cut. There would be no trains, no ships to carry us literary people about in, no fields even. Just savagery.... More and more do I refuse to draw my income and sneer at those who guarantee it' (pp. 177–8). Margaret, like Forster, is trying to connect her sheltered and cultured existence with what guarantees it: the organising power of the Wilcoxes. She has to admit that civility rests on the measured application of brute force, and cultural refinement on economic injustice. To understand the particular resonance of this belief in *Howards End*, it will be useful to look briefly at two earlier works on similar themes: Gaskell's *North and South* (1855) and Shaw's *Widowers' Houses* (1892). Although these works helped to shape Forster's vision of the *rentier* way of life, each had its own mood and period flavour, which were quite different from *Howards End*. As usual, Forster ended up by quietly yet firmly choosing his own path. His novel became a justification of his economic status, and a vindication of the unassuming Schlegels over the ambitious Wilcoxes. The second aim of *Howards End* – and a less successful one – was to project Schlegel values into a compelling vision of what Britain's destiny might and should be.

II

Gaskell's *North and South* sets in opposition the active and the contemplative lives, North and South, men and women. These linked oppositions are all finally reconciled in the union of Margaret Hale, daughter of a Southern vicar, with Mr Thornton, a rough-hewn Northern manufacturer. Forster may well have been influenced by Gaskell's novel in conceiving *Howards End* for he uses a similar dialectical structure, contrasting the morals and economics of two sets of characters, the Wilcoxes and the Schlegels.[4] Spatially, Forster opposes town to country rather than North to South; but a more important difference between the two novels is that Forster's ends with the triumph of one side of his opposed forces, Gaskell's with a vision of complementarity. Margaret Hale and Mr Thornton have many disagreements, but at the end they are united both sentimentally and economically. Thornton has gone bankrupt in a trade recession, in spite of his competence and hard work, while Margaret has inherited money and real estate from a family friend who was a don at Oxford. She makes Thornton a formal proposal: 'if you would take some money of mine, eighteen thousand and fifty-seven pounds, lying just at this moment unused in the bank, and bringing me in only two and a half per cent – you could pay me much better interest, and might go on working Marlborough Mills.'[5] Thornton is so moved that he counters with his own proposal, that they should get married. Margaret's acceptance brings together the strong and the sweet, the entrepreneur and the rentier, North and South, industry and finance, in one of the most comprehensive of Victorian happy endings.

Margaret Hale, as a Victorian lady, need feel no qualms about becoming a passive investor in her husband's enterprise. But Forster could not rest easily with the idea of living on the fruits of his capital while others took on for him the struggle in the marketplace. It made him feel as if he were feminised – castrated, even – and his moral misgivings were equally strong. 'Ever since I have read *Widowers' Houses*', he wrote in 1934, 'I have felt hopeless about investments.'[6] He had read the play thirty-five years before as an undergraduate. Its hero is a genteel young man, Harry Trench, who has a private income but is also about to set up a medical practice. He has fallen in love with Blanche Sartorius, but is shocked when he discovers that his prospective father-in-law is a slum landlord. Trench is even more shocked to learn that his own capital is invested in a mortgage on one of Mr Sartorius's filthy hovels. Sartorius points out to him, however, that if he liquidates the mortgage and puts the money into government bonds, his income will fall from £700 to £250 a year. After consulting his conscience, Trench decides both to marry Blanche and join Sartorius in a speculation that promises to double his capital in two years. Since one cannot belong to the upper middle class without being an exploiter, he feels that he may as well be hung for a sheep as for a lamb.

Widowers' Houses demonstrates that social status is proportional to distance from economic reality. At the bottom of the play's pecking order is the despised Mr Lickcheese, the man who actually squeezes the money out of the wretched slum-dwellers. Next comes Mr Sartorius, who owns the buildings but never sets foot in them. At the top are Dr Trench (and his aunt Lady Roxdale), who have not even troubled to find out where their comfortable private incomes came from.

In his own way, Shaw too is saying 'Only connect': that is, acknowledge the economic links that implicate each member of society in the actions of everyone else. The way of the world, however, is that people who eat meat have no desire to live next to a slaughterhouse; and by the time of *Howards End*, the rentiers have removed themselves even further than in *Widowers' Houses* from the actual workings of their capital. The English investor now thinks in global, rather than just regional or national terms. So, on reaching their majority, the Schlegel sisters remove their inheritances from 'the old safe investments' and put them into what Forster archly calls 'Foreign Things' (p. 28). The safe investments would probably be Consols – British government bonds – which for many decades had yielded a steady two and a half to three and a half per cent. If we assume that Forster himself was in the same position as the Schlegels, his £8000 would have yielded about £240 a year until he reached twenty-five, when he came into control of his money and was free to invest it more adventurously. We know that one of his new investments was in British American Great Southern Railway, one of the major Argentinian railways, which yielded about five per cent.[7] The Schlegels' aunt, Mrs Munt, wants them to keep their money in Britain, if not in bonds. She persuades them to invest a few hundred pounds in her favourite 'Home Rails'; unfortunately, 'the Foreign Things did admirably and the Nottingham and Derby declined with the steady dignity of which only Home Rails are capable' (p. 28).

The popularity of 'Foreign Things' had a powerful influence on British economic development. From about 1855 to 1914, Britain exported capital on a huge scale. New portfolio foreign investment in this period amounted to well over four billion pounds. Capital export had as its correlative the relative deprivation of domestic industry, a central feature of the extended crisis of the British economy that has featured so prominently in recent historiography.[8] Two kinds of impulses promoted the shift of capital overseas. One was the straightforward economic motive that average returns were higher in foreign than in domestic investment. But there was also a cultural aversion to the root-and-branch transformation of society that would have been required to keep pace with Britain's technical and industrial rivals, especially in the United States and Germany. The possession of an Empire made it easier for Britain to avoid a head-on industrial competition with these countries, but did not fully determine that choice. In fact, sixty per cent of her overseas investment in this period went to foreign countries, and only forty per cent to the Empire.[9] The heart of the matter was that Britain's governing classes preferred a strategy of 'external' development, whereby the City of London facilitated the transfer of massive capital resources overseas, at the expense of the traditional manufacturing industries of the North.

So far as Forster is concerned, however, industry has not been deprived enough. He does not question investment in Foreign Things because it is at the expense of Home Rails, but because immoral methods must be used to organise it. When Margaret Schlegel goes to visit Henry Wilcox at his office she sees on his wall a map of Africa, 'looking like a whale marked out for blubber' (p. 196). The reader is surely meant to think of Gillray's famous cartoon of Napoleon and Pitt carving up the world like a Christmas pudding.[10] If in *Widowers' Houses* the issue is domestic exploitation, in *Howards End* it is Imperialism, and the application of the Imperial mentality to class rule in Britain.

Henry is a self-deceiving Social Darwinist, who speaks complacently of 'the battle of life'; and cuts down the salaries of his clerks in the name of the 'survival of the fittest' (pp. 192–3). Margaret becomes steadily disillusioned with him; she comes to believe that he does not stand for the control of savagery, but is himself an expression of it. Social Darwinism gives Henry an excuse to spurn Leonard Bast, the aspiring but unlucky working man. It encourages him to exploit the 'subject races' for England's benefit, affronting Margaret's (and Forster's) anti-imperial or 'Little England' sentiments. And at home, the creed of the 'battle of life' leads to the destruction of the cherished past, the pollution of the countryside by the noise and stink of the motor car, and the loss to the English people of what they most need –

a sense of being securely rooted in their own particular corner of the earth. Margaret begins by contrasting the Wilcoxes' manly vigour with her own lack of worldly purpose; but she ends up repelled by the amoral use that the Wilcoxes make of their strength.

III

Howards End repudiates the Wilcox way of life as hopelessly philistine, materialist, and brutal. But Forster is left with the task of imagining a coherent alternative to the Wilcox culture of 'red [i.e. red-brick] houses and the Stock Exchange' (p. 170). He seeks to *disconnect* from 'the inner darkness in high places that comes with a commercial age' (p. 322), to find a way for the Schlegels to avoid complicity in any of the Wilcox undertakings – that is to say, with commerce, imperialism, modernity itself. The obvious candidate for an alternative British culture is pastoralism, such as Forster described in the conclusion of 'The Abinger Pageant':

> Houses and bungalows, hotels, restaurants and flats, arterial roads, by-passes, petrol pumps and pylons – are these going to be England? Are these man's final triumph? Or is there another England, Green and eternal, which will outlast them? I cannot tell you, I am only the Woodman, but this land is yours, and you can make it what you will. [11]

Martin Wiener has told us how pervasive such sentiments have been in English culture since 1850, and even how constitutive of it. But Wiener says relatively little about the functional linkages between anti-industrialism and such distinctive features of English society as the dominance of the City over industry, the export of capital – that is to say, the displacement of industry overseas – and the emergence of an influential rentier class. This syndrome, if we may call it that, has allowed England to have its cake and eat it too: to enjoy the fruits of modern industry while preserving, in the South at least, an archaic and congenial mode of life modelled on a country-house (or country cottage) ideal.

   C. K. Hobson's book *The Export of Capital*, published in 1914,[12] is refreshingly explicit about the structural changes in the British economy that are the direct and intended results of capital export. He notes, for example, that 'the decay of British agriculture [was] largely attributable to the development of railways in new countries' (p. xxv). These are the same railways that Forster personally invested in. Furthermore, the depopulation of the British country-side after the Corn Laws was precisely what made it possible for the bohemian fringe of the middle class to move into their country cottages and play at being rustics. Foreign investment may contribute to the decline of British manufacturing, Hobson notes; but when the profits are repatriated they are 'likely to mean an increased demand for labour in certain kinds of industry – e.g. for artists, printers, dressmakers, domestic servants, gardeners, chauffeurs' (p. 236). In recent years, the familiar chorus of lamentation about the relative decline of Britain tends to ignore the segment of the economy that is based on internationally-oriented finance capital, and that has continued to be viable, prosperous, and politically dominant.[13] If Britain has been in decline, one can only say that large parts of it are declining in style.

Forster's pastoralism, however, seeks to be a true alternative to modernity, rather than a self-serving myth of finance capital. An essential part of his case against the Wilcoxes, that Imperial family, is that they can enjoy their traditional English comforts by doing their dirty work overseas and out of sight. And if the Schlegels were to invest their capital in British industry rather than in Foreign Things, Forster would only see this as dirty work at home. His problem is how to uphold the civic and cultural virtues intrinsic to the rentier way of life, yet avoid complicity with commerce or technology.

He begins by sidestepping the charge that the rentier is a parasite who consumes, but does not produce. Helen Schlegel believes, like G. E. Moore, that 'personal relations are the important thing for ever and ever' (p. 176). Work is thus assigned a purely instrumental value, in providing the comfort and leisure that are required for agreeable personal relations. If one can have the comfort without work, so much the better for 'the important thing' in life. The Schlegels' younger brother Tibby *is* stigmatised, but for emotional rather than physical laziness. As his name suggests, he is a rather epicene young man, who warms the teapot 'almost too deftly' (p. 55). He is also a surrogate for Forster himself; as with Rickie in *The Longest Journey*, the author passes a stern sentence on those whose deficiencies are closest to his own. Tibby's languid existence contrasts with the striving Wilcoxes, but morally he is no better than them:

> Unlike Charles [Wilcox], Tibby had money enough; his ancestors had earned it for him, and if he shocked the people in one set of lodgings

he had only to move into another. His was the leisure without sympathy – an attitude as fatal as the strenuous: a little cold culture may be
raised on it, but no art. His sisters had seen the family danger, and had
never forgotten to discount the gold islets that raised them from the
sea. Tibby gave all the praise to himself, and so despised the struggling
and the submerged.

(p. 302)

Tibby is damned for his cold self-sufficiency, whereas his sisters are
redeemed by their sympathy, their eagerness for connection with the
world. These are specifically female traits, of course, and it is part of
the female image that they are not *expected* to work. Middle-class
women of this period can be thought of as rentiers by biological destiny; their vocation is to display their accomplishments, to *be* rather
than to *do*. No one would expect them to be anything but passive
investors.

Still, they have some work to do in the world – of an appropriate
kind. One of their callings is to *prevent* change, which in Forster is
almost always for the worse. In 1907, the year before he began
Howards End, the Georgian mansion of the Thornton family,
'Battersea Rise', had been torn down and its site 'completely covered
with very small two-storey houses'.[14] Forster had given money to a
campaign to save the house and garden, but nothing could be done.
Howards End is named after a house which *is* saved – even if the red
tide of semi-detached houses is lapping at its fringes – and which
ends up in the hands of those who have the moral right to inherit it,
the Schlegels.

What is at stake here is the principle of cultural continuity.
Property that is rightly transmitted and cherished from one generation to another has its own 'aura' (to borrow Walter Benjamin's
term); it contrasts, in the novel, with dwellings that are merely
passed around by the marketplace and torn down when they cease
to be profitable, like the London houses where the Schlegels are
living at the beginning of the book. The rentier is a preserver of the
aura, the precious 'spirit of place' that is threatened by the onrush-
ing chaos of modernity. A society dominated by 'new men' would
have no traditions, no landmarks to guide the succession of generations; the rentier does not build, but she guards the ancestral rites,
like the pigs' teeth embedded in the elm at Howards End.[15] She may
live on the wealth amassed by previous generations, but she can
mitigate this guilt by being a better custodian of England's heritage
than the *nouveaux-riches* Wilcoxes.

In the concluding scene of the novel the Schlegel sisters have gained a far more substantial vocation than their earlier life of concert-going and tea-drinking in London. They have become traditional female providers of nurture: Helen cares for her infant son by Leonard Bast, Margaret cares for her husband, who breaks down after his son's conviction for Bast's manslaughter. They are farmers, raising hay on the meadows around the house. And Margaret will be a philanthropist, giving away half her capital over the next ten years. When she dies the house will pass to her nephew, the living symbol of union between the bourgeois Schlegels and the proletarian Basts. As R. N. Parkinson has pointed out, Forster upholds the principle of inheritance, but according to poetic rather than formal justice: in each generation, Howards End is held by those who morally deserve to have it.[16]

Forster's own life imitated his art. His inherited capital was greatly increased by his earnings as a writer after the success of *Howards End* in 1910; but he gave away much of what he had, either to charities or to his friends.[17] In 1931, after some ups and downs in his financial affairs, he joked that 'I am not again making the mistake of investing, or even of letting it lie in the Bank. I shall bury it to be disinterred as wanted.'[18] In 1934 he started a lively controversy on the issue of ethical investment in *Time and Tide*.[19] He described how he went to South Africa in 1929 and was appalled by the treatment of black workers in the mines at Kimberley; on his return, he sold his shares in a Belgian mining company. Now, he wanted to encourage the readers of *Time and Tide* to get rid of investments in arms companies. Several readers wrote in to point out flaws in this advice, but Forster stuck to his guns. 'You can bowl anyone out on his investment list', he responded, 'but I deny that all lists are equally harmful or harmless and that one need not bother, and I think it would be healthier if people talked openly about the contents of their lists and did not conceal them like illegitimate children.'[20]

Still, a code of personal conduct does not necessarily provide the basis for a credible vision of society as a whole. The Schlegels' retreat into pastoralism is not really an adequate solution to the 'Condition-of-England' issues that are presented in the body of the novel. Margaret's strategy for dealing with the modern world is simply to wait until it renounces its own vital principle:

> 'Because a thing is going strong now, it need not go strong for ever',
> [Margaret] said. 'This craze for motion has only set in during the last

hundred years. It may be followed by a civilisation that won't be a movement, because it will rest on the earth. All the signs are against it now, but I can't help hoping, and very early in the morning in the garden I feel that our house is the future as well as the past'.

(p. 239)

Again, the contrast with the more positive outlook of *North and South* is instructive. When she revisits her old village in the South, Margaret Hale is at first dismayed not to find the rural Eden she had remembered in her Northern exile:

A sense of change, of individual nothingness, of perplexity and disappointment, overpowered Margaret. Nothing had been the same; and this slight, all pervading instability, had given her greater pain than if all had been too entirely changed for her to recognise it....

Wearily she went to bed, warily she arose in four or five hours' time. But with the morning came hope, and a brighter view of things.

'After all it is right', said she, hearing the voices of children at play while she was dressing. 'If the world stood still, it would retrograde and become corrupt.... Looking out of myself, and my own painful sense of change, the progress of all around me is right and necessary. I must not think so much of how circumstances affect me myself, but how they affect others, if I wish to have a right judgement, or a hopeful trustful heart.'

(pp. 488–9)

Margaret Schlegel gives *Howards End* its moral centre, and she is its most sympathetic character; but her social perspective, at the end, is that of a hermit in the Dark Ages. Although she has remained true to her mission of connecting classes and sexes, almost all of the novel's significant actions have been initiated by more vital characters: the Wilcoxes, Leonard Bast, her sister Helen. At the end, Forster turns Henry Wilcox into a cipher in order to remove an inconvenient force from the plot, much like the sudden deaths of unwanted characters in other Forster novels. And Henry's personal defeat is made into a facile allegory of the withering away of the class he belongs to. 'I'm broken – I'm ended' he whimpers to Margaret (p. 324); but what he represents surely is not. The device recalls D. H. Lawrence's crippling Clifford Chatterley, to point a similar moral; and it shows the artist's traditional condescension to the managerial classes, denying them any real moral or psychological complexity.[21]

Good liberal that he was, Forster was well aware of the case that could be made against his pet causes. He feared that those on the frontier of scientific thought would 'abandon literature, which has committed itself too deeply to the worship of vegetation'.[22] We can see another danger too: that English literature would waste away on its vegetarian diet – clinging to archaism and nostalgia while failing to engage the contemporary passions of the ordinary citizen. In his creative career, Forster remained a perpetual Edwardian, even though he lived until 1970. That period was the golden age of rentier culture in England – which is why it figures so prominently in England's nostalgia industry today. Everyone wants 'a room with a view'; but England is peculiar in its insistence that the view should be of the eternally sunlit meadows of the past.

From *English Literature in Transition*, 31 (1988), 285–96.

NOTES

[This essay examines Forster's politics and looks towards *A Passage to India* in taking imperialism as an issue of the text. The rentier class represented by the Wilcoxes is involved with imperialist projects abroad (e.g. Paul Wilcox works in Nigeria and the novel refers to India and South Africa); its capital goes overseas, which would not have been the case with Mr Thornton, the Manchester-based manufacturer hero of Mrs Gaskell's *North and South*, a novel that Delany brings in for comparison with *Howards End*. A consequence of capital going overseas was the increase of working-class poverty which the novel calls 'the abyss'. Socialism is referred to several times in *Howards End*, alongside the statement which opens chapter 6: 'We are not concerned with the very poor. They are unthinkable...' The furthest the novel can think about is Leonard Bast, who is petit-bourgeois, not working class, and the same chapter mocks Bast's 'hope to come to Culture' – that which liberalism, since the time of Matthew Arnold's *Culture and Anarchy* (1869), held out to be an important way of 'connecting', of bringing classes together. Delany's essay discusses the limitations of Forster's own class position and his association with the rentier class. Liberalism in Forster becomes complicity with imperialism, and with an escape towards a pastoral world (noted already in Kaplan's essay above on *The Longest Journey* and obvious in *Maurice*), with which Forster tries to evade the 'red rust' (ch. 44) of 'creeping' suburbia. The escapism seems part of the reason why in 1910 Forster virtually stops writing novels – he does not become the modernist, but remains committed to an older nostalgic form of living. Ed.]

1. 'The Challenge of Our Time', in *Two Cheers for Democracy* (Harmondsworth, 1965), p. 65.

2. O. Stallybrass (ed.) *Howards End* (Harmondsworth, 1975), p. 134. Citations in the remainder of my article are to this edition.

3. Pp. 72–3. In an earlier draft of the novel Forster gave the Schlegel sisters twice as much income, and Tibby £1500.

4. Forster paid tribute to Gaskell in 'The Charm and Strength of Mrs Gaskell', *Sunday Times*, 7 April 1957, p. 10. He mentions having met Gaskell's daughters when he was a boy.

5. Elizabeth Gaskell, *North and South* (1854–5, Harmondsworth, 1970), p. 529.

6. 'Notes On The Way', *Time and Tide*, 2 June 1934, p. 696.

7. P. N. Furbank, *E. M. Forster: A Life* (London, 1977), I, 159.

8. Martin Wiener, *English Culture and the Decline of the Industrial Spirit 1850–1980* (Cambridge, 1981). For an important revision of Wiener's view see also Geoffrey Ingham, *Capitalism Divided: The City and Industry in British Social Development* (London, 1984).

9. Matthew Simon 'The Pattern of New British Portfolio Foreign Investment, 1865–1914', in A. R. Hall (ed.), *The Export of Capital From Britain 1870–1914* (London, 1968), p. 24.

10. 'The Plumb-pudding in Danger', 1805.

11. *Abinger Harvest* (London, 1953), p. 399.

12. *The Export of Capital* (London, 1914).

13. For a recent survey of the issue, see Perry Anderson, 'The Figures of Descent', *New Left Review*, 161 (Jan./Feb. 1987).

14. *Marianne Thornton* (New York, 1956), p. 9.

15. The attitude to such rites in *North and South* is quite different. When Margaret Hale goes back to visit her old village in the South, she is shocked to hear that one of the villagers had tried to control the 'powers of darkness' by roasting alive her neighbour's cat (pp. 477–8). This 'practical paganism' is contrasted to the more progressive attitudes of the industrial North.

16. 'The Inheritors; or A Single Ticket for *Howards End*', in *E. M. Forster: A Human Exploration*, ed. G. K. Das and John Beer (London, 1979), pp. 55–68.

17. For example, £10,000 to Bob and May Buckingham in 1964. His major asset, the copyright in his writings, was left to King's College, Cambridge.

18. *Selected Letters of E. M. Forster*, ed. Mary Lago and P. N. Furbank (Cambridge, Mass., 1985), II, 107. Compare J. M. Keynes on the

'gradual disappearance of a rate of return on accumulated wealth' (the 'euthanasia of the rentier'): 'A man would still be free to accumulate his earned income with a view to spending it at a later date. But his accumulation would not grow. He would simply be in the position of Pope's father, who, when he retired from business, carried a chest of guineas with him to his villa at Twickenham and met his household expenses from it as required.' *The General Theory of Employment, Interest and Money* (London, 1973), p. 221.

19. Issues of 2 through 23 June, with associated letters to the editor.

20. *Time and Tide*, 23 June 1934, p. 797.

21. As usual, Forster himself anticipated this criticism: 'there is a huge economic movement which has been taking the whole world, Great Britain included, from agriculture towards industrialism. That began about a hundred and fifty years ago, but since 1918 it has accelerated to an enormous speed, bring[ing all sorts of changes into national and personal life....It has meant the destruction of feudalism and relationship based on the land, it has meant the transference of power from the aristocrat to the bureaucrat and the manager and the technician. Perhaps it will mean democracy, but it has not meant it yet, and personally I hate it. So I imagine do most writers, however loyally they try to sing its praises and to hymn the machine.' *Two Cheers for Democracy*, p. 278.

22. *Commonplace Book*, ed. P. Gardner (London, 1985), p. 37.

5

Gesturing Towards an Open Space: Gender, Form and Language in *Howards End*

ELIZABETH LANGLAND

E. M. Forster is a difficult writer to approach because he appears simple. His work presents none of the stylistic resistance and technical virtuosity characteristic of his notable contemporaries like Joyce and Woolf. Further, he seems to have recourse to a nineteenth-century liberal humanism in resolving his novels, an emphasis that sets at naught the complexities of literary modernism.[1] So, at best, Forster claims a precarious stake in the twentieth-century canon. But Forster accomplished something difficult and important in his novel *Howards End* that a gendered politics of reading can uncover. In his personal embattlement with gender and his embattlement with patriarchal culture, Forster exposes the constructed nature of gender and his own ambivalent relationship to traits coded 'masculine' and 'feminine' in his culture.

This gendered politics of reading begins with an acknowledgment of Forster's homosexuality and outspoken misogyny, a textual politics that is tied to a sexual politics. There is substantial evidence that Forster was deeply troubled and preoccupied by his own gender identity during this period. He had spent his own childhood largely in the female company and sheltering presence of his mother and aunt, who no doubt gave him his 'knowledge' of women and female friendship. At the same time, he was uncertain of his own sexual orientation and uncertain of even the basic facts of male–female reproduction, which Forster claimed he never fully grasped until his thirties. The conviction of his homosexuality came shortly after publication of *Howards End* when George Merrill, the working-class homosexual lover of Forster's friend Edward Carpenter, 'touched Forster's backside "gently and just above the buttocks"'. Forster continued: 'The sensation was unusual and I still remember it.... It seemed to go straight through the small of my back into my ideas, without involving my thoughts.'[2] That touch conceived *Maurice*, Forster's novel about homosexual love published only posthumously.

It wasn't until 1916 that Forster found 'total sexual fulfilment – or, as he put it, "parted with respectability"'[3] – and not until 1917 that he finally fell in love: with an Egyptian tram conductor, Mohammed-el-Adl. After that fulfilment, Forster wrote to Florence Barger: 'It isn't happiness.... it's rather – offensive phrase – that I first feel a grown up man.'[4] The offensiveness lies in the implication that a man becomes grown up through sexual mastery.

Thus, in 1910, while composing *Howards End*, Forster was in a great deal of confusion, which we can understand more fully if we consider the Victorian notion of homosexuality: *anima mulieris in corpore virile inclusa* or 'a woman's soul trapped in a man's body'.[5] Ironically, that confusion and dissatisfaction precipitated a misogynistic homosexuality, which I suggest we see in light of Forster's fear of the feminine in himself.[6] This understanding also gives us some insight into the process by which the confusions that produced this misogyny in Forster also fuelled a desire for something other than the classical opposition between male and female, masculine and feminine, and so initiated his embattled relationship with patriarchy. In *Howards End* we see this relationship played out through the narrator, the leading female characters, certain thematic oppositions, and the connections between all of these and the dramatic structure of the novel.

At a first glance, Forster appears to offer neither a radical literary practice nor a liberal sexual practice in this story of a younger woman's conventional marriage to an older and successful business-man, who looks upon women as 'recreation'. But textual evidence suggests that this conventional image is an anamorphosis reflecting Forster's attempt to manage a site of conflict in himself. A close analysis of the textual manoeuvres in *Howards End* discloses a radical sexual politics that has been obscured by psychobiographical approaches and by assumptions about Forster's literary allegiance to the nineteenth century. We may begin to excavate the layers of the text through its narrative stance, which is ambiguous, uneasy, and defensive. The following passage from the middle of the novel first brought me to examine *Howards End* because of the ways it makes problematic the omniscient narrator's voice:

> Pity was at the bottom of her [Margaret's] actions all through this crisis. Pity, if one may generalise, is at the bottom of woman. When men like us, it is for our better qualities and however tender their liking, we dare not be unworthy of it, or they will quietly let us go. But unworthiness stimulates woman. It brings out her deeper nature, for good or for evil.[7]

The problem emerges from the 'us', which initially appears to refer back to 'woman', used to essentialise all women, with whom the narrator seems to identify.[8] A closer reading suggests that 'us' simply refers to all people, that is, 'when men like people....' The temporary confusion arises here because, previously, the events have been focalised through the female protagonist, Margaret Schlegel, and 'us', the first-person-plural pronoun, invokes the feminine perspective.[9]

The 'us' feels problematic, too, because the narrator's previous narrative intrusions have been characterised by an uneasy authority that hovers between irony and sympathy, creating an overall impression of indefiniteness.[10] The narrator opens deferentially: 'One may as well begin with Helen's letter to her sister' (p. 3). Shortly thereafter we are told: 'To Margaret – I hope that it will not set the reader against her – the station of King's Cross had always suggested Infinity' (p. 12). The special pleading is intrusive here and later: 'That was "how it happened", or, rather, how Helen described it to her sister, using words even more unsympathetic than my own' (p. 25). Comments on the underprivileged seem to attempt sarcasm but end up sounding defensive: 'We are not concerned with the very poor. They are unthinkable' (p. 45); or, 'take my word for it, that [poor woman's] smile was simply stunning, and it is only you and I who will be fastidious and complain that true joy begins in the eyes' (p. 48). Later addresses to the reader fail to achieve either authority on the one hand or familiarity on the other: 'It is rather a moment when the commentator should step forward. Ought the Wilcoxes have offered their home to Margaret? I think not' (p. 98); and, 'Margaret had expected the disturbance.... Good-humour was the dominant note of her relations with Mr Wilcox, or, as I must now call him, Henry' (p. 177).

Forster is more assured when he avoids omniscient comment and focuses on Margaret Schlegel, from whose perspective we see the events of the novel. It is not merely that we share the point of view of a woman here (although that is important to Forster's ends) but also that we tend to take her perspective as representative of the female point of view in general. As the novel develops, Forster complicates this identification of Margaret with the 'female' or the 'feminine', but initially it undergirds the binary oppositions informing the novel. The novel is built upon a dialectical opposition between male and female, under which several others are subsumed.[11] The most significant oppositions for this analysis are those of class – rich and poor; those of philosophy – logic and vision; and those of language – word and intuition. Under the male side of the equation fall wealth, logic, and the word; under the female, poverty, vision and intuition. These oppositions are worked out on the level of theme and plot.

On the level of theme, that resolution is fairly straightforward, although we should note that those terms subsumed under the aspect of male and female perpetuate a hierarchical tradition that relegates women to an inferior status. We may want to applaud Forster for attempting to redress the balance by privileging the feminine, but we are still caught in a net of stereotypes that perpetuate hierarchy and binary opposition, ideas that inscribe male perspectives in the world, as we shall see in a moment.

Although I have relegated wealth to the male side of the equation and poverty to the female, in fact, the female protagonists of the novel, Margaret and Helen Schlegel, are well-to-do women. Their sympathy with the poor, however, initiates Forster's interrogation of class distinctions. The Schlegels are distinguished from the Wilcoxes, the masculine protagonists, by their recognition of the privilege that money confers. Margaret asserts that the rich 'stand upon money as upon islands' in the sea of life (p. 61). As a result of this perception, she and Helen are able to look beneath the social surface of a poor individual like Leonard Bast to the 'real man, who cared for adventure and beauty' (p. 316).

Yet, even as the novel attempts to redress the imbalance between rich and poor, it cannot transcend certain class attitudes which are implicit in Forster's uneven characterisation of the workingman and explicit in Margaret's discovery that Jackie Bast has formerly been Henry Wilcox's mistress. She writes to Helen that 'The Basts are not at all the type we should trouble about' (p. 241), and Helen, 'who is ready enough to sympathise with Leonard Bast, condemns Jackie as 'ready enough to meet' Henry Wilcox and laments that such women 'end in two ways: either they sink till the lunatic asylums and the workhouses are full of them ... or else they entrap a boy into marriage before it is too late' (p. 253). That Jackie is a victim of patriarchy is understood imperfectly, although Margaret strenuously criticises Henry's double standard. Helen's disclaimer, 'I can't blame her', sounds unconvincing as the novel seeks to deconstruct sexist and class values on the level of theme, which it then reconstructs on the level of plot when Helen has a sexual relationship with Leonard – a woman's classic offering of her body in sympathy – and then arrogantly seeks to compensate him with cash, admitting that 'I want never to see him again, though it sounds appalling. I wanted to give him money and feel finished' (p. 313). Both of these episodes play out basic patriarchal expectations about relationships between men and women, between the rich and the poor. The pattern we see here, where plot reconstructs what the theme interrogates to deconstruct, will be replicated in working out Forster's other binary oppositions.

Thematically, vision is privileged over logic, intuition over word. Of course, logic and the word are related: They are in this novel the logos, the word of the fathers. Forster is committed to an ideology that seeks to defy the phallic mode and, from the novel's opening, logic and the word are made to appear irrational. Charles Wilcox's blustering question to his brother, Paul, about his engagement to Helen Schlegel – 'Yes or no, man; plain question, plain answer. Did or didn't Miss Schlegel' – is corrected by his mother's response: 'Charles, dear Charles, one doesn't ask plain questions. There aren't such things' (p. 22). When Henry Wilcox confronts Margaret over Helen's seemingly irrational behaviour at the end of the novel, he echoes his son: 'Answer my question. Plain question, plain answer' (p. 284). Henry's plan to trap Helen like some hunted animal and Margaret's resistance provoke her recognition that the plan 'is impossible, because – ... it's not the particular language that Helen and I talk' and his counterclaim that 'No education can teach a woman logic' (p. 284). Margaret's later rejoinder – 'leave it that you don't see.... Call it fancy. But realise that fancy is a scientific fact' – refuses Henry's reductive dichotomies. Margaret is given the final word in the novel as she reflects that, 'Logically, they had no right to be there. One's hope was in the weakness of logic' (p. 339), and she is vindicated in the conclusion as the Wilcox clan gather to hear the word of the father – 'And again and again fell the word, like the ebb of a dying sea' – which belatedly, yet inevitably, affirms the intuitive vision of the mother in seeing that Margaret is the 'spiritual heir' she seeks for Howards End.

And yet Margaret's 'final word' is problematic because definitive answers belong to the male-inscribed discourse the novel seeks to deconstruct. We might want to argue that the apparent difficulty is only a matter of semantics. But, in fact, my introduction of a teleology of final word here anticipates the deeper problems we discover on the level of plot.

Forster's central opposition between man and woman would seem, initially, to be played out between Henry Wilcox and Margaret Schlegel. It begins on the level of houses. Margaret recognises that 'ours is a female house.... It must be feminine and all we can do is to see that it isn't effeminate. Just as another house that I can mention, but I won't, sounded irrevocably masculine, and all its inmates can do is to see that it isn't brutal' (p. 44). This summary prepares us for the dialectic to follow, but Forster's feminist vision removes Margaret as a single term within the traditional dialectic, replaces her with Helen, and reinterprets Margaret as the principle that will complicate the hierarchical oppositions and provide a new kind of connection. That new connection is not the old androgyny, a merging or blurring of terms and traits;[12] it is a condition that preserves difference.

Whereas Henry Wilcox remains inscribed in a male mode of discourse, set within masculine imagery of dominance and conquest, Forster's descriptions of Margaret transcend the traditionally feminine and reinscribe her within a rhetoric of reconciliation and connection. Through Margaret Schlegel, the traditional terms of masculinity and femininity are scrutinised and subjected to the demands of higher integration. Margaret's point of view, then, is ultimately not representative of a view we might code as essentially female or feminine. Forster is sensitive both to essentialist conceptions of the female and to the social coding of the feminine. He subverts both in his characterisation of Margaret Schlegel, who can calmly state, for example, 'I do not love children. I am thankful to have none' (pp. 337–8), thus debunking ideas of a natural, maternal female.

And Margaret remains constantly alert to social expectations of feminine behaviour, decoding those expectations. She turns the notion of 'reading the feminine' into a lever against the men who are dependent on and limited by its convenient categories. When Henry proposes, Margaret has anticipated his action, but 'she made herself give a little start. She must show surprise if he expected it' (p. 164). Later, when a man hits a cat with his automobile and Margaret jumps out of the car, we learn that 'Charles was absolutely honest. He described what he believed to have happened.... Miss Schlegel had lost her nerve, as any woman might.' But the narrator reveals that 'His father accepted this explanation, and neither knew that Margaret had artfully prepared the way for it. It fitted in too well with their view of feminine nature' (p. 215). Later, in response to a question, Margaret 'knew ... but said that she did not know' (p. 221) because 'comment is unfeminine' (p. 240).

Throughout the novel, Margaret resists being controlled by this dichotomous thinking and instead manipulates the terms with the goal of dismantling and transcending them. From the beginning, she is suspicious of hierarchies, as we discover in her mediation of the English and German claims to superiority. She announces, 'To me one of two things is very clear; either God does not know his own mind about England and Germany, or else these do not know the mind of God' (p. 30). The narrator pronounces her, ironically, 'a hateful girl', acknowledging that 'at thirteen she had grasped a dilemma that most people travel through life without perceiving' (p. 30). That dilemma focuses on the logic of binary thinking. Margaret resists such dichoto-mous thought and chastises Helen's binary oppositions as 'medieval', telling her 'our business is not to contrast the two, but to reconcile them' (p. 104). Not surprisingly, it is Margaret who is capable of con-cluding that 'people are far more different than is pretended. All over the world men and women are worrying because they cannot develop as they are supposed to develop' (p. 339).

In his reconceptualisation of Margaret, Forster generates a new integrative principle that is associated with a woman but not ideologically coded as feminine.[13] Part of his success here depends, as I have suggested, on using Helen to re-evaluate the traditionally feminine by associating her with emotion and the inner life.

Helen Schlegel, in contrast to Margaret, is emotional, impulsive, impatient of logic, impatient of all restraint on her generous impulses. She scoffs at moderation and is incapable of balance; she is first seduced by the Wilcox men and then violently rejects them. She extols the 'inner life' and, unlike Margaret, refuses to acknow-ledge the value of Wilcox energy, which has created a civilised world in which her sensibilities and the inner life can have free play. When Margaret must protect a pregnant and unmarried Helen from the interference of Wilcox men, Margaret herself codes the struggle as a sexual one: 'A new feeling came over her; she was fighting for women against men. She did not care about rights, but if men came into Howards End, it should be over her body' (p. 290). Although Margaret prefers not to be locked into a struggle between opposed faces, under duress she will privilege what Helen represents. Forster has anticipated this moment earlier in the novel when Margaret and Helen disagree over the older sister's impending marriage to Henry Wilcox. Their 'inner life was so safe', we are told, 'that they could bargain over externals.... There are moments when the inner life actually "pays", when years of self-scrutiny, conducted for no ulterior motive, are suddenly of practical use' (p. 195). The narrator adds that 'Such moments are still rare in the West; that they can come at all promises a fairer future'. Forster codes the inner life within another set of oppositions – Eastern mysticism versus Western pragmatism – but he reverses the usual hierarchy to privilege the East and the inner life.

In contrast to Helen, Henry is associated with an imagery of war, battle, and self-defence. When Margaret discovers that Jackie Bast was Henry's mistress, the narrator claims that, 'Expelled from his old fortress, Mr Wilcox was building a new one' (p. 244). Margaret is forced to play 'the girl, until he could rebuild his fortress and hide his soul from the world' (p. 246). Henry believes that 'Man is for war, woman for the recreation of the warrior, but he does not dislike it if she makes a show of fight. She cannot win in a real battle, having no muscles, only nerves' (p. 259). At the end of the novel, in the crisis over Helen, Henry speaks 'straight from his fortress', and Margaret at first fails to recognise that 'to break him was her only hope'. It is only when 'Henry's fortress [gives] way' that Margaret can initiate the process that leads to the integration, the connection, she enacts in the novel's conclusion by bringing Henry and Helen together at Howards End.

It is significant in *Howards End* that the most moving scene occurs between two women, Helen and Margaret.[14] When the sisters meet at Howards End and Margaret discovers Helen is pregnant, she asserts, 'It all turns on affection now' (p. 291). Although at first they feel themselves in antagonism, unconsciously they move toward communion:

> The triviality faded from the faces, though it left something behind –
> the knowledge that they never could be parted because their love was

rooted in common things. Explanations and appeals had failed; they had tried for a common meeting-ground, and had only made each other unhappy. And all the time their salvation was lying round them – the past sanctifying the present; the present, with wild heart-throb, declaring that there would after all be a future, with laughter and the voices of children. Helen, still smiling, came up to her sister. She said: 'It is always Meg'. They looked into each other's eyes. The inner life had paid.

(p. 299)

In stark contrast stands Charles Wilcox's relationship with his father:

The Wilcoxes were not lacking in affection; they had it royally, but they did not know how to use it. It was the talent in the napkin, and, for a warm-hearted man, Charles had conveyed very little joy. As he watched his father shuffling up the road, he had a vague regret – a wish that something had been different somewhere – a wish (though he did not express it thus) that he had been taught to say 'I' in his youth. He meant to make up for Margaret's defection, but knew that his father had been very happy with her until yesterday. How had she done it? By some dishonest trick, no doubt – but how?

(p. 329)

The traditionally feminine mode is clearly affirmed in these final contrasting scenes that sanction the inner life and 'voiceless sympathy'.

In privileging the inner life, as we have seen, Forster reverses the usual hierarchy in the oppositions of inner/outer, female/male, East/West, intuition/logic. This affirmation is a part of Forster's achievement. More significant, he takes a further step and sets up through Margaret a double reading in which the poles indecidably include each other and the *différance* of this irreducible difference. It is a process made familiar to us by Derrida.[15] We are forced to think or imagine the 'inconceivable', what we have seen as mutually exclusive; we are forced to form conceptions of that for which we have no concepts. The novel's epigraph – 'Only connect' – stands at the heart of this difficult process through which Margaret hopes to enable Henry's salvation: 'Only connect! That was the whole of her sermon. Only connect the prose and the passion, and both will be exalted, and human love will be seen at its height. Live in fragments no longer' (pp. 186–7). At Howards End, Margaret senses this connection of comrades between the house and the wych elm tree: 'It was a comrade, bending over the house, strength and adventure in its roots, but in its utmost fingers tenderness.... It was a comrade. House and tree transcended any similes of sex' (p. 206). Significantly, Forster has chosen representative terms – a house and a tree – that resist hierarchical placement and the classical oppositional structure of patriarchal thinking. Margaret reflects that, 'to compare either to man, to woman, always dwarfed the vision. Yet they kept within limits of the human.... As she stood in the one, gazing at the other, truer relationship had gleamed' (p. 206). Margaret also argues for connection – this discovery of mutual inclusivity – in her conception of proportion: 'truth, being alive, was not halfway between anything. It was only to be found by continuous excursions into either realm, and though proportion is the final secret, to espouse it at the outset is to insure sterility' (p. 195). Finally, in the novel's conclusion, Margaret looks toward an 'ultimate harmony' (p. 330).

To summarise, the connection that Margaret seeks is obviously not born out of an attempt to merge or to blur or reverse oppositions. She fights the 'daily grey' of life, the blending of black and white. Rather, she seeks to dismantle the hierarchical privileging of one term over another. She expresses it as a celebration of 'Differences – eternal differences, planted by God in a single family, so that there may always be colour; sorrow perhaps, but colour in the daily grey' (p. 338).

Ironically, however, although the resolution thematically insists on connections and although the patriarch Wilcox is unmanned, the plot appears to encode the patriarchal structures that the novel seeks to escape. I began this essay with the narrator's ambiguous sexual identification. I then quoted a paragraph which is followed by one that reads,

> Here was the core of the question. Henry must be forgiven, and made better by love; nothing else mattered.... To her everything was in proportion now.... Margaret fell asleep, tethered by affection, and lulled by the murmurs of the river that descended all the night from Wales. She felt herself at one with her future home, colouring it and coloured by it, and awoke to see, for the second time, Oniton Castle conquering the morning mists.
>
> (p. 243)

We notice the imagery of proportion, of connection, of mutuality monopolising the paragraph which, nonetheless, concludes with an image of domination, 'Oniton Castle conquering the morning mists'. It is possible Forster is being ironic because Oniton is not to be Margaret's home and she is, perhaps, mistaken in so valuing it. Yet, if this is irony, it is irony of a very subtle sort.

I suggest instead that the pattern is not ironic; rather, it anticipates the resolution of the novel where the value of connection, represented by the presence of Henry and Helen at Howards End, is enacted in the plot by Margaret's conquest of Henry. Henry, in masculine style, has earlier told Margaret, 'fix your price, and then don't budge', and she has responded, 'But I do budge' (p. 155). Nonetheless, on the issue of connection, she, like her masculine counterparts, won't budge: 'He had refused to connect, on the clearest issue that can be laid before a man, and their love must take the consequences' (p. 331). And in the novel's closing paragraphs, Margaret reflects, 'There was something uncanny in her triumph. She, who had never expected to conquer anyone, had charged straight through these Wilcoxes and broken up their lives' (p. 341). Margaret has triumphed, conquered, and broken up their lives. This conclusion to a novel about connection is ironic although not, I would suggest, deliberately so.

The irony arises because Forster inscribes the value of connection within the patriarchal dialectic of conquest and defeat, domination and submission, and within a narrative form that demands a resolution instead of 'continuous excursions into either realm' (p. 195). Although the themes of the novel indicate a desire to deconstruct the patriarchal ideology, ultimately, it seems, Forster is forced to reconstruct that ideology in the structure of the novel, in Margaret's 'victory' over Henry. Plot has demanded a hierarchical ordering of terms for a resolution to conflict even though the novel's themes have argued for replacement of conquest with connection. Forster's often trenchant interrogation of patriarchal language and perspectives appears to give way before the resistless temptation to expropriate the authority available to him in patriarchy. What he *wants* to assert, of course, is the value of the feminine perspective as a first step to dismantling hierarchy, but in the *act* of assertion, he affirms the value of the masculine mode, remaining dependent on patriarchy's hierarchical structures for authority, resolution, and conclusion. Ultimately, Forster recuperates an authority that would thematically seem to be repudiated.

Reaching this point in my argument – where the need to conclude a paper definitively is as imperative as the requirement to resolve a novel – I nonetheless stepped back from my own recuperation of authority, stepped from form to language. Perhaps Forster's critique of patriarchal modes and binary thinking was more trenchant and thoroughgoing than I first perceived. Forster had certainly appropriated the language of conquest, but he had also recontextualised it and, in the process, forestalled expropriation by that masculine terminology. A deep suspicion of conquest in its most notable manifestations – imperialism and war – lies at the very heart of *Howards End*. The narrator simply asserts, contrasting the yeoman who is 'England's hope' to the Imperialist who 'hopes to inherit the earth', that 'the Imperialist is not what he thinks or seems. He is a destroyer. He prepares the way for cosmopolitanism, and though his ambitions may be fulfilled, the earth that he inherits will be grey' (p. 323). Strong biblical cadences underline this apocalyptic vision of a world shaped in a masculine mode.

Perhaps, then, Forster is having his joke when Margaret characterises her success as a conquest. 'She, who had never expected to conquer anyone, had charged straight through these Wilcoxes and broken up their lives' (p. 341). In fact, she has not 'charged through'; she has simply done what 'seemed easiest' (p. 334). 'No better plan had occurred to her' (p. 335). She confesses, 'I did the obvious things' (p. 339). 'Conquer', in this context, is not an act of self-assertion and dominance but is redefined as non-assertion, an opening up of space, a refusal to accept the exclusivity of opposition, between Henry and Helen. 'Everyone said [living together at Howards End] was impossible' (p. 338), but Margaret defies this patriarchal logic.

The futility of binary thinking appears in the lives of both Henry and Helen, both of whom declare they are 'ended'. Henry confesses, 'I don't know what to do – what to do. I'm broken – I'm ended' (p. 334).[16] As if in echo, Helen rejoins, 'I'm ended. I used to be so dreamy about a man's love as a girl, and think that, for good or evil, love must be the great thing. But it hasn't been' (p. 337). The man of action and the woman of emotion reach the bankruptcy implicit in their exclusive positions. Margaret's conquest or victory, then, is not the patriarchal one demanding suppression of an other but one that emerges as the traditional oppositions destroy themselves and clear a space for difference.

Forster has anticipated this conclusion, as we have seen earlier, in identifying a warfare mentality with Henry Wilcox. But we may now discover a further step Forster has taken. While Henry Wilcox persistently refers to casualties such as Leonard Bast as 'part of the battle of life' (p. 191) as if such casualties were in the 'nature' of things, Margaret decodes his metaphor: 'We upper classes have ruined him, and I suppose you'll tell me it's part of the battle of life' (p. 224). Margaret herself is a master of words, as we see in her first encounter with Leonard Bast when her speeches 'flutter away from him like birds' (p. 40). But Margaret's strength lies in recognising the way ideologies are encoded in language and in acknowledging the social privilege behind her 'speech'. She early argues 'all our thoughts are the thoughts of six-hundred-pounders, and all our speeches' (p. 61), underlining both the intensity and the futility of Leonard Bast's desire 'to form his style on Ruskin' (p. 49). Ruskin's style cannot 'speak' Leonard Bast's life.

When Margaret rejects Henry's language and metaphor of life as a battle, she rejects his patriarchal ideology and introduces new terms into the novel. She reflects that 'Life is indeed dangerous, but not in the way morality would have us believe. It is indeed unmanageable, but the essence of it is not a battle. It is unmanageable because it is a romance, and its essence is romantic beauty' (p. 107). This passage informs the entire novel and encourages us to reread the metaphors of conquest concluding the novel within a romance topos put into play by the figure of Ruth Wilcox, Henry's first wife.

Margaret's own sense of victory is severely qualified when she learns that Ruth Wilcox had 'willed' Howards End to her, had designated her as its 'spiritual heir', many years earlier: 'Something shook [Margaret's] life in its inmost recesses, and she shivered' (p. 342). Ruth Wilcox is introduced into the novel as one who always 'knew', although no one 'told her a word' (p. 27). Ruth Wilcox is represented as beyond language deployed as power, beyond the words that cripple communication among the other characters, implicated as they are in ideology. Margaret ultimately asserts to Helen: 'I feel that you and I and Henry are only fragments of that woman's mind. She knows everything. She is everything. She is the house, and the tree that leans over it' (p. 313).

Miss Avery, who after Mrs Wilcox's death becomes her representative, prophesies to Margaret: 'You think you won't come back to live here [at Howards End], but you will' (p. 272), and Margaret, who has discounted her words, is disturbed to find them fulfilled when she and Helen sleep in the house: 'It is disquieting to fulfil a prophecy, however superficially' (p. 302). She will, of course, fulfil it much more deeply, making Howards End her permanent home, as, increasingly, Margaret herself recognises the 'power of the house. It kills what is dreadful and makes what is beautiful live' (p. 300).

As Margaret moves toward insight and vision, she, too, moves away from language. The narrator comments, for example, that Margaret's 'mind trembled toward a conclusion which only the unwise will put into words' (p. 205). And later we learn that Margaret 'had outgrown stimulants, and was passing from words to things', an inevitable process 'if the mind itself is to become a creative power' (p. 262). Finally, Margaret admits to Helen, who calls her life 'heroic', 'No doubt I have done a little towards straightening the tangle, but things that I can't phrase have helped me' (p. 339).

At best, because of its ideological character, language can take characters to the brink of understanding as it does when Margaret exposes Henry's hypocrisy in committing adultery himself and refusing to forgive it in Helen. Margaret confronts Henry: 'I think you yourself recommended plain speaking'. And the narrator reveals that 'they looked at each other in amazement. The precipice was at their feet now' (p. 307). Language takes them to the abyss, but it cannot reconstruct their lives on a new basis because they cannot form conceptions of that for which there is no concept. Margaret simply relies on 'the power of the house'.

As we reconsider Forster's resolution in light of Mrs Wilcox and the spiritual heir she seeks for Howards End, we notice that the novel moves toward resolution, but it is a resolution that existed from the beginning as a 'part of Mrs Wilcox's mind' (p. 315). In that respect, the plot subverts its own commitment to hierarchy and sequence, to prior and subsequent events. In addition, the power that has 'defeated' Henry Wilcox, the patriarch, is diffused over the universe. At the end of the novel, Henry Wilcox lies suffering with hay fever, confined to the house, recalling Miss Avery's words with their echoes of battle imagery: 'There's not one Wilcox that can stand up against a field in June' (p. 273). The patriarch is 'shut up in the house', and his wife pronounces, 'It has to be.... The hay-fever is his chief objection to living here, but he thinks it worth while' (p. 336).

As previously noted, the novel's last words belong to Helen, who rushes into the house with her child and the neighbour boy accompanied by 'shouts of infectious joy': 'We've seen to the very end', she cries, 'and it'll be such a crop of hay as never' (p. 343). To see 'to the very end', in this scene and in the novel as a whole, is to discover the beginning of possibility: 'such a crop of hay as never'. The last phrase is appropriate, too, concluding with a 'never' that has already been subverted. In its closure, the novel gestures toward an open space, like a field in June, that 'not one Wilcox ... can stand up against'. It is a 'closure' that echoes Hélène Cixous on *écriture féminine*. Though Cixous is speaking of women writers, she describes what I am arguing that Forster has achieved:

> [Writers] must invent the impregnable language that will wreck partitions, classes, and rhetorics, regulations and codes, they must submerge, cut through, get beyond the ultimate reserve-discourse, including the one that laughs at the very idea of pronouncing the word 'silence', the one that, aiming for the impossible, stops short before the word 'impossible' and writes it as 'the end'.[17]

This reading seems more true to the narrative and linguistic procedures of Forster's *Howards End*. But it raises further questions. Can Forster thus evade the connection between discourse and power by postulating an unspoken knowledge? Indeed, the pressure of resolution may seem inevitably to produce an evasion as Forster gestures toward an alternative to binary thinking, a 'conclusion that only the unwise will put into words'. It is, at best, an uneasy truce. And this final inaccessible metaphysics may leave us frustrated by our own discontinuing embattlement with language, power, and patriarchy.

From Laura Claridge and Elizabeth Langland (eds), *Out of Bounds: Male Writers and Gender(ed) Criticism* (Amherst, Mass., 1990), pp. 252–67.

NOTES

[This essay begins with the point that Forster was not part of the literary and cultural movement called 'modernism', associated with Eliot, Woolf, Pound, Joyce, etc. Langland, however, negates the importance of this apparent limitation by suggesting that there is something new in *Howards End* – an attempt to defy patriarchal logic and rationality through writing in a feminine mode, even as though the narrator was a woman. This is a feminist reading of *Howards End* which has begun with the question whether male writers can undo patriarchy in their own writings, and the answer here seems to be positive: the text comes down on the side of the feminine – 'deconstructing' the terms which place male above female, and which marginalise the terms which in ideology belong to the feminine – the inner life, intuition, for instance. 'Deconstruction' comes from the theorist Jacques

Derrida, whose work aims at showing how structures of thought privilege certain powerful Western myths – including, of course, myths sanctioning imperialism. At one point Langland argues that Forster returns to patriarchal/ imperialist ideology, but then concludes by finding in his adherence to and investment in the *mother*, Ruth Wilcox, and his sense of the importance of what cannot be put into language – a commitment to unspoken knowledge – ways in which the text sides with the feminine. The question remains, however. Delany (essay 4) fastens on the text's political limitations: Langland fastens on its strengths with regard to gender politics, about which Delany said nothing. The question of the critical status of *Howards End* remains, depending on which reading is found to be more satisfactory. Can an undoing of patriarchy mean a change in politics? Does an attention to the feminine entail changes that make a difference in public life? Langland leaves the question open. Ed.]

1. After the early, enthusiastic appreciation of Forster's work set in motion by Lionel Trilling, *E. M. Forster* (New York, 1943), and Trilling's identification of *Howards End* as 'undoubtedly Forster's masterpiece', because it develops to their full the themes and attitudes of the early books and connects them 'with a more mature sense of responsibility' (pp. 114–15), other critics have not been content to rest with the thematic coherence of his work and have disagreed with Trilling's assessment. They have located Forster's reliance on nineteenth-century modes as a source of the novel's weakness. See, for example, Frederick Crews, who feels that Margaret's '"connection" with the Wilcoxes is merely diagrammatic' and that Forster's 'plot must finally retreat to an un-convincingly "moral" ending' (*E. M. Forster: The Perils of Humanism* [Princeton, NJ, 1962], p. 122). See also Wilfred Stone, who claims that 'The forces of value do not "connect", but pursue each other in a lonely and circular futility. And the circle is especially vicious because Forster seems to see only its "proportion" and not its "emptiness"' (*The Cave and the Mountain: A Study of E. M. Forster* [Stanford, Cal., 1966], p. 266).
   I hope my own analysis identifies a new way to see the narrative strengths and challenges of Forster's novel, to perceive those techniques and questions that align him with other literary modernists. At the same time, my goal in this essay is to give another perspective from which to assess the novel's difficulties, which have been too readily grouped under the rubric of Forster's return to a nineteenth-century liberal humanism.

2. Francis King, *E. M. Forster and His World* (New York, 1978), p. 57.

3. Ibid., p. 64

4. P. N. Furbank, *E. M. Forster: A Life*, 2 vols (New York and London, 1977, 1978), II, 40.

5. D. A. Miller, *The Novel and the Police* (Berkeley and Los Angeles, 1988), pp. 154–5.

6. Eve Kosofsky Sedgwick, *Between Men: English Literature and Male Homosocial Desire* (New York, 1985), p. 20, has made an important connection here between misogyny and fear of the feminine. She argues that 'homophobia directed by men against men is misogynistic, and perhaps transhistorically so. (By "misogynistic" I mean not only that it is oppressive of the so-called feminine in men, but that it is oppressive of women).' Sedgwick also notes that, although antihomophobia and feminism are not the same forces, the bonds between them are 'profound and intuitable'.

7. E. M. Forster, *Howards End* (New York, 1921), p. 243. All subsequent references are from this edition, and page numbers are provided in the text.

8. One critic who has observed that the narrator is female is Kinley Roby, 'Irony and Narrative Voice in *Howards End*', *Journal of Narrative Technique*, 2 (May 1972), but his argument differs sharply from mine because he uses the evidence that Forster has created a female narrator to argue for Forster's separation from and *condemnation* of the narrator's narrow and biased attitudes: 'The contrast between the action of the novel and the narrator's view of that action suggests that the narrator and the group for whom she claims to speak see the world neither steadily nor as a whole.... Forster seems to be suggesting that the narrator and those like her cannot have their "islands", their illusions and, at the same time, a world worth inhabiting' (p. 123).

9. There is some evidence from contemporaneous reviews that Forster's narrator and the narrative point of view were problematic. Indeed, some reviewers were persuaded that E. M. Forster must be a woman who had adopted a male pseudonym. Elia Pettie of the *Chicago Tribune*, in support of her argument that Forster was female, wrote: 'In feeling the book is feminine' (cited in Philip Gardner [ed.], *E. M. Forster: The Critical Heritage* [London and Boston, 1973], p. 160). Gardner also notes in his introduction that Pettie's conviction had British precedent: 'The idea [that Forster was female] had already been whispered in passing' (p. 5).

10. Philip Gardner, *E. M. Forster* (London, 1977), has also noted of *Howards End*, identifying Forster with his narrator, that 'at times Forster's [comments] to the reader lack his usual authority and aplomb' (p. 25).

11. It is a commonplace to recognise that Forster's novel is built upon oppositions. He himself said about the book's composition: 'I am grinding out my novel into a contrast between money and death' (cited in King, *Forster and His World*, p. 49). Other critics have generally cited the clash between the material and spiritual lives, the seen and the unseen, Bentham and Coleridge, Lloyd George liberalism and classical liberalism. My own interpretation takes the gender conflict as pre-eminent.

12. The subject of androgyny has become a vexed one in contemporary feminist discourse. In early stages of the feminist movement, the argument for equal treatment of women and men seemed to depend on detecting similarities: the masculine in the feminine and the feminine in the masculine. Then androgyny seemed the ideal. Subsequently, women have wanted to argue for the authority of the female perspective and values, and androgyny as a concept has become less attractive. It is interesting, in this light, that Forster doesn't advocate the merging of traits androgyny implies but instead insists on preserving distinctions. He is, in that regard, closer to the spirit of a contemporary discourse that speaks of escaping hierarchies.

13. Glen Caveliero suggests a similar point but does not develop it in *A Reading of E. M. Forster's Novels* (Totowa, NJ, 1979). Caveliero writes: 'Although it is possible to detect an anti-female bias in his work, it is really in the interests of feminine values and fulfilment that he writes, and the kind of wisdom he advocates goes well beyond the contemporary sexual polarisations. Even as a homosexual he was ahead of his time' (pp. 127–8). Also, Anne Wyatt-Brown, in '*Howards End*: Celibacy and Stalemate', *Psychohistory Review*, 12: I (Fall 1983), 29, argues that Forster lends 'his own feelings to Margaret; surely the pressures of virginity that drove her into Henry Wilcox's arms were his own'.

14. Contemporaneous reviewers testify to Forster's success at representing female friendship. An unsigned reviewer in the *Atheneum* wrote: 'the great thing in the book is the sisters' affection for each other.... personal relationships ... have never, we venture to say, been made more beautiful or more real' (cited in Gardner, *Critical Heritage*, p. 151). Forster's success here, and I would argue that he does succeed, is the more remarkable if we consider that Virginia Woolf wrote in *A Room of One's Own* (New York, 1929): '"Chloe liked Olivia", I read. And then it struck me how immense a change was there. Chloe liked Olivia perhaps for the first time in literature' (p. 86). Woolf argues that the representation of female friendship depends on female writers and so seems to forget Forster's novel. But his treatment of women must have impressed her at one time. Vanessa Bell invited Forster, after the publication of *Howards End*, to speak at the Friday Club on 'The Feminine Note in Literature'. According to Furbank, 'Virginia told him [Forster] afterwards it was the best paper the Club had heard so far' (*Forster: A Life*, 1, 193).

It is an interesting, if small, point that critics Wilfred Stone, *Cave and Mountain*, p. 239, and Elizabeth Heine, 'E. M. Forster and the Bloomsbury Group', *Cahiers d'Etudes & de Recherches Victoriennes & Edouardiennes (CVE)*, 4–5 (1977), 47–8, have pointed to Virginia and Vanessa Stephen as models for the Schlegel sisters although Forster himself claimed the three sisters of Goldsworthy Lowes Dickinson as his models ('The Art of Fiction', *Paris Review*, 1 [1953], 37).

15. Although I find *différance* a fruitful concept for allowing us to see Forster's achievement in a new light – for allowing us to perceive a radical dimension to his art obscured by previous insistence that he belongs to a nineteenth-century tradition of liberal humanism – I am not doing a Derridean deconstruction on this text. Indeed, the conclusion I postulate – Margaret's ultimate spiritual insight outside language – Derrida would probably see as a metaphysics. I am, however, inevitably led to see the parallels between Forster's conception of connection and Derrida's notion of *différance*, both of which are crucial to the problem of sexual difference.

16. The tendency among critics has been to pose the Schlegel sisters together in opposition to the Wilcoxes. Frederick Crews is one critic who appreciates the distinctions Forster has drawn between Helen and Margaret and the similarities between Helen and Henry: 'Henry and Helen together are people who isolate and simplify rather than allowing their imaginations to play across a broad range of related circumstances.... Both the Wilcoxes and Helen are unwilling to come to grips with prosaic reality' (*E. M. Forster*, p. 120).

17. Hélène Cixous, 'The Laugh of the Medusa', in *New French Feminisms: An Anthology*, ed. Elaine Marks and Isabelle de Courtivron (New York, 1981), p. 256.

6

Edward Carpenter and the Double Structure of *Maurice*

ROBERT K. MARTIN

Maurice remains E. M. Forster's least appreciated novel largely because it is also his least understood novel. Because of the wide attention paid to the book's revelation of Forster's homosexuality, readers have not accorded it the serious attention they have paid to Forster's other works. The novel has been taken simply as a plea for homosexual rights on the part of a homosexual writer. And, as a didactic work, it has been thought to lack the qualities of subtlety and irony that mark Forster's other novels.

Despite Forster's acknowledgment that *Maurice* 'was the direct result of a visit to Edward Carpenter',[1] readers have not fully explored the significance of that source. It has regularly been supposed that the novel is concerned primarily with an opposition between homosexuality and heterosexuality and that the views expressed by Clive in the first half of the book may be taken to represent the author's.[2] In fact, the novel opposes two kinds of homosexuality – one that is identified with Cambridge and Clive, and one that is identified with Alec and the open air – and uses the opinions on homosexual love expressed by Clive to indicate a stage in Maurice's development, but one that does not represent the author's concept of the final stage of development: this Maurice can achieve only through the encounter with Alec. *Maurice* is not a plea for homosexual rights, but an exploration of the growth in awareness of a homosexual protagonist, who moves from a false solution to a truer one.

The novel is divided into roughly equal parts, each of which is then again divided in two, to provide the four parts identified by Forster. The first half of the book is devoted to the Maurice–Clive relationship, to suburban life, and to Cambridge. Similarly, the second half of the book is devoted to the Maurice–Alec relationship, to the opposition of gentry and servants, and to the country house, Penge. The first is dominated by Plato and, indirectly, by John Addington Symonds and the apologists for 'Greek love',[3] the second is dominated by Edward Carpenter and his translation of the ideas of Walt Whitman. The two sections run almost exactly parallel: Part I ends with Maurice entering Clive's window in response to his call; Part III concludes with Alec entering Maurice's room in response to a similar call. Part II concludes with dawn, the hoped-for new light that ironically brings the death of the love between Maurice and Clive; Part IV ends with sunset, the apparent darkness that ironically brings life and the survival of the love of Maurice and Alec.

Although Forster's concept of homosexuality was not fully developed until he had absorbed the ideas of Carpenter, some of the elements that are present in *Maurice* can be traced back at least a decade earlier. For instance, the story 'Ansell', probably written in 1902 or 1903, treats in abbreviated version some of the important themes of the later novel. Ansell himself recurs in *Maurice* as George, the garden boy about whose departure Maurice's mother lies and who serves as a foreshadowing of Alec. By the time of the composition of this story, Forster had already come to see a possible link between a homosexual love that crossed class barriers and the questioning of the assumptions based on class, including the expectation of worldly success.[4] Although we do not know the exact date at which Forster first read Whitman's poetry (the first diary mention we know of is for 1907), the story is similar in its implications to a number of poems from the 'Calamus' sequence, notably 'When I heard at the close of the day' with its opposition of the satisfactions of a personal love to those of fame.[5]

During the early years of his awareness of himself as a homosexual, Forster was concerned with understanding the nature of a homosexual literary tradition. Signs of this are evident in *The Longest Journey*, his novel conceived in 1904 and published in April 1907. The allusion to Theocritus, whom Rickie 'believed to be the greatest of Greek poets',[6] underscores the novel's ironic contrast between the actualised pastoral of Stephen, the 'real' shepherd, and the pseudo-Greek spirit of late-Victorian England and its public schools. Rickie fails to understand Theocritus' significance as a poet of pastoral love between two men, but the reader makes use of the allusion as a way of measuring Rickie's lack of self-knowledge and the gap between Theocritus' time and the present. The reference to Shakespeare's Sonnet CXVI, when Rickie is reported to think 'he wished there was a society, a kind of friendship office, where the marriage of true minds could be registered',[7] serves to heighten and dignify Rickie's plight, as well as to remind us of the way in which homosexual art can be turned to the purpose of a heterosexual society.

Forster's means of establishing a homosexual tradition was the one that has often been followed: he made a list of famous homosexual authors. Such a list is in part a gesture toward the alleviation of the radical loneliness that may confront the homosexual following the acknowledgement of his or her own nature. It is also the raw material out of which can be built a sense of history, an understanding of how others have dealt with a similar situation. Because Forster limited his list-making to homosexual artists, it is clear that he was especially aware of the problems he would face if he were to deal with his homosexuality in his art (as he had begun to do in a conscious manner in *The Longest Journey*). Forster's list (an entry in his diary for New Year's Eve 1907) is given in part in a footnote in Furbank's biography. Furbank terms it simply 'a further book list', but a glance at the list makes its real purpose clear. The names are: Sturge Moore, A. E. Housman, Symonds, Pater, Shakespeare, Beddoes, Walt Whitman, E. Carpenter, Samuel Butler, Fitzgerald, Marlowe.[8] Forster's reading during this period was directed in part toward discovering a homosexual literary tradition. What he found in his own time was largely the schoolboy novel, with its celebration of a wistful and impossible love between boys. He knew at least four examples of such novels: A. E. W. Clarke's *Jaspar Tristram*; H. N. Dickinson's *Keddy*; H. O. Sturgis' *Tim*, published anonymously, and Desmond Coke's public school and college novels, pseudonymously published as by 'Belinda Blinders'. Something of their spirit may well have contributed to the Cambridge scenes of *The Longest Journey* and *Maurice*. Forster's knowledge of this tradition contributes to our recognition that the homosexual allusions and implications of *The Longest Journey* were intentional. The schoolboy novels display a characteristic emphasis on hopeless love, one which Forster retained for *The Longest Journey* but abandoned for *Maurice*.

What sent Forster back to this material six years later was his celebrated visit to Edward Carpenter and George Merrill at Milthorpe. It was this visit that caused Forster to, as it were, rewrite *The Longest Journey*. In its new version the character of Ansell is transformed into Clive, and that of Stephen into Alec. As in the earlier version, it is neither Cambridge nor Sawston that shall prevail, but Wiltshire (Penge is on the border of Wiltshire and Somerset, and Sawston is not unlike Alfridge Gardens in its embodiment of suburban values). Rural England, under the surface of its county families, retains a heritage that is close to that of rural Greece, as the characters of Stephen and Alec demonstrate. What Carpenter's influence meant for Forster was a re-examination of the homosexual tradition he had been constructing, and a revision of it. In the first half of *Maurice* the attitudes of Symonds prevail: homosexuality is defined as a higher form of love, and its spiritual superiority is preserved by its exclusion of physical consummation. In the second half of the book, which presents homosexual love as viewed under the influence of Carpenter, homosexuality is seen to include physical love, and whatever superiority it may possess over heterosexuality is now related to its social consequences, to its provision of an outlaw status for even its most respectable adherents. It seems likely that in depicting these two aspects to Maurice's development Forster is working out of his own life. For it was surely Carpenter more than anyone who helped Forster to an awareness of his own need for a relationship at once spiritual and physical.

The first half of *Maurice* is concerned with tracing the false vision of an idealised homosexuality. We perceive its falseness, however, only after we have followed Maurice through his sense of confusion and his apparent salvation in the arms of Clive. By adopting a narrative method that is related to James's 'point of view', but with considerably more authorial intrusion, Forster forces the reader to follow Maurice up his wrong path and to feel with him the pain that ensues upon its dead-ending.

Part I illustrates the unreliability of school and university as guides to conduct in the sexual realm. The first chapter, for instance, exposes Mr Ducie as a pious fraud, who asserts a brave sexual honesty but is actually embarrassed at the thought that someone may find his sexual diagram in the sand. Maurice knows enough to recognise Ducie as a liar and coward, but not enough to know the truth about sexuality. Thus the act of betrayal, when Ducie promises enlightenment but offers none, opens a world of darkness: 'the darkness that is primeval but not eternal, and yields to its own painful dawn' (p. 9). Teachers cannot give Maurice the light that he needs, and when Ducie invites Maurice *and his wife* to dinner in ten years' time, he not only expresses the conventional assumption that everyone is heterosexual, but also prepares for one of the central ironies of the book. For it is precisely ten years later that Maurice meets Alec, and although the two do not take Ducie up on his invitation, they do meet him in the British Museum.[9] On that occasion Mr Ducie gets his facts wrong again, calling Maurice Wimbleby, and Maurice finally renounces his past, his previous identity, by momentarily assuming Alec's name. Cambridge provides no higher standard of intellectual integrity: at the Dean's translation class, a passage is omitted because it is 'a reference to the unspeakable vice of the Greeks' (p. 42). The same Dean will send Maurice down because he sees it as his duty 'to spoil a love affair' between two students when he has the chance (p. 70). One of the ironies on which Forster insists throughout this section is that such attitudes persist in a culture that is officially so classicising. Maurice, we recall, gave the Greek Oration on his school's Prize Day, delivering a speech in praise of war ('The Greek was vile: Maurice had got the prize on account of the Thought', p. 18) and receiving a copy of Grote's *History of Greece* as his prize. Thoroughly inbued with things Greek, and thus bolstering its own imperialism and militarism, English culture has nonetheless totally ignored the most striking fact about Greek society: its institutionalisation of homosexual relationships.

As Maurice comes to recognise the inadequacy of education as a moral guide, he also comes to an understanding of his own sexual nature. This nature has been present since his earliest memories and is manifested in his two dreams, the one of the naked garden boy leaping over the woodstacks and the other of a face and a voice saying 'That is your Friend'.[10] It is also present in his schoolboy crushes, and it reasserts itself in his recognition of his need for friendship with Risley. Although he is not sexually attracted to Risley, he recognises that the two share something, even though he is not yet able to give a name to it. Clive suggests that Maurice read *The Symposium*, but even this is apparently not enough to transform his suburban soul. His rejection of Clive, however, leads him to re-examine himself and come to terms with his own nature. He acknowledges the degree of self-deception that he has engaged in: his agony 'worked inwards, till it touched the root whence body and soul both spring, the "I" that he had been trained to obscure, and, realised at last,

doubled its power and grew superhuman' (p. 51). This rediscovery
of the personal self below the social self leads him to his resolve: 'He
would not – and this was the test – pretend to care about women
when the only sex that attracted him was his own. He loved men
and always had loved them' (p. 53).[11] Part I concludes with the dramatisation of what we would now call Maurice's 'coming out'. But,
because of his education, in which sexuality remains clandestine and
unspoken, his emotional coming out is not accompanied by a similar
physical expression. Clive remains his only model, and Clive's model
is Plato. Thus, the groundwork is laid by the false climax of Part I
for the developing disaster of Part II.

Clive's expression of their love to Maurice in Part II reflects the
language of the late nineteenth-century apologists for homosexuality. It is an argument derived essentially from *The Symposium*:
'I feel to you as Pippa to her fiancé, only far more nobly, far more
deeply, body and soul . . . a particular harmony of body and soul
that I don't think women have even guessed' (p. 81). For Clive this
higher love depends upon the renunciation of physical passion: 'The
love that Socrates bore Phaedo now lay within his reach, love
passionate but temperate, such as only finer natures can understand
. . .' (p. 89). The snobbishness of his responses is evident and seems
an accurate depiction of the mainstream of homosexual defence at
the turn of the century, and indeed up until the very recent past. The
failure of Maurice's relationship with Clive provides an opportunity
for Maurice to develop beyond these attitudes. Homosexuality, as
expressed by Clive and as lived by Maurice and him, is a state
reserved for a tiny elite of those with highly developed sensibilities.
It effects no change in the homosexual. It encourages misogyny –
Clive is, Forster tells us, even more misogynistic than Maurice. It
allows the life of the 'suburban tyrant' (p. 92) that Maurice is about
to become. Its only concession to itself is a small part of time,
apportioned off and reserved for the lover:

> But every Wednesday he slept at Clive's little flat in town. Weekends
> were also inviolable. They said at home, 'You must never interfere
> with Maurice's Wednesdays or with his weekends. He would be most
> annoyed.'
>
> (p. 93)

Despite Maurice's resolve not to go back on his nature, he lives his
life as if he were heterosexual. Homosexuality remains a small,
secret vice at the heart of an otherwise conventional life.

Although it is Clive's conversion to 'normal' sexuality that brings an end to Maurice's dream for a time, everything has led the reader to expect such a failure. Even those images that seemed most positive are, upon closer inspection, often ironic. Take, for instance, the ride in the cycle and side-car. The apparently ecstatic prose conceals a sense of warning: 'They became a cloud of dust, a stench, and a roar to the world, but the air they breathed was pure, and all the noise they heard was the long drawn cheer of the wind' (p. 66). In the self-absorption of their love, they fail to see the consequences of their action. Their reliance upon a machine, something that creates dirt, noise, and stench, should warn us of Forster's wry use of this scene. The escapade comes to an end when 'the machine comes to a standstill among the dark black fields' (p. 67), Forster's cold term ('machine') signalling the opposition between nature and the products of an industrial society. Clive's recollection of the scene completes the irony: 'Bound in a single motion, they seemed there closer to one another than elsewhere; the machine took on a life of its own, in which they met and realised the unity preached by Plato' (p. 71). The absurdity of the motorcycle and its side-car as image of the Platonic egg warns us of the inadequacies of this kind of 'poeticising' idealism as a guide to behaviour, just as Ansell's realism (in *The Longest Journey*) ought to have served as a warning to the idealism of Rickie.

If the second section of the novel is devoted to an exploration of homosexual love in the atomosphere of late-Victorian Cambridge, the third part turns to an investigation of lust, the element totally excluded from the earlier relationship. Two episodes help to remind Maurice of his own sexual desires: once when he sees Dickie Barry asleep, 'embraced and penetrated by the sun' (p. 134), and a second time when a handsome French client invites him to lunch. On the second occasion Maurice's refusal to respond to the invitation is due to the influence of the Clive relationship: 'The ethereal past had blinded him, and the highest happiness he could dream was a return to it.' This past includes the rule that 'their love, though including the body, should not gratify it' (p. 139), and so he is prevented from realising the possibilities that confront him. Clive, too, although embracing heterosexuality, retains a prudishness about sexuality that makes his marriage shallow: 'He never saw her naked, nor she him. They ignored the reproductive and digestive functions. [Here one should recall Maurice's nursing of Clive during his illness, which includes cleaning out his chamber pot. Their love does provide something of a triumph over squeamish respectability, at least for Maurice – Clive prefers a trained female nurse.] He had never itched to call a spade a spade, and though he valued the body the actual deed of sex seemed to him unimaginative, and best veiled in night. Between men it is inexcusable, between man and woman it may be practised since nature and society approve, but never discussed nor vaunted' (p. 151).

Maurice's visit to Penge demonstrates the extent to which he is unmoved by his sexuality. He remains an unbearable snob, and his snobbery is directed ironically at the man who will become his lover. His hard-heartedness is a response to his own misery: unwilling to face his own situation, he develops a philosophy of toughness that takes his personal defences and applies them to the world. One may help the poor, he asserts, but only because poverty may injure society. Not because one loves the poor: that kind of soft-heartedness he leaves to the priest, Mr Borenius. As Glen Cavaliero has remarked, Maurice confronts the 'four guardians of society – the schoolmaster, the doctor, the scientist and the priest. All four in different ways condemn him, and not one of them can offer any help.'[12] The irony of Mr Borenius as an exponent of the gospel of love, while Maurice and Alec are about to make actual love in the Russet Room, is delightful, and it anticipates the central irony of 'The Life to Come'. Penge itself serves two simultaneous functions: as a house it represents the values of the English upper middle classes, values that are in serious disrepair but nonetheless muddle on in their unthinking, oppressive way; but as a place Penge is part of the English landscape and provides a way back into the natural world. Maurice is called outside by the scent of the primrose bushes and accidentally bumps into Alec. When he returns to the house, his head is covered with pollen.

The final scenes of Part III indicate a major change in direction. The first two parts were, as we saw, dominated by the image of dawn. Light was seen as a positive figure toward which Maurice was groping, and yet the only dawn that came was the one that culminated Part II, Clive's vision of his new heterosexuality. In the encounter with Alec, Maurice becomes aware of a new darkness: 'not the darkness of a house which coops up a man among furniture, but the darkness where he can be free!' (p. 178). It is the darkness that calls Maurice to sensuality, the darkness that allows for Alec's visit to Maurice's bed. The light that prevails over their room at Penge is not of the sun but the moon. As Maurice's pollen-covered head indicates, the transformation in Maurice is in part a shift from Apollo to Dionysus, from light to darkness, from sun to moon, from science to art, from head to heart.

The Dionysian spirit evoked by Alec is subversive of all the values Maurice had lived by. He recognises that events at Penge have paralleled those at Cambridge ('Risley's room had its counterpart in the wild rose and the evening primroses of yesterday, the side-car dash through the fens foreshadowed his innings at cricket' (p. 191). But the episodes with Clive have not served to question any fundamental assumptions of society or even of their own lives. The affair with Clive was, in the common phrase, just a phase. The affair with Alec goes far deeper and is far more disturbing:

> ... all that night his body yearned for Alec's, despite him. He called it lustful, a word easily uttered, and opposed it to his work, his family, his friends, his position in society. In that coalition must surely be included his will. For if the will can overleap class, civilisation as we have made it will go to pieces.
>
> (p. 191)

The cricket game re-establishes the fundamental class structure of England, momentarily overturned by the night Maurice and Alec have spent together. Maurice comes to realise that his sympathies will finally be with his lover, not with his class (just as in his famous statement, so often used against him, Forster asserted his loyalty to his friend over his country). Maurice's love for Alec frees him from the stifling values of middle-class England and offers him the possibility of spiritual growth. Maurice confronts this when he sees the King and Queen passing and, following convention, removes his hat. The choice he sees is between the office and Sherwood Forest. It is Alec who provides the occasion, and the courage, to choose the Forest.[13]

The novel thus depicts three stages in Maurice's development. In the first, Maurice comes to accept homosexuality as an idealised friendship, as the expression of a pure and spiritual love. In the second he moves toward the acceptance of lust in the physical expression of homosexuality. In the final stage he begins to accept the social and political consequences of homosexuality. In this final stage he realises that the outlawed state of the homosexual provides the privilege of a radical perspective on society. By creating a hero who is completely unexceptional, Forster calls attention to the possibility that homosexuality may provide growth for even the most conventional. Forster came to recognise the importance of this third stage largely through the influence of Carpenter. As we have seen, Forster was already aware of Carpenter by 1907, if not earlier; and he had an apparently intuitive grasp (based on personal experience) of the possible connections between homosexuality and democracy. Such views were by no means common at the time Forster was writing. They were limited almost exclusively to Whitman and his English disciple Carpenter. But Forster's visit to Carpenter, and his reading of him and Whitman, provided the basis for a novel that would attempt not to analyse the passage of a man from confused or repressed homosexuality to a blissful ideal homosexuality, but to juxtapose that development with another, much more significant one from the homosexuality of the *fin de siècle* aesthetes to the robust political homosexuality of Whitman and Carpenter.

A brief examination of *Love's Coming of Age* will shed some light on the role Carpenter played in the conception of *Maurice*. Carpenter's essay 'Man the Ungrown' seems particularly pertinent. In it he concerns himself with 'the men of the English-speaking well-to-do class' whose learning stops after public school. These men are, in Carpenter's analysis, permanent schoolboys who continue to run society by the rules of their school days. These men see no reason for equality in marriage, since for them, according to Carpenter, 'it seems quite natural that our marriage and social institutions should lumber along over the bodies of women, as our commercial institutions grind over the bodies of the poor and our "imperial" enterprise over the bodies of barbarian races'.[14] The character of Clive is particularly influenced by Carpenter's analysis. He is Forster's illustration of the 'ungrown' man, who has never learned to question any of the values of his class. Clive's marriage in *Maurice* is an illustration of the marriage of such a man. The novel's final words, '[he] returned to the house, to correct his proofs and to devise some method of concealing the truth from Anne' (p. 231), illustrate not the failure of marriage, but the failure of such a marriage, based on inequality and ignorance. Thus Norman Page's complaint that 'it is surely a limitation of Forster's that he finds himself unable simply to make a place for the acceptance of homosexual love as an equal to heterosexual love, but must claim that it is superior and thus involves himself in the disparagement of marriage'[15] seems less than fair. The novel clearly rejects the idea of the superiority of homosexuality, an idea that is specifically Clive's and derived from Plato, while keeping the idea that homosexuality may provide the occasion

for a growth in spiritual awareness. It is not, of course, that hetero-
sexuals are denied the possibility of such growth; it is that they lack
the impulse toward it, and that the institutions of heterosexuality,
such as marriage, specifically work against growth. Marriage in Carpenter's view is linked to property, whereas homosexuality exists
outside of class and ownership. Maurice's realisation, 'They must
live outside class, without relations or money; they must work and
stick to each other till death' (p. 233), is pure Carpenter – and, in
turn, pure Whitman: recall the closing stanza of 'Song of the Open
Road'.

> Camerado, I give you my hand!
> I give you my love more precious than money,
> I give you myself before preaching or law;
> Will you give me yourself? will you come travel with me?
> Shall we stick by each other as long as we live?

To the ungrown man of the middle class, Carpenter opposes the
energetic workman, who provides 'sympathy and affection' lacking
in the upper classes. Something of this analysis lies behind the depiction of Alec, although there is also a great deal of Forster's personal
mythology (after Alec, 'now he knew very well what he wanted with
the garden boy', p. 191) and something of the mythological structures one finds in other novels of this period (Alec as Dionysus or
Pan). But above all, Carpenter gave him personal testimony to a love
between two men, a love that had survived by moving outside
society and through which a man of the upper middle classes had
come to question the dominant image of homosexuality presented
by the homosexual apologists.

Edward Carpenter thus brought an end to Forster's search for a
homosexual tradition. For Carpenter seemed to create his own tradition, to offer a world where the homosexual could build a new
social order. In the crucial passage in which Clive and Maurice discuss the role of desire in beauty and oppose Michelangelo to Greuze
(copies of Greuze turn up in Dr Barry's office, along with a Venus de
Medici), Forster writes, 'Their love scene drew out, having the ines-
timable gain of a new language. No tradition overawed the boys.
No convention settled what was poetic, what absurd' (p. 83). Page
has complained that this passage 'works against'[16] the Greek references, but he ignores the way in which the novel itself works against
these references. They are Clive's, not Maurice's, although Maurice
will adopt them for a time, just as Michelangelo is an appropriate

enthusiasm of Clive's, as of Symonds'. Whitman and Carpenter were the means by which Forster came to go beyond those traditions. Do Alec and Maurice have a cast of David in the boat-house? One assumes that their love does not require such appeals to authority, which would in any case be contrary to its spirit, in which two men face the world alone, free to create their lives as they please. That is the revolutionary part of *Maurice*, not its homosexuality, and it was that which Carpenter praised in his congratulatory letter to Forster: 'I am so glad you end up on a major chord. I was so afraid you were going to let Scudder go at the last – but you saved him and saved the story, because the end tho' improbable is not impossible and is the one bit of real romance – which those who understand will love.'[17] That 'major chord', Forster's 'happy ending', which he found 'imperative', is a sign of Maurice's growth from the false values of Clive to the truer values of Alec. Successfully transforming the conventions of marriage fiction, Forster moves his Austen-like protagonist toward wisdom through courtship and concludes with a marriage that seals his moral growth. It was Carpenter who confirmed Forster in his sense of the 'new' homosexual and who proposed the terms for Forster's dual perspective on homosexual love.

From *Journal of Homosexuality*, 8 (1983), 35–46.

NOTES

[Homosexual acts between men were criminalised in 1885: the trial of Oscar Wilde followed ten years later. Michel Foucault argues in *The History of Sexuality* (1976) that the category of 'the homosexual' as a character, as a personality type, emerged during the nineteenth century, the word first appearing in 1870. Much current criticism, inflected by interest in how gender is constructed, has suggested the importance of homoeroticism as the basis of male friendships (however unacknowledged within patriarchy and renamed 'homosociality'). Eve Kosofsky Sedgwick's *Between Men: English Literature and Male Homosocial Desire* (New York, 1985) is a classic statement of this. Roland Barthes thought of writing a book called 'The Discourse of Homosexualities' (*Roland Barthes by Roland Barthes* [New York, 1977, p. 150]) – the idea being that homosexuality itself is plural, not one identifiable phenomenon, just as heterosexual behaviour has multiple characteristics.

Martin in this essay also suggests that Forster distinguishes between different types of homosexuality. He also finds positive aspects in *Maurice* in its utopianism about class and about love which is not based on property, derived from the inspiration given by Edward Carpenter (1844–1929); nonetheless, we can still see Forster's attitude to homosexuality to be reactive in character, accepting the marginal status of homosexuality (cf. Maurice's words to the doctor: 'I'm an unspeakable of the Oscar Wilde sort' – ch. 31), and not constructing or self-fashioning an alternative identity for himself. In contrast, Wilde, in being camp, finds a means to stage his homosexuality in a way that makes it a challenge to heterosexuality. Significantly, then, Wilde might be regarded as postmodernist (abandoning a belief in deep subjectivity, for instance, in favour of the cultivation of the surface) whereas Forster remains trapped in an older set of identity problems – diagnosable by Foucault – accepting the truth of homosexuality as being the ultimate clue to identity and closely definable. Ed.]

1. E. M. Forster, *Maurice* (Toronto, 1971), 'Terminal Note' (1960), p. 235. All further citations are to this edition, a Canadian printing of the Edward Arnold edition, and are indicated in the text.

2. One example of this confusion may be seen in Glen Cavaliero's complaint that although Maurice's relationship with Clive 'disguises his true nature instead of revealing it', Forster 'appears to endorse it for more than it proves to be worth' (*A Reading of E. M. Forster* [London, 1979], p. 134). An earlier, and more hostile, view is expressed by Jeffrey Meyers, who calls Maurice '*a roman à thèse* whose aim is to defend homosexual love' (*Homosexuality and Literature 1890–1930* [Montreal, 1977], p. 101). His essay on *Maurice* repeatedly confuses Clive's and Maurice's statements.

3. On Symonds, see Jeffrey Weeks, *Coming Out: Homosexual Politics in Britain, from the Nineteenth Century to the Present* (London, 1977), pp. 47–56, and Symonds' *A Problem in Greek Ethics* (1883). In an 1893 letter to Carpenter, however, Symonds praised homosexuality as a leveller of social classes. The 'nobler' view of homosexuality was one of the most striking aspects of the Uranians. See Timothy d'Arch Smith, *Love in Earnest* (London, 1970).

4. See my essay on 'Ansell'; 'Forster's Greek: From Optative to Present Indicative', *Kansas Quarterly*, IX (Spring 1977), 69–73. It is worth noting, given the emphasis in *Maurice* on the protagonist's being twenty-four years old when he meets Alec, that Forster was twenty-four in 1903, the probable year of composition of 'Ansell'.

5. See my *The Homosexual Tradition in American Poetry* (Austin, Texas, 1979).

6. E. M. Forster, *The Longest Journey* (New York, 1962), p. 4.

7. Forster, *Journey*, p. 69.

8. P. N. Furbank, *E. M. Forster: A Life* (New York, 1978), I, 159, n. l. An examination of the actual diary entry reveals Forster placed a small

question mark above Sturge Moore, and marks whose significance is unclear above Symonds, Shakespeare, and Butler. Above this list in the diary, but not reprinted by Furbank, is another list of four names: A. E. W. Clarke, Desmond Coke, H. N. Dickinson, Howard Sturgis. All of them are authors of schoolboy novels. Below the main list is a third list, one three lines: Tuke/Luca Signorelli? Michelangelo, Cellini/Loti. There are marks above Signorelli and Cellini. (Forster's diary is in King's College Library, Cambridge.)

9. The scene in the British Museum treats comically the schoolmaster's ignorance of sexuality by referring to the statue of the five-legged Assyrian bull, a joke not unlike that of 'The Classical Annex'. It also takes the British Library to task, calling it 'supposedly catholic' (p. 209), an apparent reference to the library's refusal to include Carpenter's *The Intermediate Sex* in its catalogue until forced to do so in 1913, the year of the first composition of *Maurice*.

10. One source of this dream, as well as of the dawn imagery, is almost certainly Kenneth Grahame's *The Wind in the Willows*. Grahame is another example of the idealised, ethereal homosexuality that Maurice will grow beyond. Grahame's domestic/prophetic voice may be the source of the ecstatic prose that is partially parodied in *Maurice*.

11. Again the analogies to Whitman are striking. Many poems in the 'Calamus' sequence deal with the discovery of the real self beneath the facade of a social self. And the image of the root may well be a reference to the calamus itself ('Calamus' 4). Consider also Whitman's resolve in the second 'Calamus' poem, 'I will escape from the sham that was proposed to me, I will sound myself and comrades only'.

12. Cavaliero, *A Reading*, p. 137.

13. Norman Page complains, '... if Forster believed, as he seems to have done right up to the time of the Wolfenden Report, that toleration of the homosexual's condition was still a distant dream, there is nothing in *Maurice* to bring home to the reader that the question is an urgent and continuing one' (*E. M. Forster's Posthumous Fiction* [Victoria BC, 1977], p. 84). Page completely misses the point. Forster sees only a choice between a world of hypocrisy in which the homosexual 'passes' and the world of the outlaw. It is precisely because he thought that an elimination of homosexual oppression was 'a distant dream' that his novel is not primarily concerned with the question of political change. In any case, Page apparently fails to see that the novel is concerned with personal development, not with politics in the narrow sense (although earlier he calls it a *Bildungsroman*). The novel's 'politics' derive from the radical perspective that Maurice may achieve through his homosexuality.

14. Edward Carpenter, *Love's Coming of Age: A Series of Papers on the Relations of the Sexes* (New York and London, 1911), pp. 34–7. The

book was first published in 1896, and editions after 1906 include *The Intermediate Sex*, Carpenter's essay on homosexuality.

15. Page, *Posthumous Fiction*, pp. 92–3.

16. Ibid., p. 82.

17. Unpublished letter from Carpenter to Forster, 23 Aug. 1914, King's College Library. Carpenter may well have in mind the Epilogue rather than the present ending. (See Philip Gardner, 'The Evolution of E. M. Forster's *Maurice*', in *E. M. Forster: Centenary Revaluations*, ed. Judith Scherer Herz and Robert K. Martin [London, 1982], pp. 204–21.) In any case, Forster 'saves' Alec and ends on 'a major chord'.

7

Forster's Friends

RUSTOM BHARUCHA

I

It is a sad photograph that should have faded with time. Perhaps it should not have been taken in the first place. The camera catches the two figures in a blank moment, their faces stiff, their eyes wide and vacant. The men seem to belong together like a married couple, but there is a rift between them. Outwardly, they resemble men of property, utterly respectable; their hair parted neatly on the side, their moustaches trimmed. Yet it is not a club that they belong to but a universe – of oblivion, separation, and death. Almost as a sign, the photographer has left an enormous space above their heads, a nothingness that seeps into the gulf between the men.

Looking at the photograph many years after it was taken, Forster observed that he looked 'starry-eyed' in it, 'very odd indeed'. Significantly, he tore up all the letters that he had written to his mother from Tesserete, Switzerland, where the photograph had been taken. It was a time he would rather forget, reminding him of a relationship that hadn't worked out. As he put it, the holiday in Tesserete was like 'a honeymoon slightly off-colour'. The man who lost interest in him, preferring to flirt with a waitress, was Syed Ross Masood, Forster's lifelong friend to whom *A Passage to India* was originally dedicated. He is the other figure in the photograph.

Otherness is what initially attracted Forster to Masood. This 'oriental' was unlike anyone he had met. In the suburban milieu of Weybridge, where Forster lived with his mother, Masood must have appeared like a sultan from the *Arabian Nights* – an alluring, exotic figure, well over six feet tall, regal in style, histrionic in manner, and very handsome. When he got bored with the Latin Forster attempted to teach him, he would pick up his tutor bodily and tickle him. When his fellow students at Oxford ragged him about using scent, he simply 'wiped the floor with one of them in a wrestling match'. Masood was everything Forster was not – physically, socially, and culturally – and it is perhaps for that very reason that Forster came under his spell. On New Year's Eve, 1910, he confessed his love in his diary:

> Let me keep clear from criticism and scheming. Let me think of you and not write. I love you, Syed Masood; love.

These lines illuminate Forster's style of thought. First, the individual utterance – 'I love you, Syed Masood' – then a break, an intake of breath signified by a semicolon, and then the thought itself – 'love'. Rooted in a person, and yet anonymous, detached. On reading the details of Forster's love for Masood so intimately recorded by P. N. Furbank in his celebrated biography – an intimacy so natural that Forster himself seems to be speaking to us – one realises how much turmoil there was within Forster not only because Masood did not reciprocate his love, but because their friendship itself was based on differing conceptions of love, enigmatic, and left unexplained. Forster loved Masood and Masood loved Forster, but not in the same way.

It is too easy to use the dichotomy of East and West to explain the incompatibility of love between Forster and Masood. For one thing, if Masood was an 'oriental', a man of the East, he was also an unqualified wog. And like all wogs, he was and was not Indian. He was the grandson of Sir Syed Ahmed Khan, the great Muslim reformer, but he was also the devoted foster son of Theodore Morrison, the principal of the Muslim Anglo-Oriental College at Aligarh which resembled Eton in its early years. Masood's sentiments were eastern, but his education was almost entirely western. On the one hand, he was entranced by Urdu poetry, particularly by the verse of Ghalib and Hali, but he also played the banjo and read the French symbolists. He never found time to attend meetings of the India Society at Oxford, but he was invariably free for a game of tennis. So how 'oriental' was Syed Masood?

It would seem that Masood played with oriental images, fully aware of their stereotypes. Never embarrassed to indulge in grandiloquence, he once said: 'Ah, that I had lived 250 years ago when the oriental despotisms were in their prime!' Clearly, he lived before Wittfogel and Said had their say about orientalism, and at a time when the British could still be tolerated by educated Indians. Masood enjoyed his role as an 'oriental' and frequently wrote to Forster in the epistolary style of a Scheherazade: '... let it be known to thee that thy slave's house was this day brightened by the arrival of an epistle from thee – the source of all his happiness.' Even in jest, it is ironic for Masood to speak of himself as the 'slave' (and of Forster as his 'master'), because it was he who dominated the friend-ship. In fact, Masood was possessive of all his friends, whose attention he commanded in a vehement way. Not surprisingly, by the time he graduated from Oxford, his only friends were Indian with the exception of Forster and another Englishman. It seems that Masood's English 'friends' could no longer accept his despotic view of friendship.

Forster learned to accept it in time. But in the early years, he must have been confused by Masood's protestations of love, particularly when they were yearning and not in the least possessive. For instance, in a letter written to Forster eight months before they went to Tesserete, Masood writes:

> Dearest boy if you knew how much I loved you & how I long to be alone with you. ... Let us get away from the conventional world & let us wander aimlessly if we can, like two pieces of wood on the ocean & perhaps we will understand life better. ... I only wish that you & I could live together forever & though that is a selfish wish I feel sorry that it will not come to anything. Did you see the eclipse, how beautiful it was!

What was this? Rhapsodic 'oriental' rhetoric or true sentiment? It would seem that Masood had the latter in mind because in a sub-sequent letter he tells Forster: '... you are about the only Englishman in whom I have come across true sentiment & that, too, real sen-timent even from the oriental point of view.' He then urges Forster to cultivate a faculty that every 'true and well bred oriental' possesses – *Tarass*. For Masood, *Tarass* is that capacity to enter the feelings of another and absorb the atmosphere of a place. The orien-tal senses are always ready '*to receive* & quivering to receive some impression'.

If Forster had possessed or had been possessed by *Tarass*, he would have embraced Masood when they once parted company at the Gare du Nord in Paris. He would have understood why Masood was so 'extraordinarily sad'. When Forster defended his crisp English goodbye by saying that they would be meeting in three days, Masood wailed: 'But we're *friends!*' A parting had to be lingered over for Masood, otherwise how could friendship be savoured? What was the point of saying goodbye if there was no sentiment attached to it?

Not only are the signs of friendship different for Forster and Masood, but their acceptance of sentiment in relation to love is also at odds. For Masood, sentiment seems to be the grace of love, and in its excess of feeling, it becomes the raison d'être of friendship. It is beautiful in itself and does not have to lead anywhere or prove anything. Like a verse by Ghalib whose sounds hang in the air, waiting to be received and then fading away, it becomes that moment of intimacy which true friends share. In contrast, it would seem that for Forster sentiment is merely an attribute of friendship. In itself there is no guarantee of intimacy. No wonder he felt compelled to clarify his relationship with Masood. When he eventually confessed his love, Masood merely said, 'I know', and allowed the moment to pass. For Masood, the intimacy of their friendship lay in the exchange of sentiment itself, not in the physical act of love. Many years later, Forster was to understand this. There is that inexplicable moment in *A Passage to India* when Aziz quotes Ghalib, and Forster reflects:

> The poem had done no 'good' to anyone, but it was a passing reminder, a breath from the divine lips of beauty, a nightingale between two worlds of dust. Less explicit than the call to Krishna, it voiced our loneliness nevertheless, our isolation, *our need for the Friend who never comes yet is not entirely disproved.*

As Masood knew, his friend Forster would find *Tarass* in his art.

II

It is actually quite amazing that Forster and Masood were able to share as much as they did because the world they belonged to had a very rigid conception of how men should behave with men, and more specifically, how white men should treat black men. Colonialism, one might say, did not approve of intimacy between the rulers and the ruled. Not only did familiarity breed contempt, it also undermined the fundamental premises of authority and separatism that characterised the colonial administrative system. This position is staunchly upheld by Turton, the prototype of the *burra sahib* in *A Passage to India*, who says, 'I have never known anything but disaster result when English people and Indians attempt to be intimate socially. Intercourse – yes. Courtesy – by all means. Intimacy – never, never'. The sexual racism of the British is even more conspicuous in McBryde who assumes that 'the darker races are physically attracted by the fairer, not vice versa'. The intimacy he envisions, of course, is between a man and a woman. What would he have thought – and this is merely a perverse hypothesis on my part – if Aziz had made sexual advances to Fielding (or vice versa)? It is more than likely that this 'crime' would have outraged not only his sense of decency and morality, but his very idea of manhood – not only his own sense of being a man, but his absolute faith in the masculine identity of his culture.

An ethos of masculinity developed during the British Raj of India, first in England, and then later, through a process of imitation, within India itself. Whether a man was serving his country at home or abroad, he was required to be 'manly' – aggressive, competitive, and in control of his emotions and duties. The Empire had no particular use for women or for the values associated with femininity. Homosexuals were tolerated only insofar as they remained discreet about their activities and functioned within the strict confines of marginal societies like Bloomsbury and Oxbridge. It was among select and 'understanding' members of these societies that Forster circulated his homosexual novel *Maurice*, which he knew could not be published 'until his death or England's'. While Forster was to have a fairly active homosexual life in England, particularly after he returned from India, he was no doubt aware that he belonged to the silent minority, a secret society of the sensitive, whose sexual ambivalence was symptomatic of their innate resistance to the authoritarian and paternalistic rule of their government. Fundamentally, Forster was caught within a system that upheld norms of manhood that contradicted his own.

Even in India he could not entirely escape these established norms, because they had been adopted by Indian men as their only alternative to defeating the British at their own game. In psychoanalytic terms, Indians had begun to 'identify with the aggressor'. Elaborating on this phenomenon in his brilliant study *The Intimate Enemy*, Ashis Nandy situates the opposition between *purusatva* (the essence of masculinity) with *klibatva* (the essence of hermaphroditism) as the essential conflict in the colonial psychology of Indians. 'Femininity-in-masculinity', he claims, 'was perceived as the final negation of a man's political identity, a pathology more dangerous than femininity itself.' In reaction to this 'pathology', there was an upsurge of 'manly' sentiments and attitudes, martial acts of defiance, and frequently humiliating attempts to emulate the 'tough politics' of the British. In *A Passage to India*, Ronnie speaks derisively of this nascent masculinity among the Indians, which his own government has unconsciously enforced. 'They used to cringe', he says, 'but the younger generation believe in a show of manly independence.... Whether the native swaggers or cringes, there's always something behind every remark, and if nothing else he's trying to increase his *izzat* – in plain Anglo-Saxon, to score.'

The kind of 'native' who asserted his masculinity was more often than not semi-Westernised. Masood, of course, was so Westernised that 'manliness' was second nature to him. There is the famous story of his abrasive encounter with a British officer who ordered him out of a railway compartment. With his legs stretched out, Masood coolly said, 'D'you want your head knocked off?' whereupon he and the officer became 'excellent friends'. The anecdote reveals the kind of tolerance, even camaraderie, that could develop between Indian and English men, particularly if the former imitated the manners of manhood assumed by the latter.

The real antagonists of Indian men were not their sahibs but the memsahibs who formed a minuscule society of their own. Excluded from any kind of meaningful social activity, they increasingly saw themselves, as Nandy puts it, as 'the sexual competitors of Indian men with whom their men had established an unconscious homo-eroticised bonding'. Though this 'bonding' is suggestively, though not explicitly, explored in the relationship between Fielding and Aziz, there can be no doubt of Mrs Turton's racist abhorrence of Indian men. 'They ought to crawl from here to the caves on their hands and knees whenever an Englishwoman's in sight, they oughtn't to be spoken to, they ought to be spat at, they ought to be ground into the dust.' Significantly, this invective is aimed primarily at the white men in the room, Mrs Turton's men, whom she considers 'weak, weak, weak'.

What is so astonishing about *A Passage to India* is that it reson-ates with these colonial attitudes and tensions while remaining a novel 'set out of time'. Forster scrupulously avoids specifying dates, though the imaginative space of the novel suggests an India that has passed through the Swadeshi Andolan and the Partition in Bengal. Now there is a deceptive calm, a scarcely controlled tension that threatens to break out into a national uprising. The novel is set within this tension and maintains a precarious equilibrium. Certainly, when Forster visited India for the first time in 1912, he became fully aware of the resistance to British rule, particularly through his meeting with two radical Muslim leaders, the brothers Shaukat and Mohammed Ali. Joint editors of an anti-imperialist journal, the *Comrade*, they condemned the British endorsement of Italian rule in Tripoli and supported the pro-Turkish movement among Indian Muslims. It is possible to see traces of this radical fervour in the 'manly' Indian characters of *A Passage to India*, particularly in Aziz after the trial, when he becomes 'an Indian at last'. But Aziz's resistance to the British is deeply confused not only because he is a Muslim before he is an Indian, but because he doesn't know how to get rid of the British. All he has is rhetoric, emotion, and manliness. His cheers at the end of the novel, 'Hurrah for India! Hurrah! Hurrah!' are like the echoes of the Empire mocking him.

> And Aziz in an awful rage danced this way and that, not knowing what to do, and cried: 'Down with the English anyhow. That's certain. Clear out, you fellows, double quick, I say. We may hate one another, but we hate you most. If I don't make you go, Ahmed will, Karim will, if it's fifty or five hundred years we shall get rid of you, yes, we shall drive every blasted Englishman into the sea.'

Clearly, the novel was written before Gandhi's advocacy of non-violence had acquired a national dimension. He needed less than fifty years not to 'drive every blasted Englishman into the sea', but to convince them that it was time that they left. He alone knew how to deal with the manliness of the Turtons and the Burtons, not to mention Sir Winston Churchill. With his deceptively childlike and gentle manner, he strategically debunked the ethos of *purusatva* not to capitulate to the British, but to defeat them with another concept of manhood that brought the feminine instincts of man to the surface. As Ashis Nandy so accurately perceives, 'Gandhi was clear in his mind that activism and courage could be liberated from aggressiveness and recognised as perfectly compatible with womanhood, particularly maternity'. Though this alternative to the Western concept of manhood is something that Aziz has yet to learn, there is a moment in the novel when he does assert his manhood, not in

Gandhian terms, but in the deeply personal tone of his author. It occurs when Hamidullah is talking to him man-to-man about 'sticking to the profession' and earning the respect of European doctors. Aziz listens to the spiel, then winks and says, 'There are many ways of being a man: mine is to express what is deepest in my heart'. This is my moment of *Tarass* in the novel.

III

In *A Passage to India*, Forster attempted to express what was deepest in his heart. The writing of the novel was not easy. It wasn't just the incompatibility between East and West that proved to be an obstacle; Forster had reconciled himself to the fact that 'most Indians, like most English people, are shits, and I am not interested whether they sympathise with one another or not'. The novel was hard to write for personal rather than political reasons: it followed the death of a friend, another Muslim, Mohammed-el-Adl.

They had met in Alexandria in 1916 when Forster worked for the Red Cross and Mohammed was employed as a tram conductor. Not only was Mohammed Forster's first true lover, he was also the first man who challenged Forster to cross 'a big racial and social gulf'. He was Egyptian, a race more despised by the British than the Indians, and he belonged to the working class. He had more reason to be anti-British than Masood, particularly when in 1920, at the height of British colonialism in Egypt, he was sentenced to six months' hard labour in prison on a false charge of attempting to buy firearms.

'They shaved the hair they used a filthy basket instead of a towel, took off my civil clothes and gave me a prisoner's clothes', he wrote incoherently to Forster who was 'wrecked' by the news. The political forces of his country had humiliated his friend. There is some reason, I believe, for Forster to have written the notorious statement many years later in *What I Believe*: 'If I had to choose between betraying my country and betraying my friend I hope I should have the guts to betray my country.'

On returning from his second visit to India in 1922, Forster stopped over in Port Said to spend a few days with Mohammed, who was dying of consumption. He arranged for his friend to live in a health resort, bought a silk shawl for his wife, and made provisions for the family. This extension of friendship to the family of his friend is typical of Forster's later relationships with men. Mohammed's world mattered to Forster as much as did Mohammed himself. On returning to England, Forster simply waited for his friend to die. In his diary, he confided: 'I want him to tell me that he is dead, and so set me free to make an image of him.'

Mohammed died within four months, bequeathed a ring to Forster, and *A Passage to India* was well under way. If this sounds somewhat ruthless, an exploitation of life in the pursuit of art, it should be remembered that Forster also wrote a private 'letter' to Mohammed after his death that contains some of the most poignant autobiographical writing that I have ever read. Through recollections of dreams and a confrontation of the struggle involved in making a dead person live, Forster forged his way to an acceptance of his friend's death in the larger context of being alive in the universe.

In the spring of 1923, he went for a walk in Chertsey Meads, wearing Mohammed's ring, and found that he could no longer remember his friend. He acknowledged the sad truth of this experience in his diary, and in the process of recording it, he crystallised his vision of friendship.

> You are dead, Mohammed, and Morgan is alive, and thinks more about himself and less of you every word he writes. You called out my name at Beebit el Hagar station after we had seen that ruined temple.... It was dark and I heard an Egyptian shouting who had lost his friend: Margan, Margan – you calling me and I felt we belonged to each other, you had made me an Egyptian. When I call you on the downs now, I cannot make you alive, nor can I belong to you because you own nothing. I shall not belong to you when I die – only be like you.

There is no otherness in this friendship. The categories of 'you' and 'me' are dissolved; Forster can be Egyptian. Or more precisely, he can be made Egyptian by his friend. Ultimately, these national distinctions are of no consequence because in death, there is nothing to own – neither a name nor a country. Even friends no longer belong to each other: they *are* each other.

This magnanimous view of friendship had evolved over time. Certainly, it would be wrong to assume that Forster had always upheld it or had been guided by it in his attitude to men. During his second trip to India, for instance, we have a document of his relationship with an Indian boy called Kanaya that disturbingly reflects an

authoritarian view of friendship based on the principle of ownership. Forster had met 'this barber-boy' while serving as the secretary
to the Maharaja of Dewas Senior. Unable to control his homosexual
instincts ('the heat provoked me sexually') and oppressed by his
constant masturbation and vacancy of mind, Forster eventually
found comfort in Kanaya, whose services were arranged by none
other than the Maharaja himself. While officially an 'anti-sodomite'
(unlike the Maharaja of Chatrapur whose attachment to boy-actors
was well known), the Maharaja of Dewas sympathised with
Forster's problem.

> 'Why a man and not a woman?' he once asked. 'Is not a woman
> more natural?'
> 'Not in my case', replied Forster. 'I have no feeling for women.'
> 'Oh, but then that alters everything. You are not to blame.'

Not only was the Maharaja Forster's active accomplice in his sex
life, he even advised Forster to accept homosexual jokes made at his
expense and, at all costs, to avoid passivity, 'for a rumour of that
kind would be bad'. In a more tantalising way, he revealed Forster's
age to his courtiers under the dubious assumption that 'at forty-two
any properly constructed Indian is impotent or nearly so and can
dally no more with maiden or boy'.

While the Maharaja appears to us, quite literally, as a character –
he is whimsical and delightfully absurd in his manoeuvrings and
strategies – one should also keep in mind that he embodies power.
As the ruler of the state, he *owns* Kanaya's life. In his manuscript,
Forster reveals that Kanaya was 'terrified of H.H., whose severity
towards his class seemed notorious'. And significantly, as His High-
ness's friend, Forster also assumes an ownership of Kanaya who has,
in his words, 'the body and soul of a slave'. When Kanaya eventually attempts to exploit the relationship by endearing himself to the
Maharaja, Forster reacts sharply:

> I hesitated not but boxed his ears.... He had been such a goose – had
> done himself and the rest of us in because he couldn't hold his tongue.
> What relationship beyond carnality could one establish with such
> people?

The petulance of Forster's tone and his very English dismissal of
Kanaya as a 'goose' indicate that he wrote his description of Kanaya
to be read by or to friends in the Bloomsbury Memoir Club. It is for

the amusement of these friends that Kanaya himself becomes a character, a source of entertainment.

Needless to say, one has no idea who Kanaya is apart from what we learn from Forster. Even his appearance implies ridicule: 'Somewhat overdressed in too yellow a coat and too blue a turban, he rather suggested the part and his body was thin and effeminate and smelt of cheap scent.' Kanaya hardly speaks, and when he does, he sounds as real as any slave in the *Arabian Nights* talking to his master. We have no way of knowing what he really felt and thought about being sexually involved with a sahib, because Forster does not permit him a point of view. It is possible that the value judgements made by Forster on Kanaya's behalf are a reaction to the 'little racial vengeance' that he received from the local people in Dewas, who teased the sahib for liking boys. But there is no justification, I think, for the peremptory tone adopted by Forster in the conclusion of the piece:

> I resumed sexual intercourse with him, but it was now mixed with the desire to inflict pain. It didn't hurt him to speak of, but it was bad for me, and new in me, my temperament not being that way. I've never had that desire with anyone else, before or after, and I wasn't trying to punish him – I knew his silly little soul was incurable. I just felt he was a slave, without rights, and I a despot whom no one could call to account.

Despite the self-criticism which actually hints of selfishness ('it didn't hurt him, it was bad for me'), this attitude is undeniably despotic. I cannot help wondering how Kanaya reacted to this change in attitude by Forster. What happened to Kanaya anyway? And who *was* he in the first place?

I see a very slight and ineffectual Indian beginning to speak, but then, absurdly, there is an image of Forster's barber-boy 'skipping away through the sunshine holding up a canvas umbrella to protect his complexion'.

IV

The inherent problems in representing Kanaya are symptomatic of the contradictions faced by Flaubert when he represented the Egyptian courtesan Kuchuk Hanem as the prototype of Oriental womanhood. Kanaya's misrepresentation seems inconsequential in comparison, but it echoes what Edward Said has said about Kuchuk Hanem: 'She never spoke of herself, she never represented her emotions, presence, or history. [Flaubert] spoke for and represented her.' It seems that representation in itself poses an unavoidable paradox: on the one hand, we have reason to be concerned when we believe that something or someone has been misrepresented, and yet, can there be a true representation of anything? What is the truth in a representation? Is it an essence that has been faithfully reproduced in the re-presentation? Or is it, less ambiguously, a point of view that you happen to share with the author?

It is well known that the representation of the Anglo-Indian characters in *A Passage to India* was strongly criticised by many Anglo-Indian readers as 'unfair' and 'inhuman'. 'Your Collector is impossible', wrote a retired Indian civilian of 'thirty years' experience' (as opposed to Forster's 'year-and-a-half'). 'All the fuss about the bridge-party is hopelessly out of date', wrote another. Ultimately, as Forster was to acknowledge with daring candour, 'I loathe the Anglo-Indians and should have been more honest to say so'. But does the fact that he 'loathes' the Anglo-Indian imply that he doesn't *know* them? I think not, but then I speak as an Indian. Turton is not a one-dimensional caricature for me: he represents a particular combination of pomposity and power that was known to exist in colonial India. In fact, we still have Turtons in India today, only now their skin is 'coffee-colour' as opposed to 'pinko-gray'. The *burra sahib* mentality is not obsolete at all: it is a living presence in post-Independence India and can be traced to the behaviour of company directors and bureaucrats. In fact, replicas of Turton can be found all over the world, notably in members of Margaret Thatcher's party and in immigration officials at Heathrow Airport.

If I seem to be arguing as an 'oriental' here, it is because I know when I like or dislike certain people, not unlike Mrs Moore and her author. 'Sympathy is finite', as Forster once remarked. As for 'fair-mindedness', it was to be commended as a 'rare achievement' in art, but 'how sterile in one's soul'. What mattered to Forster most of all as a writer was what he called the *accent* in a work of art. 'If I saw more of Anglo-India at work', he explained to a critical reader, 'I should of course realise its difficulties and loyalties better and write about it from within. Well and good, but you forget the price to be paid: I should begin to write about Indians from without. My statements about them would be the same, but the accent would have altered.' It seems that the 'accent' involves a great deal more than a change in emphasis of tone or point of view. In the case of Forster's depiction of the Indian characters in *A Passage to India*, notably Aziz, it becomes a sympathetic link that an author feels for a particular character that transcends the objectivity of his representation. The author may criticise this character, but fundamentally, he is linked to him rather like a friend.

One could say that Forster wrote *A Passage to India* as an 'oriental', which in the context of the book signifies 'a friend of the East'. This does not mean, of course, that he wrote the book as an Indian. How could he? Like any author, his sympathies were circumscribed by his intellectual milieu, his personal and political commitments, and his sense of history – all of which had been unavoidably shaped by his English upbringing, education, and cultural inheritance. Obviously, the truth to be found in Forster's novel is something that has been shaped by Forster himself. It is not a metaphysical essence of India that has simply been borrowed and absorbed into the book. Therefore, in asking the inevitable (and problematic) question, How true is the book to India? one should keep in mind that the truth represented in the book is itself a representation. In other words, we have to examine it, as Said advises in *Orientalism*, not in relation to 'some great original', but more concretely through the book's style, figures of speech, and narrative devices. The very exteriority of a text is what constitutes its truth.

Upholding this critical premise, Said quotes the famous ending of *A Passage to India* (perhaps more famous now after its rendition in David Lean's film) and comments that it is *this style* that 'the Orient will always come up against'.

> But the horses didn't want it – they swerved apart; the earth didn't want it, sending up rocks through which riders must pass single-file; the temples, the tank, the jail, the palace, the birds, the carrion, the Guest House, that came into view as they issued from the gap and saw Mau beneath: they didn't want it, they said in their hundred voices, 'No, not yet', and the sky said, 'No, not there'.

It is almost as if Forster's language is setting up a barrier which prevents the East and West from coming together. Otherness seems to be affirmed through the rhetoric itself. One is left, in Said's words, with 'a sense of the pathetic distance still separating "us" from an Orient destined to bear its foreignness as a mark of its permanent estrangement from the West'.

My problem with this interpretation is that it is much too strategic in its focus and situation in the wide spectrum of Orientalist thought. Yes, there is separation in the final moments of *A Passage to India*, but it is so subtly juxtaposed with intimacy that one might say that Aziz and Fielding have acquired a mutual understanding of each other for the first time – perhaps because of the separation. Let us not forget that before the horses 'swerve' apart, the language is steeped in a physical detail that totally contradicts the 'distant' style of the conclusion. Aziz is shouting,

> 'We shall drive every blasted Englishman into the sea, and then' – he rode against him [Fielding] furiously – 'and then', he concluded, half kissing him, 'you and I shall be friends.'
> 'Why can't we be friends now?' said the other, holding him affectionately. 'It's what I want. It's what you want.'

The irony that Forster suggests so seductively is that Aziz and Fielding *are* friends at the moment of parting. If history and the universe are bent on separating them, Forster seems to imply that it is 'not yet' time for them to be permanently united.

For me, the ending is not 'disappointing' as Said claims. If Aziz and Fielding had galloped away into the sunset, it would have been as unconvincing as their gentlemanly handshake in Lean's film. Forster, I believe, is attempting something a great deal more complex than an orientalist vision of irreconcilable differences between East and West. One could say that he is juxtaposing three kinds of friendship: the friendship between friends, between nations, and between friends and (their friends') nations. The struggle between these different kinds of friendship is most richly textured in the final exchange between Aziz and Ralph. As Mrs Moore's son, Ralph has to be Aziz's friend:

> 'But you are Heaslop's brother also, and alas, the two nations cannot be friends.'
> 'I know. Not yet.'
> 'Did your mother speak to you about me?'
> 'Yes.' And with a swerve of voice and body that Aziz did not follow he added: 'In her letters, in her letters. She loved you.'
> 'Yes, your mother was my best friend in all the world.'

Truly, it is in language that the ambivalent truths of books are ultimately conveyed. In the passage quoted above, we find so many of the tussles within Forster's characters – their allegiance to themselves, to their friends, and to their nations – all cohering in an irresolute conflict. It is the words that carry this irresolution through to the end of the novel. It is 'not yet' time for the nations to be friends. But more subtly, in Ralph's '*swerve* of voice and body', I sense a movement *toward* Aziz and the very counterpoint of the final separation between Aziz and Fielding when the horses swerved apart. In the separation, I hear an echo of the earlier movement.

Separating and uniting, giving and receiving, the novel moves between these states of being. The possibilities of friendship that lie at the very core of Forster's vision may be questioned, but they are absolutely denied. As Ralph instinctively knows, even a stranger can be a friend. He is white and, in a sense, unavoidably related to the Turtons and Burtons (on a racial level) and to Ronnie (through his mother's first marriage), but he can also be an 'oriental'. And not through manipulative or exploitative means but by feeling something extraordinary about India of which Aziz himself is unaware. Stella also feels 'that link outside either participant that is necessary to every relationship' – a link that she discovers after experiencing the Hindu celebration of Krishna. Forster poses here a controversial paradox in making Mrs Moore's children seem more 'oriental' than Aziz through their insight into Hinduism. As a Muslim whose allegiance is to Babur and Alamgir, the poetry of Ghalib, and the spirit of Islam, which is 'more than a faith' for him, Aziz seems excluded from India in a significant way. While he is an 'oriental' by birth (though he has no 'natural affection' for his motherland), Ralph and Stella feel connected to their colony on a spiritual level. Forster may be criticised for mystifying the 'link' felt by the Moores, but it is gratifying that he does not uphold the orientalist dichotomy of 'them' and 'us' in a rigid way.

This does not mean, of course, that all Westerners can be 'orientals'. Good old Fielding remains committed to his 'Mediterranean norm'. As for the other Anglo-Indian characters, they are orientalists by profession for the most part and are in India 'to do justice and keep the peace'. Their necessary commitment to recording, controlling, administering, and defining the Orient in their own terms is what prevents and forbids them from being 'oriental'. Forster's dislike of these orientalists is what prevents him from celebrating the 'marriage' of East and West that Walt Whitman affirmed in his own *Passage to India*. Written to memorialise the opening of the Suez Canal in 1869, the poem has nothing in common with the novel but the title. In fact, it seems that Forster has quite deliberately debunked almost every ideal rhetoricised in the poem.

The 'doubts to be solv'd' and 'blanks to be filled' mentioned in Whitman's poem are neither solved nor filled in the novel. 'Old occult Brahma' becomes nothing and 'reason's early birth' seems the very antithesis of the 'muddles' that Forster's India seems to generate. The 'great achievements of the present' which Whitman glorifies are conspicuous by their absence in Forster's world. Technology cannot explain the echoes in the Marabar Caves. Ultimately, what Forster refutes in Whitman's vision of 'the marriage of continents, climates, and oceans' is its assumptions of global order and universal brotherhood. The poem reeks of belief, an abstraction odious to Forster. All he really believed in, as he mentioned in a famous essay, was personal relationships. It is not surprising, therefore, that he did not share the grandiose vision of man symbolised in the building of the Suez Canal.

This ambitious project was unanimously heralded as a revolutionary step in uniting the peoples and nations of the world. 'Now we will be one' is what Ferdinand de Lesseps must have envisioned. Not inappropriately, his investment company for the project was called the *Campagnie universelle*. 'The whole earth' seemed to be involved in the project. On its completion, 'this cold, impassive, voiceless earth', in Whitman's words, 'would be completely justified'. The truth, of course, is that it was the 'engineers, architects, and machinists' from the West who 'justified' the project. They were the initiators of this vision for the unification of the world. Their missionary zeal is very clearly reflected in a prize-winning poem on the Suez Canal written by Bornier. In the poem, it becomes clear that the Suez Canal has been created not only 'pour l'univers', but 'pour le Chinois perfide et l'Indien demi-nu'. And inevitably, 'Pour ceux à qui le Christ est encore inconnu'. In such sentiments one realises the racist dimension underlying global missions and projects.

A Passage to India does not share this global mission. The only oneness that is alluded to in the novel is one that an individual may find on coming to terms with Nothing. But apart from this uncertain tryst with the unknown, there are no solutions provided by Forster for the oneness of the world. Unlike de Lesseps, he would not, in all probability, believe that 'le rapprochement de l'occident et de l'orient' could be achieved through building a canal. But perhaps, if a Brahmin schoolteacher with clocks on his socks remembered a wasp once observed by a white 'oriental' lady – perhaps it was at such moments that the East and West could enter each other's minds. Now this preoccupation with wasps may seem precious to Forster's critics, but even the severest among them would have to agree that there is nothing orientalist about it.

Minute in detail, it is symptomatic of Forster's distrust of big events – a distrust that challenged the pomp and ceremony of the Raj, its laws and proclamations, its edicts and messages. There is no colonial fervour in Forster to change India, no humanist scheme of progress imposed on a country ridden with problems. Forster accepted India for what it was, and therein lies the extraordinary strength and love of his novel. One can say that India was like so many of his friends. If he saw faults in them, they became part of his love for them. And as in any true friendship, his friends were 'his for ever and he theirs for ever: he loved them so much that giving and receiving became one'.

Forster's love for India endured and deepened over the years. It did not fade with time. When he finally returned to India in 1945 to attend a conference of writers, he again visited Hyderabad, Masood's home city, and realised 'how much of his heart had gone into the place'. Now he was a famous writer and Masood was dead. Seeking refuge from all the attention he received as a dignitary, Forster retreated to a hillside one evening and watched the sun set. Later, he revealed that he had been thinking of Egypt. In his memory, Egypt and India had coalesced, and his friends, too, Mohammed and Masood, were one. Forster never wrote about this moment. Perhaps he realised that some accounts of friends can be written only in the heart.

From *Raritan*, 4 (Spring 1986), 105–22

NOTES

[This essay, which leads into discussion of *A Passage to India*, works by discussing Forster's attitude towards friendship, which is a dominant theme throughout his work, especially here in the reference to 'our need for the Friend who never comes yet is not entirely disproved' (*Passage*, ch. 9). The first friend discussed is Syed Ross Masood, to whom *A Passage to India* was dedicated. But can friendship exist when the relationship is one of power – between colonised and coloniser? In such circumstances, is not talk of friendship a liberalism which ignores inequality? And how do sexual relations map onto an ideal of friendship? Do they materially affect power relations, and if so, do they do so necessarily? These questions, which are equally implicit in Sara Suleri Goodyear's essay (9) are basic to this essay.

Bharucha also explores Forster's attitude to the 'other', both relating to him (Forster's homosexuality means that it is a 'him') and representing him. Representing the other is a theme raised by Edward Said's *Orientalism* (New York, 1978), referred to early in the essay by Bharucha, along with Karl August Wittfogel, whose *Oriental Despotism* (New Haven, Conn., 1957) is an early denial of the idea that the whole world may be understood in terms of the development of Western societies. (On *Orientalism*, see the Introduction, pp. 7–9, above.) Bharucha reads Forster as denying otherness in some of his personal relationships – and these were all that he said he believed in – but also reads Forster positively, as responding to otherness, his homosexuality allowing him to do this, which implies something more positive in that than has been noted about *Maurice*. If masculinity is the key quality required to govern an empire, Forster's subversion of that, which Langland discusses in her essay (5) on *Howards End* in noting its gender-positioning, becomes the source for a form of oppositional politics to the 'England' that Forster felt kept back, by its hegemonic values, the publication of *Maurice*.

In discussing gender, Bharucha refers to the Indian intellectual Ashis Nandy and his *The Intimate Enemy: Loss and Recovery of Self under Colonialism* (Oxford, 1983), which makes a few interesting incidental comments on Forster, while noting how the white woman is marginalised by the homoerotic bonding of colonial men and Indians (pp. 8–10). The point holds for Suleri Goodyear's essay below, though this does not refer to Nandy. Whereas British rule imposed masculinity (*purasatva*) as hegemonic, Nandy finds older Indian forms of femininity and androgyny which had been repressed by colonial rule brought back and reaccentuated, for example by Gandhi (Nandy, p. 54). This deployment of different gender-terms may be linked with Forster's undoing of patriarchy through a questioning of masculinity in *A Passage to India*. Ed.]

8

The Politics of Representation in *A Passage to India*

BENITA PARRY

> Perhaps the most important task of all would be to undertake studies in contemporary alternatives to Orientalism, to ask how one can study other cultures and peoples from a libertarian, or a non-repressive and non-manipulative perspective. But then one would have to rethink the whole complex problem of knowledge and power.
>
> Edward Said, *Orientalism* (1978) p. 24

> This pose of 'seeing India' ... was only a form of ruling India
>
> *A Passage to India*, xxxvi, 301

I

The discussion on *A Passage to India* as a political fiction has for long been dominated by the followers of a mimetic theory of literature, whose quest for empiricism tied to didacticism is achieved when they find the narrative content to be an authentic portrayal of India and a humanist critique of British–Indian relations during the last decades of the Empire. Since the accession of critical methods concerned with representation as an ideological construct, and not a truthful, morally inspired account of reality, however, the politics of the novel have demanded another mode of analysis, where the articulations of the fiction are related to the system of textual practices by which the metropolitan culture exercised its domination over the subordinate periphery; within this theoretical context, *A Passage to India* can be seen as at once inheriting and interrogating the discourses of the Raj. In common with other writings in the genre, this novel enunciates a strange meeting from a position of political privilege, and it is not difficult to find rhetorical instances where the other is designated within a set of essential and fixed characteristics: 'Like most Orientals, Aziz overrated hospitality, mistaking it for intimacy' (xiv, 154); 'Suspicion in the Oriental is a sort of malignant tumour' (xxxi, 276); and so on. It is equally possible to demonstrate that while the idiom of Anglo-India is cruelly parodied, the overt criticism of colonialism is phrased in the feeblest of terms: 'One touch of regret – not the canny substitute but the true regret from the heart – would have made him a different man, and the British Empire a different institution' (v, 70).

Yet to interpret the fiction as an act of recolonisation which reproduces the dominant colonial discourse would be to ignore – egregiously – the text's heterogeneous modes and its complex dialogic structure.[1] Even the most superficial consideration of the 'India' construed by Western texts, an India which was virtually conterminous with the European consciousness of it, will show that this canon of historical, analytical, propagandist and fictional writings (official minutes, political treatises, scholarly studies, geographical surveys, missionary tracts, journalists' copy, memoirs of civil servants and army officers, educational manuals, school text books, adventure stories, children's books, Anglo-Indian romances, the works of Kipling) devised a way of dividing the world which made British rule in India appear a political imperative and a moral duty. The strategy of discrimination and exclusion can be deduced from the series of meanings produced by the word 'exotic': dissimilar, unrelated, extraneous, unconformable, untypical, incongruent, eccentric, anomalous, foreign, alien, abnormal, aberrant, deviant, outcaste, monstrous, fantastic, barbarous, grotesque, bizarre, strange, mysterious, unimaginable, wondrous, outlandish. Only by wilfully suppressing its initiation of an oppositional discourse is it possible to insert *A Passage to India* into the hegemonic tradition of British–Indian literature.

Written from within the liberal–humanist ideology, and in its realist aspect using the style of ironic commentary and measured ethical judgement, the fiction does act to legitimate the authorised cultural categories of the English bourgeois world. Indeed, so far as it imitates 'the beauty of form... the harmony between the works of man and the earth that upholds them, the civilisation that has escaped muddle, the spirit in a reasonable form' (xxxii, 278), the narrative organisation underwrites the value of Western cultural norms. Other rhetorical modes converge, however, to subvert the certainties of the fiction's own explanatory system as these are put into confrontation with foreign codes. It has been repeatedly alleged in the critical literature that Forster's India is an amorphous state of mind, a figure of inchoate formlessness, a destroyer of meaning. This is to substitute the firm stance on epistemology discernible in traditional fiction for the ontological puzzlement of a modernist text, where India's difference is represented not as a Manichean opposition threatening Western precepts and practices, but as an original system of knowledge and an alternative world view. Without embracing or consolidating the cosmic perspectives and aspirations institutionalised in some of India's major cultural traditions, the novel does, in its triadic structure of Mosque, Caves and Temple, undermine the politically constructed concept of India (as well as refusing the scented East of legend, and the India to be seen as pageant or frieze from the seat of a dogcart) to produce instead a set of radical alternatives to the meanings valorised by an imperialist civilisation.

Thus, within the novel's colloquy, the gestures of performance and force are countered by icons of restfulness and spiritual silence; the rhetoric of positivism, moral assurance and aggression is transgressed by the language of deferred hope, imponderables and quietism. Against the grain of a discourse where 'knowing' India was a way of ruling India, Forster's India is a geographical space abundantly occupied by histories and cultures distinct from the Western narrative of the world and the meanings this endorses. But if *A Passage to India* can be seen to act as an ideological catalyst, it can also be seen as constrained by its conditions of production. What is absent is a consciousness of imperialism as capitalism's expansionist, conquering moment, and the enunciated critique of the Raj is consequently toned down. Imperialism's triumphalist rhetoric is present, but modulated and made safe by irony. Lampooned in the conversations of the Anglo-Indians, it is without the danger such declamations arouse in Conrad's writings, where a language extolling might, force, domination and supremacy, conflating a mystical zeal for conquest with a utilitarian preoccupation with exploitation, engenders a ruthless criticism of imperialism's beliefs, practices and styles. All the same, given the evasions in the novel's articulations of imperialist ideology, *A Passage to India* is the limit text of the Raj discourse, existing on its edges, sharing aspects of its idiom while disputing the language of colonial authority. Forster's reputation as the archetypal practitioner of the domestic, liberal–humanist, realist English novel, has inhibited contemporary readers from engaging with A Passage to India as a text which disrupts its own conventional forms and dissects its own informing ideology. Where criticism has not applauded the novel's humanist political perceptions, it has scorned its equivocations and limitations; it should now address itself to the counter-discourse generated by the text, which in its global perspective refuses the received representation of the relationship between the metropolitan culture and its peripheries, and interrogates the premises, purposes and goals of a civilisation dedicated to world hegemony.

II

The symmetrical design and integrative symbolism of A Passage to India confirm Forster's wish to make a coherent statement about human realities through art – for him the one internally harmonious, material entity in the universe, creating order from the chaos of a permanently disarranged planet[2] – while the deeper structure to the novel holds open-ended, paradoxical and multivalent meanings, discharging ideas and images which cannot be contained within the confines of the formal pattern. In a text consisting of a political fiction, an allegory, a philosophical novel, a social tragedy and a metaphysical drama, both centrifugal and centripetal forces are at work: the themes diverge from the axis and realign, the literary forms radiate and join, the ostensibly poised whole emitting ambiguity, dissonance and contradiction which are formally repossessed and transfigured in an affirmative if allusive coda. The novel's mythopoeic mode strains after models of universal and ahistorical order, composing an archetypal symbolism intimating that there exists a metaphysical wholeness of all the antinomies in physical reality, social formations and the psyche. Countermanding this cosmic vision of vistas beyond the time–space world is a pessimism which perceives a universe apparently random and inhospitable to habitation, a disjunctive historical situation and the human mind divided against itself. The one orientation points towards an escape from the dislocations in the material world to the timeless womb of myth, the other confronts the present disarray in all its specificity and contingency. But finally, in the 'not now, not here' (xxxvi, 309), 'not yet, not there' (xxxvii, 316), another direction is indicated, one which forecasts that the visionary and the secular will be reconciled. This anticipation of a future still to emerge, a tomorrow radically different from what exists, is rooted in the belief that institutions are not inviolable nor is consciousness fixed; with this hope, the novel's metaphoric and realist modes merge, establishing that the flight into emblematic resolutions has been abandoned, and history reaffirmed.

Forster's nonconformity was evident in his distance from both the orthodoxies and heresies of British society. Though he shared the ideology of the middle-class milieu to which he was born, he was at crucial points disengaged from it, was a part of Bloomsbury yet apart, a socialist without doctrine, a reverent humanist reassured by the sanity of rationalism and the sanctity of individual relationships, who came to speculate on the satisfactions of sacred bewilderment and the dissolution of self in a transcendent other. With the accelerated disintegration of the old order after 1914, Forster's refuge in liberal-humanism, never wholly proof against the elements, was drastically damaged. Confronted by the breakdown in established values, the ravages of European competition, intensified class conflict within British society and growing disaffection amongst the colonial peoples, he looked outside England for a focus on this multiple disorder and, in choosing a route which passed from fiction centred on the condition of England to the global context created by imperialism, initiated a meeting with a defining condition of his times.

Forster has written of his visits to India in 1912 and 1921 as transforming experiences. For a small but significant number of English writers, brought through circumstance or choice into contact with the colonised world, the encounter exposed their consciousness to rival conceptions of civilisation, culture and community, to cosmologies postulating variant orderings to the universe, other definitions of the human condition and alternative versions of personality structure. In negotiating the contrary modes of awareness, the divergent precepts and goals devised by the West and by India, Forster produced a novel which neither fully accepts nor entirely repudiates the standards and usages of either. The text reveals the crisis of liberal–humanist ideology – its impotence as a code in an embattled social situation where moderation and compromise are not possible, its inadequacy as an explanation of a universe more extensive than the environment made by human intervention, and the insufficiency of its insights into the potentialities of mind whose experiential range exceeds ratiocination and sensory cognition. Nevertheless, although the work ventures no affirmation of its creed, it is the product of an intelligence and sensibility nurtured within the cultural and intellectual context of liberal–humanism. It is because the novel is mediated through this world view and returns there for repose that the advance into new and profoundly astonishing perceptions is accompanied by retreats to the confines of known sterilities. The narrative voice oscillates between faith and disbelief in the validity of humanist mores, observing that, within an India divided into cultural groups not always sympathetic towards each other and ruled over by aliens hostile to all, community is both a refuge and a laager; that, if immersion in mysticism wastes secular proficiency, adherence to rationalism atrophies other possible facets of personality; that, whereas empiricism can provide a rigorous arrangement of appearances, it misses essences, and, if exclusion and definition lead to functional and aesthetic excellence, only the suspension of discrimination and the abolition of barriers will facilitate the making of a total explanatory system.

To these polarities no resolution is suggested, yet, because *A Passage to India* calls on resources outside the norms and priorities of Western societies, summoning other social configurations, ethical codes and philosophical systems, evaluations which have been made of Forster's 'medium mind' and his imprisonment within a superannuated system of ideas and values should be rephrased, for this novel both articulates in ontological and moral terms a radical dissent from the conventions and aspirations of the late bourgeois world, and omits to make the critical connection between these and the social and political structures they accompanied and sustained. Because of this, there is a vacuum at the core of the political fiction. Forster, always a cultural relativist, was amused at the rhetoric of a 'high imperial vision' and came to applaud the colonial people kicking against imperialist hegemony,[3] but just as liberalism was unable to produce a fundamental critique of Western colonialism, so is a consciousness of imperialism's historical dimensions absent from *A Passage to India*. Imperialism inflicted a catastrophic dislocation on the worlds it conquered and colonised, generated new forms of tension within the metropolitan countries and brought the West into a condition of permanent antagonism with other civilisations; yet about this very epitome of contemporary conflict the novel is evasive.

But if such elisions tend to disembody the criticism, suggesting an evaluation of a superstructure uprooted from its base, the British–Indian connection is nevertheless represented as the paradigmatic power relationship, and the encounters possible within the imperialist situation are perceived as grotesque parodies of social meetings. The chilly British circulate like an ice stream through a land they feel to be poisonous and intending evil against them; British domination rests on force, fear and racism, generating enmity in articulate Indians sustained by memories of past opposition to conquest and mobilised by prospects of the independence to be regained. It is the politically innocent Mrs Moore who challenges her son's brutal pragmatism with an appeal for love and kindness, a gesture towards humanising an inhuman situation, which is repudiated in the novel's recognition that hostilities will increase as Indian resistance grows (a process to which passing references are made) and British determination to retain power hardens. Aziz, the Moslem descended from Mogul warriors, and the Brahmin Godbole, whose ancestors were the militant Mahrattas, may have conflicting recollections of an independent Deccan resisting British conquest, but they are united by their distinctively expressed disinclination to participate in their own subjugation, a shared refusal which culminates in a Hindu–Moslem entente. On the other side, the British make up their differences and close ranks, with even Fielding throwing in his lot with Anglo-India and so betraying his ideals.

The effeteness of liberal codes in the colonial situation is established in the novel by the catastrophic failure of British and Indian to sustain personal relations. The friendship between Fielding and Aziz, disturbed throughout by differences in standards and tastes, is finally ruptured when each withdraws, as he inevitably must, within the boundaries of the embattled communities, and it is Forster's consciousness that social connections will fail which sends him in pursuit of spiritual communion between Mrs Moore and both Aziz and Godbole. But perhaps the most eloquent demonstration of liberalism's impotence is its inability to offer any opposition to the enemies of its values. The obtuse, coarse, arrogant and bellicose deportment of Anglo-Indians, as realised in the novel, is the very negation of those decencies defined through Fielding: 'The world, he believed, is a globe of men who are trying to reach one another and can best do so by the help of good will plus culture and intelligence' (vii, 80). When Fielding, after his courageous stand against his countrymen and women, aligns himself with the rulers of India, he is submitting to the fact of imperialism, deferring to a mode of behaviour and feeling made and needed by an aggressive political system and conceding that his liberal principles and hopes of doing good in India exist only by favour of a Ronny Heaslop. Forster's tone can be mild, but the integrity and toughness of his pessimistic acknowledgement that here there is no middle way to compromise and reconciliation marks a break with his previous, though increasingly hesitant, appeals to rapprochement between contending social forces.

III

In an essentially speculative novel, intimating a universe which is not human-centred and departing from the romantic humanism of his earlier works, Forster – without relinquishing trust in reason – reflects on the numinous as he perceives its presence in India's religious traditions. The liberation to ecstasy and terror of the psychic energies subdued by modern industrialised societies, as represented in *A Passage to India*, is significantly different from Forster's former domesticated exhortations to connect the outer and inner life, the prose with the poetry, for the sublime now contemplated has heights and depths never discerned in 'dearest Grasmere' or artistic Hampstead, and recognition of this augurs existential possibilities still to be assimilated by the West. 'Inside its cocoon of work or social obligation, the human spirit slumbers for the most part, registering the distinction between pleasure and pain, but not nearly as alert as we pretend' (xiv, 145). The awakenings of two Englishwomen dislocated by an India that confutes their expectations take cataclysmic form and result in derangement and delusion, the one mimicking in her feelings and behaviour the ascetic stance of isolation from the world but misunderstanding its meanings as meaninglessness, the other assailed by knowledge of sexuality and misinterpreting this as a sexual assault.[4] Both are negative responses to their perceptions of India's 'otherness': Mrs Moore shrinks the august ambition of quietism to the confines of personal accidie, while Adela Quested experiences cultural differences as a violation of her person. When the urbane Fielding has intuitions of a universe he has missed or rejected, of that 'something else' he is unable to know; when he and Adela Quested, both devoted to commonsense and clarity, speculate on the possibility of worlds beyond those available to their consciousness – then they are not yielding to concepts of heaven or hell, but (stirred by an India that is difficult, intricate and equivocal) recognising the possibility of other states of awareness.

What the novel produces in its transmutations of the numinous are dimensions to experience which are authenticated by their psychological truthfulness alone – expressing a hunger for perfection, a discontent with the limitations of the present and an aspiration to possess the future. The need for the unattainable Friend 'who never comes yet is not entirely disproved' (ix, 119), the yearning after the 'infinite goal beyond the stars' (xxix, 262), the longing for 'the eternal promise, the never withdrawn suggestion that haunts our consciousness' (x, 127), these are signs of that permanent hope which will persist 'despite fulfilment' (xxxvi, 299), just as the images, substitutions, imitations, scapegoats and husks used in religious ritual are figures of 'a passage not easy, not now, not here, not to be apprehended except when it is unattainable' (xxxvi, 309).

Significantly *A Passage to India* is a novel from which God, though addressed in multiple ways, is always absent – necessarily excluded from the caves of the atheist Jains, and failing to come when invoked in the form of the Hindu Krishna or the Moslem's Friend – the Persian expression for God.[5] As represented in the novel, the numinous is not divinely inspired nor does it emanate from arcane sources; it needs no religion and meets with no God. Forster's disbelief in the power of the human spirit to 'ravish the unknown' informs his transfigurations of the mystical aspiration:

> Did it succeed? Books written afterwards say 'Yes'. But how, if there is such an event, can it be remembered afterwards? How can it be expressed in anything but itself? Not only from the unbeliever are mysteries hid, but the adept himself cannot retain them. He may think, if he chooses, that he has been with God, but as soon as he thinks it, it becomes history, and falls under the rules of time.
>
> (xxxiii, 285)

What Forster does acknowledge is that faith confers grace on the believer during 'the moment of its indwelling' (xxxiii, 282), and he affirms the gravity of religion's concerns, the fruitful discontent it speaks and the longings it makes known: 'There is something in religion that may not be true, but has not yet been sung.... Something that the Hindus have perhaps found' (xxxi, 274). This paradox signifies the meanings which Forster assigns the institutionalised routes to an understanding and changing of human existence devised by India's religious traditions.

IV

Theme and symbol in the novel's component modes converge on India. It is interesting that Forster's perceptions are in the tradition of Walt Whitman and Edward Carpenter, the one a passionate believer in popular democracy, the other a romantic socialist, both mystics and homosexuals disassociated by temperament and conviction from the conventions of their respective societies. Instead of the bizarre, exotic and perverse world made out of India by Western writers in the late nineteenth and early twentieth centuries, a compilation serving to confirm the normality and excellence of their own systems, Whitman and in his wake Carpenter found in that distant and antique civilisation expressions of transcendent aspects to experience and access to gnosis, predicting that, when connected with the secular, these would open up new vistas to democratic emancipation, international fellowship and progress.[6] But if Forster's India does have affinities with these poetic evocations, the perspectives in *A Passage to India* are informed by inquiry into, rather than new-found belief in, alternative ways of seeing, and the altogether more complex configuration centres on its difference and originality as a challenge to the authorised categories of Western culture.

It is as if the defining concepts of the major Indian cosmologies are objectified in the landscape made by the novel, and this presents to the alien a new awareness that humanity's place is within a chain of being linking it with monkeys, jackals, squirrels, vultures, wasps and flies, and on a continuum of existence extending to oranges, cactuses, crystals, bacteria, mud and stones. Drawing on Indian traditions, the text constructs an ontological scale situating the species in a universe indifferent to human purpose and intent, contiguous to an unconcerned inarticulate world, planted on a neutral earth and beneath an impartial sky. It is a position which seems to reduce existence to a respite between two epochs of dust, including a view of people as moving mud and contesting the centrality of human aspiration and endeavour. The Marabars, as a figure of eternity, and the distance behind the stars, as the sign to infinity, create mythological time–space, challenging the myopia of empirical observation and measurement. In the environs of the Marabars, where hills move, fields jump, stones and boulders declare themselves alive and plants exercise choice, hylozoistic notions formulated by archaic philosophies, and still extant in some Indian religious traditions, are confirmed. To the rationalist this failure to delineate and define, this obliteration of distinctions, spells disorientation and chaos; to the metaphysician it speaks of a continuous series accommodating disparate modes of being within one coherent structure.

It is this theoretical organisation of reality that is produced through the multiplex metaphor of India: an India which with its various cultures, religions, sects and classes, is difficult, arbitrary, intricate and equivocal, a microcosm of the 'echoing, contradictory world' (xi, 129), and an India which is the emblem of an organic entity, an all-including unity accommodating paradox, anomaly and antinomy. For if 'no one is India' (vii, 89) and 'Nothing embraces the whole of India' (xiv, 156), it may all the same be the case that 'the hundred Indias which fuss and squabble so tiresomely are one, and the universe they mirror is one' (xxix, 261). This possibility is translated in the gravitation of Aziz and Godbole towards a united front. Aziz attempts consciously to identify with India – 'I am an Indian at last' (xxxiv, 290) – and unwittingly becomes absorbed, as had his ancestors, in India; Godbole, while continuing to live obediently within the sects and castes of Hinduism, assists Aziz in moving to a Hindu Princely state and declares himself his true friend. But it is in the Hindus' ritual celebration of the entire universe of living beings, matter, objects and spirit taken into the divine embrace that the conception of a dynamic blending of opposites is symbolically enacted, that enigmas and contradictions are ceremonially resolved and fusion is abstractly attained.

Although he was not a scholar of Indian metaphysics, Forster was familiar with the myths, epics and iconography of India's varied cultures and found their innately dialectical style congenial. On re-reading the *Bhagavad-Gita* in 1912 before his first visit to India, he noted that he now thought he had got hold of it: 'Its division of states into Harmony Motion Inertia (Purity Passion Darkness).'[7] These three qualities, constituting in the classical Indian view the very substance of the universe,[8] are permuted in *A Passage to India* as Mosque, Caves and Temple, a sequence with multiple meanings – one of which is the ontological and psychological significance pertaining to three major Indian philosophical–religious systems: they are figures, respectively, of consciousness and the present, the unconscious and the past, and the emergent metaconsciousness and the future. The novel offers this triad as the form of differences contained within a whole: incorporated in the enclosing frame is the gracious culture of Islam in India, a society where personal relations amongst Moslems do flourish; the unpeopled Jain caves, place of the ascetic renunciation of the world; and the buoyant religious community of the Hindus, internally divided and internally cohesive. The approach to the component meanings of these systems is, however, profoundly ambiguous, moving between responsiveness and rejection, making the myth and subverting it.

Mystical Sufi tendencies are represented in the unmistakably Indian incarnation of Islam, a monotheistic and historically recent religion, dually committed to the mundane and the sacred. But, having confronted the more ambitious theories of older India, Forster now relegates Islam's consummation of the prose–poetry connection as too symmetrical, shallow and easy. With 'Caves', the novel passes back to the world-rejecting atheist tradition of the Jains,[9] a post-Vedic heterodoxy of the fifth century BC but, like Buddhism – with which it has historical and theoretical affinities – rooted in the ancient, aboriginal metaphysics of primal, Dravidian India. Here the novel produces a version of this uncompromisingly pessimistic outlook, one which disparages bondage to the phenomenal universe as the source of pain and suffering, and pursues liberation from all involvement with matter. The contemplation of negatives and Nothing within the text culminates in the transfiguration of the ascetic world view, and, if 'Everything exists, nothing has value' (xiv, 160) is a statement of nihilism, it has an alternative meaning, one which acknowledges the material world as verifiable but assigns significance only to Nothing, to complete detachment: 'Nothing is inside them, they were sealed up before the creation of pestilence or treasure; if mankind grew curious and excavated, nothing, nothing would be added to the sum of good and evil' (xii, 139).

There is a striking ambivalence to the imagery of the Caves; their 'internal perfection' is evoked through crystalline figures of pure emptiness. But competing with and countermanding the delicate transparency of their interiors is the opaque menace of their external form:

> There is something unspeakable in these outposts. They are like nothing else in the world and a glimpse of them makes the breath catch. They rise abruptly, insanely, without the proportion that is kept by the wildest hills elsewhere, they bear no relation to anything dreamt or seen. To call them 'uncanny' suggests ghosts, and they are older than all spirit.
>
> (xii, 137)

This speaks of the formless, primordial abyss before time and space, threatening to overwhelm consciousness, an enunciation which undermines the representation of Nothing as an authentic negative aspiration.

Moving forward to the Hinduism of India's Aryan invaders, the novel represents that tradition's ecstatic affirmation of the entire world, the ceremonial celebration of all matter and spirit as originating from and sharing in the Lord of the Universe. But if the text participates in the ambition of Hinduism – itself compounded over aeons through the assimilation and reworking of many other existing beliefs – to tie, weld, fuse and join all the disparate elements of being and existence in a complete union, it withdraws from the incalculable and unassimilable enormity of the enterprise. While *A Passage to India* applauds the refusal of the present as it is, the wish to supersede all obstacles in the way of wholeness, it rejects emblematic resolutions. The impulse to the ceremonies is shown as magnificent:

> Infinite Love took upon itself the form of SHRI KRISHNA, and saved the world. All sorrow was annihilated, not only for Indians, but for foreigners, birds, caves, railways, and the stars; all became joy, all laughter; there had never been disease nor doubt, misunderstanding, cruelty, fear.
>
> (xxxiii, 285)

But when the celebrations end, the divisions and confusions of daily life return. Just as consciousness of political conflict and social divergence transgresses against the will to union, so is there here a humanist's repudiation of symbolic concord. The allegory is over before the novel ends, the aesthetic wholeness dismembered by the fissures and tensions of the disjoint, prosaic world that the novel represents; the permanent is dissolved in the acid of contingency. In the last pages emblems of reconciliation and synthesis compete with their opposites: 'the scenery, though it smiled, fell like a gravestone on any human hope' (xxxvii, 315). The illimitable aspiration is not consummated: 'a compromise had been made between destiny and desire, and even the heart of man acquiesced' (xxxvi, 302).

V

In retrospect it is apparent that the authority of the allegory is throughout undermined by other modes within the text; as each positing of universal abstractions is countermanded by perceptions of the specifics in the historical situation, so the cosmic is cut down to size by the comic – the squeals of a squirrel, though 'in tune with the infinite, no doubt' (x, 126), are not attractive except to other squirrels; trees of poor quality in an inferior landscape call in vain on the absolute, for there is not enough God to go round; there are gods so universal in their attributes that they 'owned numerous cows, and all the betel-leaf industry, besides having shares in the Asirgarh motor-omnibus' (xxxv, 294), and a god whose love of the world had impelled him to take monkey flesh upon himself. From the infinite the novel returns to the ordinary; from eternity there is a bridge back to the mundane. The worth of human effort, ingenuity and creativity is restored in the view Mrs Moore has on her last journey across India, where the symbolic landscape is pervaded by history and culture:

> She watched the indestructible life of man and his changing faces, and the houses he had built for himself and God.... She would never visit Asirgarh or the other untouched places; neither Delhi nor Agra nor the Rajputana cities nor Kashmir, nor the obscurer marvels that had sometimes shone through men's speech: the bilingual rock of Girnar, the statue of Shri Belgola, the ruins of Mandu and Hampi, temples of Khajuraho, gardens of Shalimar.
>
> (xxiii, 213–14)

The balance is redressed, and in the retreat to the Mediterranean it is overturned in favour of the secular and the 'normal'. The relief and pleasure known by both Adela Quested and Fielding on their return voyages from India is confirmed by that narrative voice which has throughout posited and endorsed Western norms and values; and the paean to Venice is eloquent of an ambivalence within the text's discourse towards the alternatives it poses:

> the harmony between the works of man and the earth that upholds them, the civilisation that has escaped muddle, the spirit in a reasonable form.... The Mediterranean is the human norm. When men leave that exquisite lake, whether through the Bosphorus or the Pillars of Hercules, they approach the monstrous and extraordinary; and the southern exit leads to the strangest experience of all.
>
> (xxxii, 278)

But neither this tenuous repose nor the symbolic solutions, neither the inevitability of compromise nor the permanence of conflict is the final word, for these are superseded by the generation of hope in a future when the obstacles the novel has confronted will have been overcome in history. On their last ride together, Aziz and Fielding, after misunderstanding, bitterness and separation, are friends again 'yet aware that they could meet no more' (xxxvii, 310), that 'socially they had no meeting place' (p. 312). But Aziz, anticipating the time of freedom from imperialist rule, promises, 'and then ... you and I shall be friends' (p. 316); and when Fielding asks why this cannot be now, earth, creatures and artefacts intercede to reject the possibility: 'they didn't want it, they said in their hundred voices, "No, not yet", and the sky said, "No, not there." '

A Passage to India is Forster's epitaph to liberal–humanism. In search of other systems he had contemplated traditions to which ironically he had access because of the global space created and divided by imperialism, and if he withdrew from the sheer magnitude of the ambition to liberation nurtured within Indian philosophical modes, he had acquired a perspective on a transfigured tomorrow that made the social hope of his earlier fictions seem parochial. But as facism, persecution, war and the repression of the colonial struggle brought force and violence near and made the 'not yet' seem ever more distant, Forster retired to essays, criticism, biography and broadcasts, media in which it was still possible to reiterate an adherence to liberal values, an option unavailable in self-interrogating fictional texts. In 1935 Forster attended the International Association of Writers for the Defence of Culture in Paris, a meeting organised by the Popular Front to unite communists, socialists and liberals in defence of 'the cultural heritage'. It is possible in retrospect to be cynical about the political humanism which the congress opportunistically advocated and to observe that Forster would have been quite at home in such a gathering. At the time it was surely an act of integrity by an untheoretical socialist determined to demonstrate his opposition to fascism. In his address Forster used the vocabulary of liberalism – justice, culture, liberty, freedom – and conceded that the times demanded another language which he could not speak:

> I know very well how limited, and how open a criticism, English freedom is. It is race-bound and it's class-bound... you may have guessed that I am not a Communist, though perhaps I might be one if I was a younger and a braver man, for in Communism I can see hope. It does many things which I think evil, but I know that it intends good. I am actually what my age and my upbringing have made me – a bourgeois

who adheres to the British constitution, adheres to it rather than supports it ....[10]

Forster needed no critics to tell him of the ambiguities, contradictions and limitations in his intellectual stance; brought to *A Passage to India*, such categories reveal the constraints on the text's system of representation – an analysis which should not hinder the perception that this novel is a rare instance of a libertarian perspective on another and subordinated culture produced from within an imperialist metropolis.[11]

From *A Passage to India: Essays in Interpretation*, ed. John Beer (London, 1985), pp. 27–43.

NOTES

[Benita Parry's essay uses Said's book *Orientalism* and indirectly, in its second quotation at the beginning, Michel Foucault, who in *Discipline and Punish* stresses the power of apparently benign, liberal/Utilitarian surveillance as a means of social control. This surveillance was developed in the nineteenth century, and found full expression in imperialism. Parry argues, however, against taking *A Passage to India* as a colonial text, dominating India, annihilating its otherness and imposing a Eurocentric way of representing it. Her reference to the text's 'dialogic' structure recalls the literary theory of Mikhail Bakhtin (in *The Dialogic Imagination*), who argues that speech inevitably contains within it the voice of the 'other', that it breaks down a 'monological' attempt to speak with one authority-ridden voice. Parry contends that the weave of voices in the text prevents a single-subject position emerging; nonetheless she sees the text as also unable to show the historical catastrophe that imperialism entails and this limitation she associates with Forster's politics (the argument may recall Delany [essay 4] on *Howards End*). Forster in 'The Challenge of Our Time' (1946) in *Two Cheers for Democracy* said 'I belong to the fag-end of Victorian liberalism' – but liberalism itself was complicit in imperialism. While Forster could not critique some aspects of empire, he nevertheless, Parry concludes, had a sense of what the collapse of liberal values might bring, and awareness of this drove him from novel-writing altogether. Certainly there is something very prescient about Ronny, the imperialist and apparently the born Fascist, ending up in his letter to Fielding blaming the Jews. The specific reference, which Oliver Stallybrass explains in his notes to the Abinger Edition of *A Passage to India*, is to Lord Reading, the Viceroy of India from 1921 to 1926, who was Jewish, and who tried to keep down the violence of feeling after the British massacred Indians at Amritsar in 1919, and to Edwin Montagu, also Jewish, the last Liberal Secretary of

State for India, 1917–22. Montagu with Lord Chelmsford, the Viceroy before Reading, had proposed the Montagu–Chelmsford Reforms in 1918 intended to liberalise rule in the Empire: these had to be withdrawn after Amritsar. But Ronny's anti-semitism accords with Hitler's Munich *putsch* (1923), and indicates Forster's awareness of what was following the collapse of nineteenth-century Liberalism – and indeed, what Liberalism failed to prevent. Chapter and page references are to *A Passage to India* (Harmondsworth, 1961). Ed.]

1. See Sara Suleri, 'Amorphous India: Questions of Geography', paper delivered at the Session on Colonial Discourse at the Meeting of the Modern Language Association of America, December 1983.

2. E. M. Forster, 'Art for Art's Sake' (1949), *Two Cheers for Democracy*, Abinger edn (London 1972), pp. 87–93.

3. E. M. Forster, 'Our Diversions: 2, The Birth of an Empire' (1924), in *Abinger Harvest*, pp. 44–7; 'The Challenge of our Time' (1946), in *Two Cheers*, pp. 54–8.

4. Rape in British–Indian writing, both during and after the Raj, invariably represents the assailant, putative or proven, as Indian and the victim as British, an allocation of roles which inverts the historical situation. It would seem that the 'India' constructed by the Raj discourse, and egregiously apparent in Anglo-Indian romances, became a figure of sexual menace threatening to violate British values.

5. A call echoed in Forster's need for a perfect Friend.

6. Walt Whitman, 'Passage to India' (1871) in *Leaves of Grass* (New York, 1965); Edward Carpenter, 'India, the Wisdom-Land' (1890) in *Toward Democracy* (1911). In his essay 'Edward Carpenter' (1944), Forster wrote, 'As he had looked outside his own class for companionship, so he was obliged to look outside his own race for wisdom' (*Two Cheers*, p. 207). It is open to conjecture that the predominantly 'feminine' nature of India's civilisations, their cultivation of the imagination and intuitions, the pursuit of the unseen, and an eroticism in the visual arts, myths and epics which is conceptually androgynous – the Absolute as the two-in-one, the male–female principles as coexistent – may have had an especial appeal to male members of what Carpenter called the intermediate sex.

7. Quoted in P. N. Furbank, *E. M. Forster: A Life* (New York, 1978), I, 216.

8. Heinrich Zimmer, *Philosophies of India* (Delhi, 1967) p. 231 (first published 1952).

9. The significance of Jain cosmology to the ideas and images in 'Caves' is discussed in my *Delusions and Discoveries: Studies on India in the British Imagination 1880–1930* (London, 1972).

10. E. M. Forster, 'Liberty in England' (1935), in *Abinger Harvest*, pp. 62–3.

11. In addition to the works referred to in these notes I wish to acknowledge a more general debt to the following books: John Beer, *The Achievement of E. M. Forster* (London, 1962); *E. M. Forster: 'A Passage to India'. A Selection of Critical Essays*, ed. Malcolm Bradbury, Casebook series (London, 1970); Frederick C. Crews, *E. M. Forster: The Perils of Humanism* (Princeton, NJ, 1962); June Perry Levine, *Creation and Criticism: A Passage to India* (London, 1971); Edward Said, *Orientalism* (London, 1978); Wilfred Stone, *The Cave and the Mountain* (Stanford, Cal., 1966); Lionel Trilling, *E. M. Forster* (Norfolk, 1944); Peter Widdowson, *E. M. Forster's 'Howards End': Fiction as History*, Text and Context series (London, 1977).

9

Forster's Imperial Erotic

SARA SULERI GOODYEAR

I

Whether *A Passage to India* is read as an icon of the liberal imagination or as an allegory in which the category of 'Marabar Cave' roughly translates into the anus of imperialism, the novel remains one of English India's most troubling engagements in the fiction of cultural self-examination. The familiarity of its tropologies is an undiminished embarrassment to postcolonial discourse, in that the text continually prepares to address the latent infantilism within the possibility of cross-cultural friendship. If the question 'Why can't we be friends now?' concludes the unanswerability that *A Passage to India* seeks to address, it further reiterates the persistent permutations of adolescence that inform the rhetoric of subcontinental colonialism. Over Forster, the discursive ghosts of Burke and Kipling shake hands; the youthfulness that both locate as the danger of colonial power now learns that its chronology is pitiably dependent upon the mythology of 'being friends', or a fiction reliant on the dischronology of 'not now', 'not yet'.

A Passage to India translates the question of cross-cultural friendship into a more vertiginous study of how cultures both issue and misread invitations to one another. As such, Aziz's notorious invitation – 'I invite you all to see me in the Marabar Caves' – indicates the incongruity of civility within a colonial context. The oblique violence of the text points both to the fraught ambivalence with which Forster invokes the category of 'friendship' and to the absence of civil spaces upon which the possibility of friendship may be discussed. If *A Passage to India* attempts to engender an illusion of cross-cultural conversation, then it is a dialogue that is highly conscious of the limits rather than the expansiveness of cultural sympathy. As Forster himself confessed to Syed Ross Masood, 'When I began the book I thought of it as a little bridge of sympathy between East and West, but this conception has had to go, my sense of the truth forbids anything so comfortable. I think that most Indians, like most English people, are shits, and I am not interested whether they sympathise with one another or not.'[1] Even as the narrative explores mythologies of colonial friendship, in other words, it is resolutely critical of an 'only connect' rhetoric that would allow for the fiction of any transcultural male bonding.

In *Kim*, the protagonist's ability to function as a 'Friend of all the World' to the various cultures inhabiting the colonised subcontinent comes dangerously close to a promiscuous liability, and finally culminates in his silenced status as the lama's beloved. *A Passage to India*, on the other hand, disallows any distinction between friend and beloved: both terms are precariously conterminous in a colonial world where cultural reading is predicated on the passionate misinterpretation of the art of invitation. The intimacies of colonialism are thereby translated into the social and political peculiarities represented by the question, how can a people invite another people not into a home, or into a different culture, but into that alternative civil space known as a friendship? Into what caves of disappointed sublimity must such civility collapse, before it can articulate the fact that colonial friendship is never autonomous from the literal presence of the racial body?

While the homoeroticism of *A Passage to India* could be explained away with biographical reference – by reference to Forster's love for Syed Ross Masood, the friend who lent his lineaments to the shaping of Dr Aziz – it is far more productively disturbing in the context of Forster's revision of an imperial erotic. In place of the Orientalist paradigm in which the colonising presence is as irredeemably male as the colonised territory is female, *A Passage to India* presents an alternative colonial model: the most urgent cross-cultural invitations occur between male and male, with racial difference serving as a substitute for gender. As race is thus sexualised, the novel draws attention to its relentless questioning of the amorphousness of friendship, in which the visibility of race is rendered synonymous with the invisibility of sexual preference. If Forster's critique of the feminine picturesque is all too overtly available in Adela Quested's search for the 'real' India, his more haunting apprehension of a colonial aesthetic of sublimity inheres in the narrative's ability to literalise what homoerotic disappointment has signified to English India.

The erotic of race, and its concomitant cultural complications, is most clearly figured in the narrative's curious relation to the over-determination that is Aziz. From the opening chapters of the novel, it is evident that Aziz is accorded a certain mobility as a racial body which allows him an exemption from his role as complete participant in the colonial encounter. Aziz has to be punished into history through the route of his pursuit of friendship, which ultimately leads to his espousal of a nationalist rhetoric. Friendship thus functions as the conduit or the Marabar Cave that allows Aziz to transmogrify from a racial into a nationalist entity, but such evolution suggests the limits rather than the attainment of cultural autonomy. We first see Aziz after he has accepted an easy invitation into a home of his own kind, but even in such a setting, Aziz rests on the peripheries of political conversation more as an observing body than as a participant:

> He lay in a trance, sensuous but healthy, through which the talk of the two others did not seem particularly sad – they were discussing as to whether or no it is possible to be friends with an Englishman. Mahmoud Ali argued that it was not, Hamidullah disagreed, but with so many reservations that there was no friction between them. Delicious it was indeed to lie on the broad verandah with the moon rising in front and the servants preparing dinner behind, and no trouble happening.... 'They all become exactly the same, not worse, not better. I give any Englishman two years, be he Turton or Burton. I give any Englishwoman six months. All are exactly alike. Do you not agree with me?'
>
> 'I do not', replied Mahmoud Ali, entering into the bitter fun, and feeling both pain and amusement at each word that was uttered. 'For my own part I find such profound differences among our rulers.'[2]

Here, Aziz remains merely an audience to the amorous 'pain and amusement' that characterise his host's discourse: the narrative allows him a certain bodily autonomy from the debate on cultural friendship only to render his body the site upon which the exquisite costs of such friendliness shall later be determined.

If Aziz can be read as an emblematic casualty of the colonial homoerotic, then his iconic status must necessarily be released from too literal a correlation with the secrecy that attended Forster's own homosexuality. In this context, Rustom Bharucha's somewhat archly titled essay, 'Forster's Friends', is symptomatic of the unhelpful critical urge to link the sexual politics of *A Passage to India* with the idiosyncrasies of preference rather than with the imperatives that subcontinental colonial encounter generated between the cultural distinctiveness of race and gender. 'An ethos of masculinity developed during the British Raj of India, first in England, and then later, through a process of imitation, within India itself', claims Bharucha. 'Whether a man was serving his country at home or abroad, he was required to be "manly" – aggressive, competitive, and in control of his emotions and duties. The Empire had no particular use for women or for the values associated with femininity. Homosexuals were tolerated only in so far as they remained discreet about their activities and functioned within the strict confines of marginal societies like Bloomsbury and Oxbridge.'[3] Such a dichotomy relies on an almost surgical critical ability to separate masculinity from a more vexed engagement in the discourse of colonial sexuality, which necessarily implies that manliness – like friendship – is not so easily subsumed within the sexual symbolic that impels the narrative of *A Passage to India.*

If Forster's narrative is uninterested in stereotypical imperial masculinity and instead attempts to reconfigurate colonial sexuality into a homoeroticisation of race, then the keenly visual aspects of the novel require attentive reading. The discourse of friendship becomes a figure for how the imperial eye perceives race: the literal minutiae of pigmentation and physiognomy serve to rupture a more general vision of an Oriental culture. A crucial illustration of the rupturing power of the racial body occurs during the court scene, where Adela's attention is caught less by Aziz than by 'the man who pulled the punkah':

> Almost naked, and splendidly formed, he sat on a raised platform near the back... and he seemed to control the proceedings. He had the strength and beauty that sometimes comes to flower in Indians of low birth. When that strange race nears the dust and is condemned as untouchable, then nature remembers the physical perfection that she accomplished elsewhere, and throws out a god – not many, but one here and there, to prove to society how little its categories impress her. This man would have been notable anywhere: among the thin-hammed, flat-chested mediocrities of Chandrapore he stood out as divine, yet he was of the city, its garbage had nourished him, he would end on its rubbish heaps.
>
> (p. 217)

This culturally troubled passage exemplifies the colonial eye's ability to see the racial body as a specimen whose sexual aesthetics contravene principles of imperial classification. Its ostensibly casual invocation of caste further complicates the muddied gender boundaries of the text, in that the untouchability of the godlike body of the fan-puller is homoeroticised: in Forster's narrative, the untouchable no longer refers to caste alone, but is extended to include an embodiment of homosexual desire.

While the anonymity of the fan-puller can serve as a synecdoche for the troubling aesthetic posed by the colonised male racial body, the beauty that Aziz represents is touched upon far more obliquely. The second chapter of the novel describes him as 'an athletic little man, daintily put together, but really very strong' (p. 18); similarly, Mrs Moore later describes him as 'rather small, with a little moustache and quick eyes' (p. 30). In the courtroom, Aziz appears to Adela as a 'strong, neat little Indian with very black hair and pliant hands' (p. 220). His physical diminution serves as a distraction from the untouchable beauty that the text gestures toward but will not put into language: having granted Aziz a brain and a partial cultural autonomy, Forster cannot afford to linger on the articulation of attraction that Aziz represents. Here, *A Passage to India* reifies a hidden tradition of imperial looking in which the disempowerment of a homoerotic gaze is as damaging to the colonising psyche as to that of the colonised, and questions the cultural dichotomies through which both are realised.

Even though the homoerotic strategy of *A Passage to India* cannot be explained away with reference to Forster's own curiously class-conscious and cross-cultural homosexual experiences, it would be a theoretical error to ignore their relevance to the text's embodiment of the situation of alternative desire in the construction of colonial encounters. Aziz is thus both a tribute to Syed Ross Masood and a memorial to Forster's Egyptian lover, Mohammed-el-Adl, who died while *A Passage to India* was still being written. After the lover's death in 1922, Forster's diary records obsessively his dreams of Mohammed: 'I passed a young man in black with a slight but a well defined moustache. He was and was not Mohammed – not he outwardly but he in his intensity, the quality of emotion caused in my heart... [then] he leant against the edge of [my] bath, half sitting, half standing, entirely naked, his dark bush distinct, and he smiled. The effect was not physical nor was my awakening ghastly except that I awoke.'[4] In the context of the phantasmagoric quality of

Forster's diaries, the simultaneous production of *A Passage to India*
instantiates a relation of acute strain to figurative uses of the subject
of homoeroticism. As a consequence, Aziz represents a belittled
racial body whose attractions can never be literalised, and the space
upon which Forster can enact the unavoidable partition that the
longing of class creates within the context of colonial knowledge.

The death of Mohammed shapes Aziz. Aziz has hands rather than
genitalia; he is too tiny to assume the status of a godlike body. But
he is still urgently implicated in the cultural crossing represented by
the many repetitions of the trope of the Bridge Party, which remains
the central figure upon which the possibility of friendship is enacted.
While the cultural invitations generated by such encounters are too
dangerous to ignore, their inevitable misreadings signify an acute
evasion of what the anxiety of masculinity represents to the
discourse of colonialism. The phantasmagoria of cultural bonding
certainly dictates Forster's diaristic comments on colonial homoeroticism, allowing him to sustain an idealised belief in the availability of racial as well as erotic intermingling. Once Mohammed dies,
Forster can write, 'You are dead, Mohammed, and Morgan is still
alive and thinks more of himself and less of you with every word he
writes. You [once] called my name... it was dark and I heard an
Egyptian shouting who had lost his friend: Margan, Margan – you
calling me and I felt we belonged to each other now, you had made
me an Egyptian.'⁵ An extraordinarily complicated Orientalism
accompanies this claim, which implies that 'friendship' can make an
Egyptian of E. M. Forster, so that the imperial rather than the Oriental body can also be textualised. *A Passage to India*, however, functions as a wry reminder of the impossibility of such cultural and
ethnic relocations: even when dead, Mohammed cannot provide an
option for Forster's cultural belonging. His death signifies only a
moment in the imperial erotic that converts absence into an illusion
of cultural transference. In contravention of the work of mourning
and optimism that Forster's diary performs, however, *A Passage to
India* works resolutely against those commitments to transcendence
that allow Egypt to enter England.

It is hardly irrelevant that the composition of *A Passage to India*
caused Forster to burn what P. N. Furbank somewhat quaintly calls
his 'indecent short stories': 'The burning took place early in April
[1922] and was done, he told himself, not as a moral repentance but
out of a feeling that the stories "clogged" him artistically. They were
a "wrong channel" for his pen.'⁶ Whether or not such a ritual of

erotic immolation is indeed an autonomously aesthetic gesture, it surely informs the excisions of intimacy that cause the subsequent text to claim: 'We must exclude someone from our gathering, or we shall be left with nothing' (p. 38). To turn to the cross-cultural friendship that subsists between Aziz and Fielding, therefore, is in its most overdetermined sense of the term to approach a cultural 'nothing'.

II

The disembodiment and concomitant embodiment of Aziz is rarely as starkly choreographed as in chapter 7 of the opening section of *A Passage to India*, 'Mosque'. In the first physical encounter between Fielding and Aziz, the narrative informs the reader that the latter knows the former by sight; the former knows the latter 'very well by name' (p. 64). Between these discrepancies of sight and name, Aziz and Fielding attempt to articulate an alternative colonial intimacy that can escape the predictability of empowered and disempowered discourses, but is still predicated upon the licence of misreading. Neither man is in direct vision of the other: Fielding is both naked and concealed when Aziz arrives at his home. 'He was dressing after a bath when Dr Aziz was announced ... he shouted from the bedroom, "Please make yourself at home". The remark was unpremediated, like most of his actions; it was what he felt inclined to say. To Aziz it had a very definite meaning. "May I really, Mr Fielding?... I like unconventional behaviour so extremely"' (p. 63). The formalism of informality is immediately at play in their attempt to conduct conversation in an environment alternative to that of colonial communication.

What follows is perhaps the most notoriously oblique homoerotic exchange in the literature of English India. The scene is so familiar that its erotic as opposed to its cultural and colonial sartorial implications seem too obvious to read. The disastrous Bridge Party held by Chandrapore's collector has already occurred; Fielding's version of an alternative Bridge Party is designed to let the Anglo-Indian woman in search of the 'real India' literally see what Indians may be. Before the women can enter to dilute the singularity of gender, however, Fielding and Aziz have already conducted a secret gesture of intimacy that barely needs decoding. The exchange involves a transfer of an object as domestically ludicrous as a collar stud: Aziz not only wrenches his own off his collar in order to supply Fielding with what he may be missing, but further proceeds to assist Fielding in the insertion of the stud. Apart from the concluding paragraph of the novel, and the 'half-kissing' gesture with which the two protagonists part, the collar stud is the only crucially disruptive signifier through which – in a colonial configuration – men are allowed to touch men.

The exchange of the stud – in itself nothing more than a moment of irreversible cultural embarrassment – suggests an erotic interaction that demands attention to its own cultural outrage. While the counter-imperialist Western gentleman is in the act of dressing, he requires the aid of the 'little' Indian who can both charm and complicate the dialogue that follows between them. The great erotic tenderness that attends the first encounter between Aziz and Fielding is made visual only through the transfer of a stud. Aziz wrenches his own property from his body, and proffers those signs to Fielding: 'I say, Mr Fielding, is the stud going to go in?' (p. 65). What follows is an elaborate acknowledgement of what sartorial necessity may have to say to the invisibility of colonial friendship. For of course the stud will go in the collar of the Englishman, who stands, neck bowed, accepting the assistance of his new Indian friend. 'Let me put in your stud', exclaims Aziz; 'I see... the shirt back's hole is rather small and to rip it is a pity' (p. 65). It is through the paraphernalia of dressing with decorum, in other words, that erotic trust can establish its tenuous parameters: the immediate lovemaking that transpires between Fielding and Aziz suggests the prevailing cultural sadness that inhabits utopian narratives of the possibility of friendship across cultures. Aziz's domestic prophesy dangerously redounds of what political ramifications lie behind the assumption of international friendliness – the hole is indeed rather small, and to rip it is a pity.

In *A Passage to India*, however, nothing can be whole or sole that has not been rent. The novel intimacy between the two men is soon interrupted by the intrusion of Mrs Moore and Adela Quested: Aziz 'was disappointed that other guests were coming, for he preferred to be alone with his new friend' (p. 66). With the entry of the women, Aziz is rapidly Orientalised, in that he is read through the lens of the feminine picturesque – for Adela, he becomes the key through which the secrets of the real India may possibly be read. This colonial expectation is sufficient to induce a strained falsity in Aziz's discourse, causing the invitation into friendship to assume more and more phantasmagoric proportions. By reading Aziz's invitation to visit his home too literally, Adela unwittingly renders Aziz homeless:

> 'I don't know why you say [that you can give us nothing], when you have so kindly invited us to your house.'
> He thought again of his bungalow with horror. Good heavens, the stupid girl had taken him at his word! What was he to do? 'Yes, all that is settled', he cried. 'I invite you all to see me in the Marabar Caves.'
>
> (p. 74)

Here, Aziz chooses the cultural anonymity of geography in order to keep concealed the privacy of his home, and the moment is illustrative of Forster's meticulous revision of a colonialist-as-heterosexual paradigm. Rather than the male seeking to possess a feminised territory, the female seeks to enter the habitat of colonised domesticity, thereby forcing the 'little Indian' to retreat into the exotic but empty space of an unvisited cave.

Fielding's tea party thus represents a dispersal of sexual promise, or an emptying of intimacy into unintelligibility. A scene that opens with the anticipation of new modes of cultural contact is evacuated into an emblem of erotic isolation, converting each of the assembled bodies into stereotypes of colonial embarrassment. Invitation has occurred and has failed, as the song sung by Professor Godbole exemplifies. His sudden flight into song at the end of the tea party translates the submerged desire of colonial encounter into a new mode of incomprehensibility: 'His thin voice rose, and gave out one sound after another. At times there seemed rhythm, at times there was an illusion of a Western melody. But the ear, baffled repeatedly, soon lost any clue, and wandered in a maze of noises, none harsh or unpleasant, none intelligible. Only the servants understood it. They began to whisper to one another. *The man who was gathering water chestnut came naked out of the tank, his lips parted with delight, disclosing his scarlet tongue*' (p. 79, emphasis added). While Godbole proceeds to translate his song, this arresting and momentary intrusion of the male nude requires some decoding in itself. Since the scene opened with Fielding's invisible nudity, this evocation of a literal Indian nudity takes on a curious parallelism. In a colonial configuration, is a colonised body the only one that can be represented as stripping into cultural secrecy? Like the fan-puller in the later court scene, this nude embodies an act of aesthetic rupture: his appearance is singularly non-phallic, with Forster focusing instead on the mouth as an aperture that can disclose a scarlet tongue. In an encounter fraught with imperial displeasure, the nude presents an alternative if untouchable pleasure that the narrative can almost anthropologically record but into which it has no entry.

The pleasure generated by Godbole's song, of course, is further ironised by the fact that its literal subject concerns the absence of pleasure. It supplies the text with a crucial figure both for imperial longing and for the gender-crossing that gestures toward the possibility of cultural crossing. In order to sing this particular song, Godbole must ventriloquise a woman's voice:

> 'I will explain in detail. It was a religious song. I placed myself in the position of a milkmaiden. I say to Shri Krishna, "Come! come to me only". The god refuses to come. I grow humble and say: "Do not come to me only. Multiply yourself into a hundred Krishnas, and let one go to each of my hundred companions, but one, O Lord of the Universe, come to me". He refuses to come...'
>
> 'But he comes in some other song, I hope?' said Mrs Moore gently.
>
> 'Oh no, he refuses to come', repeated Godbole, perhaps not understanding her question. 'I say to Him, come, come, come, come, come, come. He neglects to come.'
>
> (p. 80)

While a critic such as Benita Parry attempts to read both this passage and the novel as a whole as illustrative of Forster's engagement in the dialogue between Islam and Hinduism in the Indian subcontinent, it is perhaps more productive to consider Godbole's song as a figure for the erotic and colonial disappointment that permeates *A Passage to India*.[7] Much as the actors on the colonial stage exchange veiled invitations to future intimacies, Krishna will decline to be invited into the sexually explicit longing of the milkmaiden. Rather than representing the alterity of polytheistic culture, Godbole's song is synecdochical of the tautological desire that vexes imperial narrative. It encompasses all the permutations of what friendship may be within the context of empire, and further anticipates the necessary deferral of desire that impels the text's conclusion.

The song that serves as the punctuation mark to Fielding's tea party suggests that imperial pleasure invariably occurs elsewhere; not yet, not here. As a consequence, the trajectory of the friendship between Fielding and Aziz is quickened by the necessary disappointment that it must continually generate. These disappointments are not necessarily the results of cultural misreadings, but indicate instead the limits of homoerotic knowledge in English Indian narrative. According to Benita Parry, the failure of friendship in *A Passage to India* can in large measure be ascribed to the barriers created by the problematic category of differences in 'national character': 'Ultimately their relationship is tainted by the context of their encounter. Fielding is instinctively patronising, as befits an Englishman in India... and Aziz, who craves an intimacy which Fielding is temperamentally incapable of meeting, is in turn importunate and easily offended, the occupational hazards of those obliged to be clients of a master-race.'[8] While characters in the text obsessively talk about what it means to be English as opposed to Indian, their discourse suggests an anxious artifice behind the desire to keep these categories intact. If both serve as accomplices in each other's alterities, then the inevitability of colonial disempowerment is equally meted out to Fielding and Aziz.

Here, it may be productive to read the friendship of the two men less as an aborted exchange between coloniser and colonised and more as an instantiation of what Kaja Silverman calls the 'double mimesis' of colonial encounter. In her perceptive reading of T. E. Lawrence's *Seven Pillars of Wisdom*, Silverman presents an alternative model for the construction of colonial identification: 'Lawrence clearly projects his homosexuality and masochism onto the Arabs he fights with, so that the sexuality he finds within them, and with which he identifies, represents a mirror image of his own... The passing of the "self" through the medium of the "other": – or, even more radically, through the medium of what has been culturally designated as "Other" – effects more than an alienation: it also holds open the possibility for a significant shift in the terms of the subject's sexuality, and hence of his or her identity.'[9] Even though Lawrence's Orientalist Arab identification was far more obsessional than Forster's with India, the comparison allows for a greater apprehension of how a homoerotic dynamic complicates the empowerment of colonialism. If Forster's diary can represent the writer as 'becoming Egypt' through his love for Mohammed, then *A Passage to India* can be read as a partial Indianisation of Fielding. More precisely, his availability to cultural intimacy problematises the interpretive usefulness of such static categories as the 'English' versus the 'Indians'.

While the exchange between Fielding and Aziz is represented in resolutely heterosexual terms – Aziz plans to visit brothels in

Calcutta; Fielding marries Stella – their friendship plays out a subterranean homoeroticism that functions as a figure for the limits of
colonial epistemology. After the gift-giving of the collar stud and the
ominous invitation to the Marabar Caves, their next conversation
takes place as a mirror image of the first. Fielding invites himself to
visit Aziz's sickbed, thus transgressing the cultural privacy that the
invitation to the caves had been designed to protect. The visit is a
humiliation for Aziz, and as Fielding is about to leave, 'rather disappointed with his call' (p. 113), Aziz confesses the real reason of
his prior coldness: '"Here is your home", he said sardonically.
"Here's the celebrated hospitality of the East. Look at the flies...
Isn't it jolly? Now I suppose you want to be off, having seen an
Oriental interior"' (p. 115). Fielding's desire for intimacy, in other
words, can register only as a violation of Aziz's space within the
colonial world: rather than heighten the cultural trust between the
two, the visit initially serves to exacerbate the distance between
them.

In keeping with the logic of an imperial erotic, in which intimacy
is always too excessive or too scant, Aziz proceeds to shift the emotional register of their encounter by suddenly evoking an image of
his dead wife. By inviting Fielding to look at her photograph, Aziz
inverts the traditional colonial paradigm in which the coloniser
seeks to penetrate the secrets of the *zenana*. As the woman's veil is
temporarily lifted, Fielding is forced into the position of a cultural
voyeur: 'She was my wife. You are the first Englishman she has ever
come before. Now put her photograph away' (p. 116). While the
oblique tenderness implicit in the symbolic exchange of the woman
may serve as the next link in the construction of friendship, it further confines Fielding to the illiteracy of his gaze. He is left in a position similar to the photographers of *The People of India*, who could
collect but could not read representations of gender and race. Aziz's
gesture both feminises the domestic space into which Fielding has
intruded and inevitably engenders an anthropological anxiety in his
friend: '"Put her away, she is of no importance, she is dead", said
Aziz gently. "I showed her to you because I have nothing else to
show. You may look around the whole bungalow now, and empty
everything"' (p. 117).

Where Fielding seeks the specificity of a localised intimacy, he
meets an imperial double bind that constrains him into an acknowledgement of his status as a colonial observer. He may have escaped
the world of Anglo-India and the ideology of the collector, but he

cannot fail to recognise that he functions as a figurative collector in his own right. Even though the photograph has been imposed upon him, it cannot but underscore the implicitly anthropological interest that he takes in Aziz: 'Fielding sat down by the bed, flattered at the trust reposed in him, yet rather sad. He felt old... Kindness, kindness, and more kindness – yes, that he might supply, but was that really all that the queer nation needed? Did it not also demand an occasional intoxication of the blood? What had he done to deserve this outburst of confidence, and what hostage could he give in exchange?' (p. 117). As in *Kim*, this enactment of the imperial erotic serves to illustrate the futility of compassion in colonial encounters. The kindness with which Fielding agrees to conduct his reading of the subcontinent cannot claim exemption from the violence of cultural intrusiveness, and the intoxication that he imagines demanded of him points less to the exoticism of the 'Orient' than to a more rarefied and internalised exoticism of cultural disappointment.

The second encounter between Fielding and Aziz closes *A Passage to India's* opening section, 'Mosque'. Functioning as a prelude to the overdetermined representations of emptiness that dominate the second section, 'Caves', 'Mosque' constructs an exquisitely hollowed-out figure for the fragility of cross-cultural friendship. For Aziz, the promising mutuality of the second encounter suggests a more long-lasting intimacy: 'But they were friends, brothers. That part was settled, their compact had been subscribed by the photograph, they trusted one another, affection had triumphed for once in a way' (p. 122). In a colonial chronology, however, such bonding cannot be settled without simultaneously implying how it can be unsettled and displaced. The compact of sexual friendship is too tenuous to sustain a dialogical discourse across the divisiveness of colonial cultures; it will be both reopened and resealed in the symbolic geography that constitutes a Marabar Cave.

III

A Passage to India opens and ends with evocations of geography. The geographic, however, does not suggest a 'natural' landscape that lies beyond the parameters of a colonial economy: it no more represents a 'real' India than do either its inhabitants or its religious and cultural mythologies. Instead, Forster turns to visualising landscape as though to an act of cultural description that is relentlessly anti-exotic in its intent. If the narratives of English India can roughly be said to have veered between sublime and picturesque representations of the colonial encounter, then *A Passage to India* collapses both modes into a reconfiguration of what disappointment may signify to divergent apprehensions of colonialism. In such a revision, geography assumes the characteristics of a hollow symbolic space upon which the limits of imperial intimacy can both be identified and articulated.

Where Forster's text most distinctly locates itself on the cusp between colonial and postcolonial narrative is in its ability to demystify the mundanities attendant on colonial exchange. *A Passage to India* opens with the productive negative that claims; 'Except for the Marabar Caves – and they are twenty miles off – the city of Chandrapore presents nothing extraordinary' (p. 7). What follows is an act of imperial cartography that adopts a curiously dispossessed and dispossessing tone toward the relationship between town and landscape, or a mapping of all the ways that both Chandrapore and its surrounding environs seem to bespeak no inherent interest. In place of the exotic, the ordinary is privileged, so that the narrative need express no desire for either overt possession or a concomitant repulsion. The brief opening chapter melds city and geography, sky and land, to conclude in a startling metaphor of embodiment: 'No mountains infringe on the curve. League after league the earth lies flat, heaves a little, is flat again. Only in the south, where a group of fists and fingers are thrust up through the soil, is the endless expanse interrupted. These fists and fingers are the Marabar Hills, containing the extraordinary caves' (p. 9). Not only is the landscape anthropomorphised, but the image of the clenched hand is further hollowed out and emptied into caves, so that the realm of the imperial extraordinary is rendered conterminous with empty space.

The emptiness of geography – or the very structure of the Marabar Caves – functions as the conduit through which each participant in the colonial encounter can come to some troubled terms with the question of historical location. In part 2 of *A Passage to India*, therefore, the symbolic geography of 'Caves' becomes the territory upon which both a colonial rape fails to occur and homoerotic desire must recognise its segregation from the story of imperial friendship. The delusional rape imagined by Adela Quested, in other words, makes of her body a further Marabar Cave through which Fielding and Aziz must delimit the historical and ethical possibilities of colonial intimacy. As in the opening chapter of the novel, 'Caves' opens with the ostensible neutrality of cultural description:

> The caves are readily described. A tunnel eight feet long, five feet high, three feet wide, leads to a circular chamber about twenty feet in diameter. This arrangement occurs again and again throughout the group of hills, and this is all, this is a Marabar Cave. Having seen one such cave, having seen two, having seen three, four, fourteen, twenty-four, the visitor returns to Chandrapore uncertain whether he has had an interesting experience or a dull one or any experience at all.
>
> (p. 124)

Such a geography denies both connection and chronology, in that it forces cultural description into a recognition of its own vacuity. The touristic experience of colonialism is deglamorised into mathematical computations of how literally banal the exotic may be.

The ready availability of the caves, however, should not lead to the conclusion that geography has no secrets: instead, it suggests that such secrecy is a further confirmation of a productive emptiness in the reading of cultures. Thus even as the narrative assumes descriptive power over the symbolic geography that it maps out, it equally questions the limits of its own claims to comprehensiveness: 'But elsewhere, deeper in the granite, are there certain chambers that have no entrances? Chambers never unsealed since the arrival of the gods. Local report declares that these exceed in number those that can be visited, as the dead exceed the living – four hundred of them, four thousand or million. Nothing is inside them, they were sealed up before the creation of pestilence or treasure; if mankind grew curious and excavated, nothing, nothing would be added to the sum of good or evil' (p. 125). Those caves that are untouchable, in other words, transmogrify into the dwelling spaces of 'chambers'; the evacuation represented by their lack of habitation accords a certain homogeneity to cultural knowledge and cultural secrecy. Once both visible and invisible caves in the hills of Marabar are rendered equally empty, then the supposed dichotomy between heterosexual and homosexual desire assumes a similarly interchangeable quality.

Aziz invites his incongruous company to visit with him in the Marabar Caves: in the course of this exposure to an unknown but erotic geography, he further invites upon himself the imperial accusation of rape and a subsequent realisation of how impossible it is to maintain the brotherhood of cross-colonial intimacy. Geography

thus functions as a cultural determinant that delimits too promiscuous a traversal of its inherent boredom, and as a consequence
becomes a figure for the inefficacy of colonial travel, whether it be
across acceptable cultural or sexual borders. Such a symbolic topo-
graphy, of course, is remarkable in its revision of received fig-
urations of the function of landscape in colonial narrative: rather
than landscape serving as the female context upon which an
imperial man can arrive at storytelling, geography in A *Passage to
India* assumes the significance of that presexual space upon which
the participants in the great game of colonial intimacy can recognise
their postsexuality.

In order to recollect what a radical shift the novel represents in the
Anglo-Indian ethos, it is perhaps helpful to juxtapose Forster's symbolic geography with that of a contemporaneous text by Richard
Sencourt, *India in English Literature*. This study, published in 1923,
reads into the geography of India little other than the tradition of
romance. The landscape is invariably feminised and exoticised; it
lies in mysterious passivity at the feet of the colonising sensibility. In
place of the meticulous emptiness of the Marabar Cave, subcontinental geography is imaged in all the fullsomeness of exoticism: 'If
India is stored with such a power of fascination, why is it that so
many have turned from her in listlessness or disgust? As she has
charmed, so has she repelled... Dusty and hideous India has often
seemed. Melancholy is her garment. She offers no home to the
Northerner: on the European she must always exert her repulsion as
well as her charm.'[10] The stale dichotomy between repulsion and
attraction is precisely that which A *Passage to India* seeks to dismantle, in order to vitalise a sense of geography that can circumnav-
igate traditional devices of colonial travel narrative. To Sencourt,
Indian terrain is inviting precisely because it is female, and can be
attributed to all the predictable lures of a family romance between
mystery and repulsion. Forster's geography, on the other hand,
articulates itself on the novel ground of disappointment, or a space
that accommodates desire but need not necessarily posit cultural disgust as the inevitable corollary to the lure of romance. It is worth
noting in passing that Sencourt's preface thanks among others who
facilitated his trip to English India one 'Mr E. M. Forster, who read
me the M.S. of a delightful novel on India on which he is engaged
and his papers on Eliza Fay which appeared in an Egyptian news-
paper'.[11] Given the secure exoticist Orientalism that impels Sencourt's reading of literature and geography, it remains only an

academic wonder as to which sections of *A Passage to India* Sencourt found 'delightful'.

For there is little delight in the longest journey of the novel, or the section that Forster titles 'Caves'. In part 2, the romance of invitation sensationally creates the delusion of accusation, allowing geography to extend its parameters in order to include within its purview the theatrical space of the court. The Marabar Caves are allowed no containment, but instead spill over their disappointment to the equal hollows represented by colonial accusations and acquittals. An imperial eye cannot confine the caves to the twenty-mile distance to which they belong from Chandrapore, but instead must watch their dangerous intrusion into the laws of the colony. Adela Quested's accusation of assault by the hands of Aziz merely converts invitation into a possible synonym for the absence of erotic exchange in the high drama of colonial metaphoricity.

The disaster of the Marabar outing has less to do with a condemnation of colonial rape than with a study of the profound fragility of colonial intimacy. After Aziz is arrested on the charge of his violation of Adela, Fielding's defence of the former must face Anglo-India's profound objection to his countenance of imperial friendship: 'I have had twenty-five years' experience of this country', the collector informs Fielding, 'and during those twenty-five years I have never known anything but disaster result when English people and Indian people attempt to be intimate socially. Intercourse, yes. Courtesy, by all means. Intimacy – never, never' (p. 164). Any alternative goegraphy described by Aziz and Fielding's intimacy is thus circumscribed by the deadening cultural perceptions that lie between Godbole's 'Come, come', and the collector's 'Never, never'.

IV

In January of 1925, Forster records in his diary a summation of what he appears to be: 'Famous, wealthy, miserable, physically ugly... [I] am surprised I don't repel more generally: I can still get to know any one I want and have the illusion that I am charming and beautiful. Take no bother over nails or teeth but would powder my nose if I wasn't found out. Stomach increases, but not yet visible under waistcoat. The anus is clotted with hairs, and there is a great loss of sexual power – it was very violent 1921–22.'[12] The violence of sexual power that Forster associates with the composition of *A*

Passage to India manifests itself in the text as both an engagement with and a denial of a colonial homoerotic imperative. Increasingly, the women play a subservient role to the friendship that barely subsists between Fielding and Aziz. They remain the peripheries upon which male discourse locates constraints upon the operation of autonomous desires.

If the concluding section of *A Passage to India*, 'Temple', sets up any dialogue with an exchange between 'Mosque' and 'Cave', it is only to reiterate the absence of a continued friendship within the parameters of colonial exchange. Forster's vision of the imperial erotic finally confines itself to the nationalism over which the two men cannot meet. Neither can claim legitimacy over the urge to disempower: 'India a nation!' jokes Fielding; 'What an apotheosis! Last comer to the drab nineteenth-century sisterhood! She, whose only peer was the Holy Roman Empire, shall rank with Guatemala and Belgium perhaps!' (p. 322). Here, the difficulty of nation is transcribed upon the possibility of sexual friendship, and allows *A Passage to India* to choose instead a geographic location of sexual belonging. The calibration of erotic exchange between cultures is elaborately articulated as a social impossibility, letting both Aziz and Fielding function as signifiers of the abortiveness of colonial exchange:

> 'Why can't we be friends now?' said the other, holding him affectionately. 'It's what I want. It's what you want.'
> But the horses didn't want it – they swerved apart; the earth didn't want it, sending up rocks through which the riders must pass single file; the temples, the tank, the jail, the palace, the birds, the carrion, the Guest House, that came to view as they issued from the gap and saw the Mau beneath: they didn't want it, they said in their hundred voices, 'No, not yet', and the sky said, 'No, not there'.
>
> (p. 322)

The longing imposed by geography cannot comply to its own complications of where the hollowness of colonial desire may end. In Forster's representation of an imperial erotic, both race and body are subjected to an awareness of colonial chronology that allows for the significance of love even when it is at its most productively dismal depths.

From Sara Suleri, *The Rhetoric of English India* (Chicago, 1992), pp. 132–48.

NOTES

[The essay by Sara Suleri (now Sara Suleri Goodyear) takes issue, incidentally, with the essays of Bharucha (7) and with Benita Parry (8). Her subject is 'how a homoerotic dynamic complicates the empowerment of colonialism' where this homoeroticism is 'subterranean' (thinking of the encounters between Fielding and Aziz) and therefore can 'function as a figure for the limits of colonial epistemology'. Suleri Goodyear sees homoeroticism not as something to be explained biographically in Forster's case (in contrast to Bharucha), but as something systemic in colonial encounters, linked to racial, as opposed to sexual, difference, and hence disturbing to the coloniser because of the way it crosses the divide. Her book suggests that a 'terror of empire' operates in the coloniser, requiring that a fear of the other (the colonised) be coded in terms of rape/conquest: the coloniser male, the colonised female, but that this rhetoric displaces fear of the other as male. It is Forster's distinction not to engage in such a coding. Terror of empire leads to the eighteenth-century politician and writer Edmund Burke recognising though not acknowledging that India is unknowable in Western terms: it is an example of the 'sublime' as opposed to the 'beautiful' – that which cannot be comprehended (Burke wrote a study of the beautiful and the sublime in aesthetics). The youthfulness of its conquerors, however, ensures the power of rule, despite this sense that India is unknowable, just as Rudyard Kipling in his novel *Kim* (1901) stresses Kim's adolescence as a force for rule in India. In Forster, there are no such consolations. The Marabar caves are not sublime nor are they feminised; they are empty and defy European representation. Kim's situation as a 'Friend of all the World' is denied here by racial difference and by desire that cannot be recognised. The absence of events in the Marabar caves evokes only the absence of exchange, of mutuality at the heart of colonialism. Ed.]

1. Letter to Syed Ross Masood, 27 September 1922, quoted in P. N. Furbank, *E. M. Forster: A Life* (Oxford, 1979), p. 106.

2. E. M. Forster, *A Passage to India* (London, 1924), pp. 10–11. (Subsequent page references included in the text.)

3. Rustom Bharucha, 'Forster's Friends', in *Modern Critical Interpretations: E. M. Forster's 'A Passage to India'*, ed. Harold Bloom (New York, 1987), p. 95. [Reprinted in this volume – see p. 115. Ed.]

4. P. N. Furbank, *E. M. Forster* (New York, 1977), p. 114.

5. Ibid., p. 114.

6. Ibid., p. 106.

7. Benita Parry, *Delusions and Discoveries: Studies on India in the British Imagination* (Berkeley, Cal., 1972), p. 270.

8. Ibid., p. 284.

9. Kaja Silverman, 'White Skin, Brown Masks: The Double Mimesis, or With Lawrence in Arabia', *differences: A Journal of Feminist Cultural Studies*, 1 : 3 (1989), 48.

10. Richard Sencourt, *India in English Literature* (London, 1923), p. 24–5.

11. Ibid., p. viii.

12. Furbank, *E. M. Forster*, pp. 134–5.

10

Periphrasis, Power, and Rape in *A Passage to India*

BRENDA R. SILVER

I

Periphrasis, defined most simply as 'the use of many words where one or a few would do', has, like all figures, a more devious side. Rooted in the Greek 'to speak around', described variously as a figure that simultaneously 'under- and over-specifies' or 'the use of a negative, passive, or inverted construction in place of a positive, active or normal construction', the circumlocution associated with periphrasis begins to suggest refusal to name its subject that emphasises the fact of its elision.[1] If we go further and describe it in Gérard Genette's terms as a figure that both opens up and exists in a gap or space between sign and meaning, a figure that is moreover 'motivated' in its usage,[2] then we arrive at the association between periphrasis, power, and rape that structures both linguistic and social relations in *A Passage to India* and provides the space for rereading E.M. Forster's most enigmatic novel.

To introduce this association, we must move immediately to the event at the heart of the novel, Adela Quested's experience in the Marabar caves that leads to the trial of the Indian doctor Aziz for attempted rape. Or so we assume: the charge, like the event, is either elided completely or referred to by the English as an 'insult', a clearly motivated circumlocution. Later, in a moment of vision during the trial, Adela returns to the caves and retracts her accusation of Aziz, but the reader never learns what, if anything, actually

171

happened there. Where we would have the naming of the crime and its perpetrator exists only a periphrasis, a gap. Continually talking around this unspecified centre, the text ironically generates more words to produce less meaning.

That Forster deliberately created this gap is clear from the original version of the scene, where the reader enters the cave with Adela and feels the hands that push her against the wall and grab her breasts, we too smash the assailant with the field glasses before running out of the cave and down the hill.[3] In the published version, not just the violent physical attack but the entire scene in the cave is elided. Into the interpretive space opened by this elision critics have not feared to rush, supported by Forster's statement that 'in the cave it is *either* a man, *or* the supernatural, *or* an illusion'.[4] 'Illusion', translated into psycho-sexual terms, has proved the most persistent choice. These critics base their reading on Fielding's description of Adela as a prig, as well as Adela's realisations just before entering the cave that she feels no love or sexual passion for her fiancé, Ronny, and that Aziz is 'a handsome little Oriental'.[5] Later, responding to Fielding's hallucination theory, she compares her experience to 'the sort of thing ... that makes some women think they've had an offer of marriage when none was made' (p. 240). Thus it is that sexual desire and repression simultaneously enter the gap at the centre of the novel. In this reading Adela becomes a later version of Henry James' governess in *The Turn of the Screw*; a hysterical, repressed, overly intellectual New Woman who fantasises and is haunted by sex ghosts. In this reading, we might add, Adela wants to be raped.[6]

That Forster used his fiction to explore and expose prevailing sexual attitudes is a commonplace. On one level, he recognised the way in which society, in Michel Foucault's terms, had appropriated bodies and pleasure and deployed a sexuality that served to control individuals; Forster certainly would have understood the strategies, including 'a hysterisation of women's bodies' that Foucault associated with this deployment.[7] At another level, however, Forster's resistance to the system and his imagination were shaped by the sexual discourse of the period, including the concept of repression. In his fiction he continually evokes a scenario in which a darker, more sensual, usually foreign and/or lower class character initiates the repressed, often intellectual English man or woman into an awareness of his or her sexuality. An explicit example occurs in the heavily ironic fantasy title 'The Torque', which hinges on the homosexual rape of a Christianised Roman by a Goth: an act that undercuts the power of institutionalised chastity (the Church) and precipitates a realm of sexual freedom and fulfilment. Rape in this story becomes the pleasurable consummation of illicit desires experienced without guilt or subsequent suffering, a transgression of racial and sexual boundaries that unites rather than separating the two races.[8]

But *A Passage to India* tells a different story. For here, as Patricia Joplin would argue, rape becomes an act of violence, a transgression of boundaries, that enacts the rivalries at work within the culture upon the body of a woman who is herself potentially silenced, elided.[9] With this in mind, we can return to Adela's 'unspeakable' experience in the cave – and the word is Forster's (p. 208) – the experience that she speaks as violation or rape, and read it not in terms of sexual desire or repression, but in terms of a deployment of sexuality within a system of power that posits a complex network of sameness and difference. Within this system, what is at stake is both gender difference and racial difference, with manifold lines of power crisscrossing the social and textual field. To read the novel from this perspective is to see it as a study of what it means to be *rapable*, a social position that cuts across biological and racial lines to inscribe culturally constructed definitions of sexuality within a sex/gender/power system.

II

In undertaking this exploration of race and gender in Forster's novel, I am keenly aware that both Forster's and my perspectives are rooted within Western, first-world, frameworks and that we both run the risk of appropriating the Indians in the novel – and defining their sexuality – for our own ends. No amount of analysis can or should alter the fact that Adela's accusation carries the weight it does because she is a white woman, a member of the colonising group, or that a more accurate representation of the colonial experience would depict the rape of an Indian woman: the repressed term in the novel.[10] To the extent that Indian women are the one group denied a voice in the novel, the text replicates the complex intersections of racism, colonialism, and sexual inequalities that have consistently worked in Western discourses to erase the other woman's experience.[11] In attempting to write the silence of 'the other woman' into my critique I wish neither to speak for her nor to substitute gender for race – or to equate them. Instead, I will explore the multiplicity of discourses and structures that doubly silence the other woman in our culture – structures that Adela begins to understand and articulate – and locate them within the process of 'social sexing' that feminist theorists associate with rape.

Starting from the assumption that the social construction of gender and the social division of power are grounded in sexuality and difference, these theories define social sexing as 'that social process which creates, organises, expresses, and directs desire, creating the social beings we know as women and men, as their relations create society'.[12] If sexuality is the product of a power over the body, then 'the system of power ... has the bodies of women as its object of privileged appropriation',[13] a *sexual* differentiation that affects every aspect of their being, including their ability to name or represent their perceptions and have them count as 'truth'. Within this epistomological system, Catharine MacKinnon notes, power includes the power to name the other as object, that which is objectively knowable and 'objectification makes sexuality a material reality of women's lives, not just a psychological, attitudinal, or ideological one'. At issue is both the construction of the female subject and the effect of this construction on women's experience of their own being: the ways in which 'women internalise ... a male image of their sexuality *as* their identity as women', making epistemology and ontology one.[14] The process of being reduced to an object, moreover, constantly aware of being looked at, acted upon, can cause women (and those placed in the feminised position) to split themselves in two, to watch themselves as women from the male perspective, affecting both their realisation and their presentation of self.[15] Women, then, materially as well as psychologically, are both object and separated from themselves as object, a thing and nothing.

Within this formulation of sexuality, gender, and power, rape plays a central role, for it illustrates clearly both the congruence of knowledge, representation, and power at work in rape law, as MacKinnon has argued,[16] and the dynamic of objectification and appropriation that informs social/sexual relations. To recognise the social meaning of the encounter, the sexual politics, is also to recognise the categories 'men' and 'women' as gender/power designations, grounded in social, not biological, distinctions: to identify rape as an enactment of power. 'Rape is sexual essentially because it rests on the *very social* difference between the sexes ... Men rape women insofar as they belong to the class of men which has appropriated the bodies of women. They rape that which they have learned to consider as their property, that is to say, individuals of the other sex class than theirs, the class of women (which ... can also contain biological men).'[17] In MacKinnon's words, 'To be rapable, a position which is social, not biological, defines what a woman is'.[18]

III

When applied to social relations in *A Passage to India*, the construction of the class, or category, woman crisscrosses racial as well as sexual lines. Illustrating Foucault's conception of power as the 'interplay of mobile and non-egalitarian relations', the intersections of race and gender have 'a directly productive role' on the discourses that simultaneously shape and sustain them.[19] Within this mobile discursive field, subject and object may shift, but the category of 'object' and the category of 'woman' remain identical.

For the first part of the novel English and Indian are locked into a power relationship and a discourse of race in which each objectifies the other, although in any direct confrontation the English maintain the position of subject. At the same time, however, English and Indian *men* share a discourse of sexuality that inscribes their subjectivity by objectifying and silencing women. After the 'insult', relations shift to place the Indians explicitly in the category of woman, where their bodies and their subjectivity are appropriated for social ends. Within this latter discourse, both Adela, the Englishwoman, and Aziz, the Indian man, are elided in the English construction of the event through a deliberate act of periphrasis said by the narrator to be the result of the rape. When Fielding, the liberal schoolteacher who sides with the Indians, produces a 'bad effect' at the English club by asking about Miss Quested's health, his transgression consists of pronouncing her name, for since the 'insult' 'she, like Aziz, was always referred to by a periphrasis' (p. 182). By reversing the figure, however, we can perceive the periphrasis as embedded in the *cause* rather than the *effect* of the rape. For periphrasis, the elision or negation of the individual human being, functions as part of a rhetoric of difference and power that objectifies the other and creates the space for rape to occur.

To a great extent, the rhetoric of power manifests itself within the novel in the use of synecdoche to reduce the other, the signified, to a physicality that denies the irreducibility and multiplicity of the

individual subject. Rather than suggesting 'relationship' or 'connect-
edness',[20] synecdochal representation opens up unbridgeable gaps.
Ironically, the Indians introduce this reductive rhetoric in the opening dialogue of the novel when they refer to Ronny, the new City
Magistrate, as 'red-nosed boy' (p. 10), a usage motivated by the
belief, stated repeatedly in this conversation and confirmed by the
text, that the English are essentially indistinguishable. '"They all
become exactly the same, not worse, not better. I give any Englishman two years be he Turton or Burton. It is only the difference of a
letter. And I give any Englishwoman six months"' (p. 11). What differences the Indians sardonically allow are physical, not moral, a
representation of the political reality that the presence of the English
in India was itself immoral: '"Red-nose mumbles, Turton talks distinctly. Mrs Turton takes bribes, Mrs Red-nose does not and cannot,
because so far there is no Mrs Red-nose"' (p. 11). Paradoxically, the
'difference of a letter' in the first figure suggests the possibility of
opening a space between signifier and signified, individual and
group, where individuals might meet, but when exceptions are introduced, they are immediately elided. As the narrator remarks, they
'generalised from [their] disappointments – it was difficult for members of a subject race to do otherwise' (p. 13).

But what of the masters, the English? Caught up in a rhetoric of
power they initiated and control, they too generalise, unwilling to
break free of the by then historically well-inscribed characteristics of
the category 'Indian' constructed through the representations of generations of Orientalists. To the English the Indians are 'types', and
they 'know' them all, as well as how to handle them. Equally important, within this conceptual and stylistic framework, the English
themselves become a type, the White Man, with a fixed set of judgements, gestures, and language; those who do not conform are not
pukka.[21] Thus the first mention of Aziz by the English, located
within the centre of linguistic and social conformity, the English
club, reduces the man, so vividly alive while chattering with his
friends and in the intervening encounter with Mrs Moore, to 'some
native subordinate or other' who had, typically, failed to show up
when needed. In the same breath Ronny is referred to as 'the type
we want, he's one of us' (p. 25).

The mode on both sides, then, is reduction, a reduction that
claims as well the privilege of totalising the other group. In addition,
both groups represent their synecdochal reductions as capturing 'the
truth', including the truth of the other's moral state. For the English,

however, the rulers, the mania for reductive categorising goes hand in hand with a dramatisation of difference and superiority inherent in their position of power: power not only to define the categories but to enforce the 'truths' they supposedly convey; for the English, knowledge, representation, and power are one. Fielding, a linguistic renegade long before the scene in the club following the 'insult', experiences the strength of this discursive system, and his alienation from it, when he comments that 'the so-called white races are really pinko-gray. He only said this to be cheery, he did not realise that "white" has no more to do with a colour than "God Save the King" with a god, and that it is the height of impropriety to consider what it does connote' (p. 62). More than a 'manner of being-in-the-world' or a style,[22] the linguistic structures practised by the English inscribe the oppression of the Indians, both individually and as a group. The Indians' subversive rhetoric, at least in the early stages of the novel, produces rhetoric alone.

Not surprisingly it is Ronny, the newcomer, who enacts most explicitly the linguistic and ideological power inherent in the racial discourse, thereby satisfying the English desire for conformity and proving the Indians' perception of their sameness correct. To Ronny, the 'higher realms of knowledge' to which he aspired were 'inhabited by Callendars and Turtons, who had been not one year in the country but twenty and whose instincts were superhuman' (p. 81). In his zeal to learn the lingo and show his orthodoxy, he continually uses 'phrases and arguments that he had picked up from older officials' (p. 33) to describe the Indians, phrases that simultaneously reduce them to a material state and equate this with their defective mental and moral character. In this way he illustrates the process by which synecdochal representation crosses the line described by Kenneth Burke between figurative language as used by poets and the scientists' belief that their representations are 'real' (p. 507). At its most extreme, as Ronny's remark during the Bridge Party that 'no one who's here matters; those who matter don't come' (p. 39), this rhetoric effectively reduces the Indians present from the status of objects to non-existence. The result is 'to wipe out any traces of individual[s] ... with narratable life histories'.[23] Ultimately, inevitably, it is Ronny who provides the most painfully ironic example of synecdochal reduction masquerading as truth: the representation of Aziz and all Indians by his missing collar stud – missing because he gave it to Fielding. To Ronny, this detail signifies 'the Indian all over: inattention to detail; the fundamental slackness that reveals the race' (p. 82).

Within the gap opened by synecdochal reduction of the other to object, rape finds its material and linguistic space. And when race is involved, the space increases exponentially. From Ronny's statement of the 'fundamental slackness of the race' it is just a short step to the policeman McBryde's theory of the depravity of Indian men, which includes their sexual promiscuity and their attention to white women. In this construction, the Indian man, reduced to his sexuality, becomes simultaneously rapist and rapable.[24] No matter that Aziz's missing collar stud signifies the space in which he and Fielding break free of the reductive generalities of the racial discourse to initiate their friendship; the established mode swallows such resistances in its representation of the Indian male. Perceived as a synecdoche, a 'penis', he falls prey to the dictum that 'whoever says *rape* says Negro'.[25]

When Adela speaks rape, however, she says more than Negro; she speaks from within a discourse of sexuality that crosses racial lines and objectifies all women. While resting on similar rhetorical strategies, this discourse shifts the axis of sameness and difference, subject and object, from race to gender. Look, for example, at the moment during the Bridge Party when Mr Turton, the highest-ranking Englishman, indicates to his wife her duty (that is, to speak to the Indian women); '"To work, Mary, to work", cried the Collector, touching his wife on the shoulder with a switch' (p. 41). The synecdochal details here, the shoulder and the switch, serve to place her in the subservient position of his horse, reducing her to a material adjunct of both the man, her master, and the empire he represents. Next to this moment we can place Turton's thought after the 'insult' when his wife, voicing her hatred for the Indians, calls for the use of violence. '"After all, it's our women who make everything more difficult out here" ... Beneath his chivalry to Miss Quested resentment lurked ...' 'Perhaps', the narrator comments, 'there is a grain of resentment in all chivalry' (p. 214). Perhaps, we could add, what we have here is the most significant aside in the novel, a glimpse into the misogyny, the contempt, characteristic of those who use '"women and children"' (p. 183) as the rallying cry for their defence of women whom they in fact subordinate and elide by touches, however light, with a switch.

What, then, do these men resent? The rare moments when women, rather than allowing themselves to be objects of protection or exchange among those who have power, resist this structure by acting or speaking for themselves? In the case of Mrs Turton and the other seasoned Englishwomen, the confinement of their roles and their limited contact with Indians evoke a racism more extreme than their husbands', but their outbursts only serve to underline the men's 'contemptuous affection for the [Indian] pawns [they] had moved about for so many years' (p. 214). The threat posed by Adela and Mrs Moore, however, differs, for their resistance threatens to destroy the status quo through intimacy, not hatred. One such moment of resistance occurs during the Bridge Party. Unlike Mrs Turton, whose knowledge of Urdu consists only of the imperative mood and whose comments in English about the Indian women are glaringly reductive (p. 42), the two newcomers attempt to initiate a conversation with the Indian women, who form a third group in the social fabric, distinct from their men and the English alike. But the attempt fails; the Indian women remain silent. For one thing, the Indian men insist on talking for them. More significant, however, is the narrator's comment that 'they sought for a new formula which neither East nor West could provide' (p. 42). Perhaps, then, men resent women as a disruption within the male discourse that controls social exchange, whether this exchange occurs officially or unofficially. Here even Fielding, capable as he is of seeing Indians as individuals, shares Turton's resentment. Motivated by his desire for the picnic at the caves to be a success for Aziz's sake, Fielding thinks, '"I knew these women would make trouble"'. Mrs Moore accurately identifies this reaction for what it is, scapegoating women: '"This man, having missed his train, tries to blame us"' (p. 158).

A similar pattern of attributing power to women who in relation to their men have little or none occurs within the Indian community as well. For the most part, Indian women in the novel are nameless and invisible, represented only through their relatives' conversation about them. When we do go behind the purdah, as in the opening scene, we find Hamidullah's wife indicating her inferiority by the endless talk she sustains in order to show that she is not impatient for the dinner she cannot eat until her husband has eaten his (p. 13). When her talk begins to worry Aziz, Hamidullah considerately '[wipes] out any impression that his wife might have made' (p. 14). The woman is left behind the purdah with nothing but empty words at her command. Yet later, when his wife refuses to see Fielding – or, more accurately, refuses to let Fielding see her – Hamidullah claims that she wields the real power in the relationship (p. 271), a power we can define as the power to choose to remain invisible and thus to disrupt, however slightly, the male bonding achieved in this novel, as

in patriarchal societies in general, through the exchange or mediation of women. Perhaps the clearest representation of women's
power as refusal or negativity, however, occurs in the discussion of
the 'queer' events surrounding Aziz's trial. Here we learn that 'a
number of Mohammedan ladies had sworn to take no food until the
prisoner was acquitted, their death would make little difference,
indeed, being invisible, they seemed dead already, nevertheless it was
disquieting' (p. 214).

Women, then, can disrupt or cause disquietude by their refusals,
but their resistance is severely limited by the dominant rhetoric of
power that reinscribes them as object of exchange or catalyst for
rivalry within male conversation and male power struggles. Thus the
alleged 'insult' of one Englishwoman becomes the occasion for clois-
tering all Englishwomen, simultaneously reducing them to objects of
protection and using them as an excuse to reassert white male power
over both their women and their potential attackers. The pattern
enacted in the novel, similar to that practised in the American South,
works to intimidate and coerce both Indian black men and women
and white women into accepting their subordinate positions.[26]
Within this context, Fielding's refusal to elide Adela's name amidst
the hysteria at the club surrounding 'women and children' takes on
heroic proportions. By speaking of her by name, by trying to reach
her directly, he resists the periphrasis that destroys subjectivity and
identity and reduces both her and Aziz to metonymic figures in a
morality play of violated innocence and evil, whose end is to reaf-
firm the power of the white male. Fielding refuses their reduction to
ciphers in the lengthening chain of periphrases leading to one possible closure only; he returns Adela to a virtual level of existence and
focuses on the particular event.

When his attempt fails, however, Fielding, knowing the code,
enacts his resistance to the group fiction by refusing to stand up for
Ronny, the 'insulted' fiancé, the 'martyr' (p. 185) in this as in every
drama of rape, in which the true victim is perceived to be the man
whose boundaries and property have been violated through the
usurpation of his woman's body. His resistance, that is, occurs
within and is contained by a social system and a discourse of
sexuality predicated on male bonding and male rivalry, in which the
woman's experience, even of rape, is elided. Forced to choose sides,
Fielding chooses Aziz, and in doing so, he reaffirms the power of
their shared gender to mediate – at least potentially – racial
difference.

Within the sexual discourse, Aziz and Fielding speak equally as subjects, as men, from the position of power, including the power to objectify and appropriate women. Thus Aziz, in his attempt to seal the intimacy between the two men, comments unabashedly that Adela '"was not beautiful. She has practically no breasts ..."', a synecdochal representation that reduces women to their physical attributes alone. For Fielding, he will 'arrange a lady with breasts like mangoes ...' (p. 120). In this scene, as elsewhere in the novel, Aziz's sexual objectification of women, the 'derived sensuality that classes a mistress among motor-cars if she is beautiful, and among eye-flies if she isn't' (p. 241), alienates Fielding, who sees Aziz's valuation of women as commodities as a sign of 'the old, old trouble that eats the heart out of every civilisation: snobbery, the desire for possessions, creditable appendages' (p. 241). But however admirable this statement appears – however blind Fielding may be to his own ethnocentric biases – in committing himself to Aziz, Fielding acknowledges as well his place within the discourse of sexuality. When Aziz initiates their intimacy by showing Fielding the photograph of his dead wife, Fielding regrets that he has no woman or story of a woman to offer in exchange. The 'compact ... subscribed by the photograph' (p. 122) is completed by Aziz's statement that had his wife been alive, he would have showed the woman herself to Fielding, justifying this transaction to her by representing Fielding as his brother. Fielding feels honoured.

It is not surprising, then, that in his attempt to reclaim Aziz from the periphrasis that threatens to engulf him after his arrest, Fielding tries to restore his status as subject by restoring his place within the sexual discourse shared by men. When McBryde, described as one of the most reflective and best educated of the English officials, offers Fielding a letter planning a visit to a brothel as evidence of Aziz's – and all Indians' – innate sexual depravity, Fielding responds by claiming that he had done the same thing at Aziz's age. 'So had the Superintendent of Police', the narrative continues, 'but he considered that the conversation had taken a turn that was undesirable' (p. 169). Why? Because by minimising racial difference Fielding is '[leaving] a gap in the line' that these 'jackals', the Indians, would exploit (p. 171). Fielding, that is, fills or bridges the gap generated by and necessary to the rhetoric of power by creating a gap in the barrier that ensures English self-representation and dominance.

But as Fielding learns from this exchange, more than racial stereotyping is in play here; social sexing is as well. In denying his complicity with Fielding and Aziz, in denying the sexual discourse that men share, McBryde refuses to recognise Aziz as man, as subject. And whatever Aziz's power to reduce women to commodities, when spoken of as Indian within the discourse of English and Indian, sahib and native, he himself is objectified; he enters the category 'woman' and becomes rapable. From the moment of his arrest, from the moment the door of the carriage is thrown open and the power of the state intrudes, Aziz is absorbed into a discourse that defines him by his sexuality alone. In contrast to the white man's position, which is conterminous with the (phallic) power of 'the law', the position of the Indian man is to be symbolically 'raped' by the accusation of rape, a position crucial for maintaining the white man's power and one that carries as much centrality in the intertwined discourses of sex and race as rape itself.

Once accused of rape, Aziz disappears as speaking subject; both his body and his possessions, including his letters, are appropriated by the police and used against him. For one thing, McBryde reduces Aziz to his body, his skin colour, by implication his sexuality, which is by definition depraved. In discussing Aziz with Fielding, McBryde asserts that while the schoolmaster sees the Indians at their best, when they are boys, he, the policeman, '[knows] them as they really are, after they have developed into men' (p. 169). Later, in Court, 'enunciating a general truth', he will state the 'fact that any scientific observer will confirm', that 'the darker races are physically attracted by the fairer, but not *vice versa*' (pp. 218–19).

From the perspective of McBryde's objective, 'scientific', epistemological system Aziz, the object known by the observer, loses his status as man and with it the power to protect women, even his dead wife. When McBryde appropriates the photograph along with Aziz's other possessions, it ceases to signify Aziz's ability to exchange women in a ritual of male bonding; instead it indicates his reduction to sexual object. In response to Fielding's identification of the photograph, McBryde 'gave a faint, incredulous smile, and started rummaging in the drawer. His face became inquisitive and slightly bestial. "Wife indeed, I know these wives!" he was thinking' (p. 172). If the Indian man is reduced to a penis, Indian women are whores.

The photograph of Aziz's wife, then, becomes emblematic of woman both as object of exchange and as object of violation – violated here by McBryde's reading of her. He 'knows' her, a metaphor that suggests clearly the relationship between knowledge, sexuality, and power – including the power to define, or name, the truth.

While McBryde's statement illustrates the specific construction that metaphorises the Orient as female, penetrated by the knowledge of the Western male Orientalist, the use of metaphors associated with sexuality or the violation of boundaries in discussions of the acquisition of knowledge is common in all 'objective' or 'scientific' – by definition 'male' – discourses.[27] Even the existence of the photograph as 'evidence' participates in the process, illustrating Susan Sontag's contention 'the knowledge gained through still photography will always be ... a semblance of knowledge, a semblance of wisdom, as the act of taking pictures is a semblance of wisdom, a semblance of rape'.[28]

Photographs, if silent themselves, can be named; and the woman in this photograph is twice named and twice silenced – first by Aziz as woman, as object of exchange, and later by McBryde as object of an object, the sexualised Indian male. As such, her circulation reveals the shifting network of signification that elides the reality of the violation of woman and Indian through the periphrases at the heart of the novel. For if as woman she signifies the way in which all women are subject to rape by virtue of their gender – their sexual objectification and powerlessness to define themselves – she also signifies the rape practised upon the Indians by virtue of their objectification and powerlessness. Her violation in her own right, however, remains an untold tale.

When Aziz regains his freedom, he reclaims his violated wife and with her his manhood (p. 261), setting the stage for the separation that ensues between Fielding and him, a separation precipitated first by Fielding's friendship with Adela after the trial and later by his marriage not to Adela – which is what Aziz mistakenly believes – but to Stella, Ronny's sister. Once the misunderstanding is cleared up, Fielding tries to recapture their previous closeness by '[forcing] himself to speak intimately about his wife' – by evoking, that is, the sexual discourse that had united them before. By now, however, Aziz no longer wishes intimacy with any English person and Fielding has 'thrown in his lot with Anglo-India by marrying' a countrywoman (p. 319). However great Fielding's initial disregard of the racial discourse, he perceives his marriage as committing him to the system that defines him as English and male, and he accepts its limitations; he can no longer, in his words, 'travel light', nor can he risk flirting with the other. Aziz is reduced to a 'memento', a 'trophy' (p. 319). Just as Fielding's defiance after Aziz's arrest was contained by the relations of power that made Ronny and him antagonists who spoke the same language, the form of his resistance corroborates rather than undermining the system. In this way it illustrates Foucault's belief that 'resistance is never in a position of exteriority in relation to power'; it exists within the power/knowledge apparatus that 'depends' upon it and is subject to its discourses.[29] In his defence of Aziz, for example, Fielding relies on the power of evidence and knowledge, which he believes will triumph, unable to recognise, as Hamidullah and the Indians do from the position of the feminised and colonised object, that even evidence and knowledge would not work to free them (p. 73; p. 269: 'If God himself descended ... into their club and said [Aziz] were innocent, they would disbelieve him'). Unable to cross the boundaries that separate subject and object, to enter fully into the category 'woman', Fielding, for all his good intentions and his exposure of the system, enacts the story of the failure to identify with otherness.

Ultimately, it is Adela Quested, the woman, not Fielding, the man, who resists the 'scientific truths' put forward by McBryde, simultaneously revealing and disrupting the mastery and violation that function as part of the rhetoric of knowledge and power. It is Adela who comes to represent the form of resistance described as 'less a resistance, a force that can be set against power, than a non-force, an absolute difference with respect to power'.[30] Edward Said has argued that the ending of the novel, where the landscape of India prevents Fielding and Aziz from bridging the gap that divides them, reinforces 'a sense of the pathetic distance still separating "us" from an Orient destined to bear its foreignness as a mark of its permanent estrangement from the West'.[31] But when viewed through the prism of gender, of social sexing, what separates the two men are their positions within the power grid that lock them into the discourse of male bonding and male rivalry, including racial rivalry. Adela, however, speaking from the gaps or interstices of the shifting power networks, speaks as woman for the category 'woman'. In this reading, the 'mark of ... permanent estrangement' that separates the two cultures is inscribed in the woman who enters the caves and returns speaking rape.[32]

IV

The Marabar caves, the site of the rape, enclose in their empty circular chambers the myth and the memory of the origin of difference that informs the novel. 'Older than anything in the world', 'flesh of the sun's flesh', the caves and the hills that surround them were 'torn from [the sun's] bosom' at the time of creation (p. 123) and figure simultaneously sameness and difference, union and rupture. In the polished walls of their interior, with their suggestion of 'internal perfection', the flame of a match becomes two flames that 'strive to unite but cannot'; '[a] mirror ... divides the lovers'. Should the two flames finally 'touch one another' in the beholder's eye, they simultaneously 'kiss' and 'expire' (p. 125). Union here becomes a form of extinction, while rupture opens the way for strife.

For Adela, the experience of the caves, the experience that she speaks as physical violation, represents her realisation of the primal separation that makes difference and hence power possible; she is forced to recognise the social sexing that appropriates her body and names her woman. She experiences, we could say, the material and psychological reality of what it means to be rapable. Before the caves, Adela had defined herself, as Fielding does, through her intelligence, her honesty, and her belief in talk. If this self-definition constitutes a will to know, it manifests itself not in the 'scientific' pronouncements endemic to the racial discourse but in a continual questioning of the givens of a situation and the desire to remove individuals from their position as figures in a frieze or typology. To the extent that Adela succeeds in having this self recognised, she believes she exists. But the obstacles are many. Ronny corrects her perceptions and language and circumscribes her actions, only a (male) background like his, he insists, produces usable knowledge in India (p. 81). Mrs Turton labels her not pukka, Fielding calls her a prig and questions her sincerity, and Aziz, although he treats her as if she were a man, defines her by her lack of beauty. Despite her will to know, she increasingly figures in the narrative as an absence, a gap, created in part by the intrusion into her consciousness of her socially constructed status as woman: a thing and nothing. Ironically, she is first alluded to in the text as Ronny's not-yet-existent wife, the 'Mrs Red-nose' who cannot accept bribes, suggesting that for women existence is inseparable from marriage. But at the end of the Bridge Party, imagining her married life under the gaze of the Marabar hills ('How lovely they suddenly were! But she couldn't touch them. In front, like a shutter, fell a vision of her married life' [p. 47]), Adela experiences a radical diminution of self, the impossibility of knowing as woman within the social confines rapidly closing in on her. After the caves, having been absorbed by the male discourse that surrounds rape, she herself disappears: 'The issues [she] had raised were so much more important than she was herself that people inevitably forgot her' (p. 216).

From this perspective, Adela's entrance into the cave affirms a crisis of identity that is both ontological and political. Coinciding with her doubts about her marriage and her perception that she lacks physical charm, it plunges her into consciousness of her place as woman: the place of sexual objectification, the place where being sexual object defines woman's existence. Within this realm, her intelligence, her desire to know, count for nothing. Within this realm, the refusal to accept her place, the refusal, for example, to marry, constitutes a refusal to be within the norms culture imposes upon her. Like the flame in the Marabar caves, she would experience union (marriage) as a form of extinction, while the rupture generated by her subversive refusal opens the space for social and political strife. That Adela ultimately represents this consciousness in the terms of a physical assault signifies both the materiality and the sense of powerlessness that accompany woman's objectification. She is, we could say, violated by the discourse, whether of rape or marriage, that reduces her to her sexuality alone.

Significantly, the words that precipitate Adela's experience by leaving her alone – her question to Aziz about the number of his wives – are not her own; they belong to Mrs Turton (p. 153) and signify the unconscious absorption into the racial discourse that makes her speech an act of ventriloquism. This absorption begins immediately after her engagement when she speaks of the Nawab Bahadur, '"our old gentleman of the car"', in exactly the 'negligent tone' desired by Ronny (p. 96), and it can be attributed to the loss of self and voice, the reduction, that accompanies her impending marriage: 'She was labelled now' (p. 94). Another way to describe her question is as an echo – an echo of the reductionism, the 'singleness of vision and voice', associated with the echo in the cave and identified by Michael Ragussis as 'the source of prejudice and egotism' in the novel.[33] By naming her experience rape, moreover, Adela activates the machinery and the discourse that violate Aziz and reduce the other Indians, even Hamidullah, to the condition of split beings, physically aware of the gaze of the other and the significance of one's self-presentation before those in the position of power – a reaction that profoundly annoys Fielding. When Hamidullah thanks Fielding for greeting him in public after the arrest, Fielding attributes this unaccustomed self-abasement to fear, not realism (p. 173).

Nevertheless, both Adela's original utterance and her subsequent withdrawal of Aziz's name during the trial can be read as a form of resistance, a resistance that resides in speaking her objectification. If the caves are for Adela 'a reflexive place in which self divides into self and other'[34] – a division that makes her aware of her status as woman – they also allow her to speak as woman, in as much as division and self-differentiation characterise woman's authentic voice. [35] After the cave, lying passively in bed with her body full of cactus spines, while they are drawn out one by one, Adela literally becomes a split being, forced by the pain both to see and to experience herself as physical object, a vulnerable body. During the trial, when McBryde's lecture on 'Oriental Pathology', the attraction of the darker races to the fairer, is interrupted by the comment, 'Even when the lady is so uglier than the gentlemen?', Adela's 'body resented being called ugly, and trembled' (p. 219). This leads to the first of the power plays initiated by the English, their insistence that Adela's and their chairs be placed on the platform at the front of the room. Adela herself, thus elevated, has the opportunity to see the Indians involved, including Aziz. This vision returns him to the material reality and the subjectivity denied him by the English, who by refusing to speak his name had made him 'synonymous with the power of evil' (p. 202). With the understanding attained through knowledge of her body, her sexuality, and the powers that control it, Adela perceives him now for what he is: devoid of evil but subject as Indian to a discourse of objectification and appropriation structured in a similar way to that she experiences as woman.

It is this insight, perhaps, that allows her to recognise that whatever existed in the caves, Aziz was not there. What was there, still unspeakable, because outside of or elided by the discourse that constructs the social/sexual category 'woman', is the ontological shock that accompanies the entrance into the gaps or interstices in the culture where she simultaneously discovers and loses her self. Enclosed by the cave, she is enclosed as well by relations of power, including gender, that make possible the discourse that represents woman as pretence for male rivalry, token of exchange for male bonding, or catalyst for male protection, even as it elides her being.

To understand the strength of her utterance it is necessary at this point to invoke Mrs Moore, the other woman who enters the caves and returns not to speak rape, but to indifference and silence. For Mrs Moore, the experience of the caves, represented by the reductive powers of the echo, reveals not so much difference as sameness

– the radical sameness of all discursive systems and their failure to escape the rhetoric of power and exclusion. From the beginning of the novel, Mrs Moore had refused the linguistic reductions that characterise the speech of both English and Indian, even that of Ronny, her son. After her first meeting with Aziz, after listening to Ronny's reading of the scene, including his horror that her tone of voice and choice of words had not indicated that she was talking to a 'native', she rejects the synecdochal mode. 'Yes,' she thinks, 'it was all true, but how false as a summary of the man' (p. 34). Later, listening to Ronny justify the behaviour of the English, she divorces the words from the 'self-satisfied lilt', perceiving, as the Indians do, 'the mouth moving so complacently and competently beneath the little red nose', but rejecting the message as the last word on India (p. 51). Mrs Moore has, moreover, an uncanny ability to hear and speak what is unspoken because unspeakable, illustrated, for example, by her naming the unknown force that attacks Ronny and Adela on the way to the caves a ghost, a naming that places her within the racial memory of the Moslems. He mode, we might say, is more metaphoric than metonymic or synecdochal; she makes no distinction between mosques and churches because 'God is here' (p. 20), she calls wasps 'Pretty dear' (p. 35), and she wishes for the union of all living things under a God who is love. At her strongest, she resists the totalising rhetoric of power that reduces individuals to types and embraces a dual vision of particularity and union.

Plunged into the cave, however, terrified by the touch of flesh on flesh and by the echo that reduces all words, all language, all systems to 'boum' (pp. 147–8), Mrs Moore's double vision folds in on itself. Perceiving the horror of the void where distinctions and values disappear, the void beyond discourse and differentiation, she perceives as well that discourse itself, no matter how multiple or mobile its forms, has the potential to obliterate rather than unify individuals, even the discourse of love and marriage that she can no longer distinguish from rape : 'Why all this marriage, marriage?... The human race would have become a single person centuries ago if marriage was any use. And all this rubbish about love, love in a church, love in a cave, as if there is the least difference' (pp. 201–2).

Despite her refusal to explain her vision ('Say, say, say ... As if anything can be said?' [p. 200]) or to declare Aziz's innocence, Mrs Moore's uncanny knowledge communicates itself to Adela during her outburst about marriage in the form of Aziz's name, which until then had been completely elided by the English (p. 202). Adela, that is, hears Mrs Moore say, 'Dr Aziz never did it', even though, as Ronny insists, 'his name was never mentioned by anyone' (p. 204). 'Aziz ... have I made a mistake?' (p. 202), the younger woman asks, but Mrs Moore no longer cares. Beyond marrying herself, encumbered by a body she feels enslaved to and children who demand things from her, including Adela, Mrs Moore turns her back on the attempt to unravel the discourse of sexuality, possessiveness, and power, choosing instead indifference and annihilation. Nothing had happened to Adela, she feels, except fright, and even if it had, 'there are worse evils than love' (p. 208). Described as a 'withered priestess' (p. 208), she becomes, through the evocation of the myth of Persephone after her departure, a disillusioned Demeter, cynical about her daughter's violation and unwilling to intervene. Instead, she withdraws into the silence of the abyss and disappears.

Adela, the daughter, chooses to speak, and what she speaks is rape, the word that remains at the centre of the novel even after she has withdrawn the charge against Aziz. Her discourse, moreover, is double, reflecting her discovery of differentiation and division. On the one hand, in speaking Aziz's name during the scene with Mrs Moore, in restoring his subjectively, she fills the gap opened by the rhetoric of power that objectifies the other and creates the space for violation to occur. She succeeds where Fielding had failed. 'Dr Aziz', she reiterates during the trial, 'never followed me into the cave' (p. 229). On the other hand, by withdrawing his name without withdrawing the accusation of rape – that is, in refusing either to specify or deny what happened in the cave, a stance she maintains to the end (p. 263) – she creates another gap, one that disrupts rather than enabling the discourse of power and knowledge. Her refusal to specify, like the Indian women's refusal to be seen, generates a counter discourse, one that opens up gaps that those in power cannot control or afford, in part by undermining their claim to knowledge and truth. She generates as well the space between the material and the representational, between referentiality and textuality, where ideology and power are located, and she associates it with rape. Being English, she has the power to speak the position of otherness denied to the Indians in general and doubly denied to the invisible and silent Indian women, whose resistance resides in absence and negativity, and she uses this power to unsettle the dominant discourse.[36] In this sense she speaks what Aziz's dead wife cannot, naming the relationship between knowledge, objectification, and violation enacted by McBryde, the relationship that is elided in

the periphrasis that surrounds Adela's experience even while it constitutes the reality of women's lives. However creative the elision of
the proper term performed by periphrasis may be in literary
speech,[37] when used as part of a rhetoric of power in *A Passage to
India*, the elision emphasises the refusal to name the reduction of
woman and Indian that makes them rapable, the refusal to name it
rape.

For Adela, then, to speak rape becomes an act of resistance. Her
double discourse brings into representation woman's experience, the
unspoken or unspeakable, that is left out of namings and ideologies
even as it refuses the rhetoric of power that denies individuality and
speech. For Forster, who spoke uneasily from within and without
the discourse that appropriated his own sexuality, the periphrasis at
the heart of the novel suggests the difficulty of his position. Unlike
Fielding, with whom he clearly identifies, Forster understands the
position of otherness inscribed in the woman, although finally
unwilling to assert it himself. At the end he tries to recuperate the
message of the caves through the marriage of Fielding and Stella and
the temporary reconciliation of Fielding and Aziz, but he is unable
to contain the woman's voice speaking from the interstices of culture
the truth beyond the discourse of 'the true',[38] the truth that echoes
throughout the novel, crisscrossing boundaries and prophesying
violence and apocalypse unless we find ways to respond when the
other – whether woman or Indian – speaks violation.

From *Rape and Representation*, ed. Lynn A. Higgins and Brenda
R. Silver (New York, 1991), pp. 115–37.

NOTES

[This is a feminist reading of *A Passage to India*, adding to Foucault's and
Said's arguments about representing the other that representation is the
work of men, so that male inscriptions of women become colonising, and
women are objectified. Thus rape, which as an issue is at the heart of *A Passage to India*, belongs to the marginalisation of women, to Adela being
reduced to a 'periphrasis', like the Indian colonised subjects of the text.
Silver uses the work of Frantz Fanon (1925–61), to discuss 'negrophobia' as
sexual anxiety (this is similar to Suleri Goodyear [essay 9] on the terror of
empire) which must be translated back into the language of dominance and
control of the other – i.e. into something which is virtually rape, or, put
another way, virtually castration (the comparison Silver uses to describe the
disempowering of Aziz after his arrest). Silver reads Adela's confusion in the

caves as an element of her alienated identity, as a marker of how she has been objectified in sexual terms according to the demands of Anglo-Indians society, and sees her and her subsequent behaviour at the trial as subversive of the authority that this society possesses. That she speaks makes her different from Mrs Moore, whose retreat into silence is seen as an acceptance of the oppressiveness of all forms of power and a belief in their identity. This is obviously not all there is to be said about Mrs Moore, but this reading which centres on Adela (as the Lean film also begins with her and focuses on her, but to very different effect), makes her speaking the opposite of male periphrasis, and constructs her as a figure of a 'counter-discourse', Ed.]

A longer version of this essay appears in *Novel* (Fall 1988), 86–105. I am grateful to Mary Childers, Louise Fradenburg, Lynn Higgins, Marianne Hirsch, Nancy K. Miller, Sandy Petrey, and Nancy Vickers for their valuable criticism and suggestions.

1. In, respectively, *Webster's New World Dictionary of the American Language*, 2nd College edn (New York, 1978); Geoffrey Hartman, 'The Voice of the Shuttle: Language from the Point of View of Literature', *Beyond Formalism, Literary Essays 1958–1970* (New Haven, Conn., 1970), p. 352; *Webster's Third New International Dictionary* (Springfield, Mass., 1971).

2. Gérard Genette, 'Figures', *Figures of Literary Discourse*, trans. Alan Sheridan (New York; 1982), pp. 47–9, 57.

3. E. M. Forster, *The Manuscripts of A Passage to India*, ed. Oliver Stallybrass (London, 1978), pp. 242–3.

4. Letter to G. L. Dickinson, 26 June 1924, quoted in Oliver Stallybrass (ed.), *A Passage to India*, by E. M. Forster, Abinger edn (London, 1978), p. xxvi.

5. E. M. Forster, *A Passage to India* (1924; reprint, New York, 1984), p. 152. Further citations appear in text.

6. The phrase 'sex ghosts' comes from Mark Spilka's analysis of the governess's 'prurient sensibility': 'Turning the Freudian Turn of the Screw: How Not to Do It', *Literature and Psychology*, 13 (1963), 105–11. V. A. Shahane, summarising various interpretations of Adela's experience, cites as 'a minority critical view' that 'Adela is sexually charmed by Aziz and that in her subconscious self she desires to be raped by him' (*E. M. Forster. 'A Passage to India': A Study* [Delhi, 1977] p. 31). But the reading of Adela's experience in terms of repression, sexual hysteria, frigidity, or fear of the body is more widespread than Shahane implies. In addition, many critics associate Adela's experience with the condition of modern rationalism and the failure to recognise the importance of the heart or the passions or the instincts (revealed in part by the 'new psychology' of Freud and Jung), but even here sexual repression enters the argument. Comparing

Adela to D. H. Lawrence's Hermione Roddice, Wilfred Stone writes: 'Both are catastrophes of modern civilisation – repressed, class-bound, over-intellectualised' (*The Cave and the Mountain: A Study of E. M. Forster* [Stanford, Cal., 1966], p. 382). A different perspective on Adela's perception of the experience as a rape, one closer to my own, associates it with the loveless or forced union symbolised by her engagement to Ronny: e.g. Gertrude M. White, '*A Passage to India*: Analysis and Revaluation', *PMLA*, 68 (1953), 641–57, and Elaine Showalter, '*A Passage to India* as "Marriage Fiction" Forster's Sexual Politics', *Women and Literature*, 5 (1977), 3–16. White also suggests an analogy between the relationship of Ronny and Adela and that of English and Indian in the novel.

David Lean's film version of the novel glaringly reinforces the view of Adela as sexually repressed. In an interview about the film, Lean remarked, 'And Miss Quested ... well, she's a bit of a prig and a bore in the book, you know. I've changed her, made her more sympathetic. Forster wasn't always very good with women': *Guardian* 23 January 1984), quoted in Salman Rushdie, 'Outside the Whale', *American Film*, 10:4 (1985), 70.

7. Michel Foucault, *The History of Sexuality*, vol. 1: *An Introduction*, trans. Robert Hurley (1978; reprint, New York, 1980), pp. 44, 47, 104–5.

8. E. M. Forster, *The Life to Come and Other Stories* (1972; reprint, New York, 1976), pp. 160–76.

9. See essay 2 in *Rape and Representation*.

10. In his critique of the Raj revival in Britain, Salman Rushdie comments: 'It is useless, I'm sure, to suggest that if a rape must be used as the metaphor of the Indo-British connection, then surely, in the interests of accuracy, it should be the rape of an Indian woman by one or more Englishmen of whatever class – not even Forster dated to write about such a crime' ('Outside the Whale', p. 70).

11. Like the black woman in Barbara Johnson's discussion of the intersections of race and gender, the Indian woman is 'both invisible and ubiquitous: never seen in her own right but forever appropriated by the others for their own ends': 'Metaphor, Metonymy, and Voice in *Their Eyes Were Watching God*', in Henry Louis Gates, Jr (ed.), *Black Literature and Literary Theory* (New York, 1984), p. 216. For the dangers inherent in Western feminist readings of 'the other women', see Gayatri Chakravorty Spivak, 'French Feminism in an International Frame', *Yale French Studies*, 62 (1981), 157, 179, and Chandra Talpade Mohanty, 'Under Western Eyes: Feminist Scholarship and Colonial Discourse', *Boundary* 2, 12/13 (1984), 333–58.

12. Catharine A. MacKinnon, 'Feminism, Marxism, Method, and the State: An Agenda for Theory', *Signs: Journal of Women in Culture and Society*, 7 (1982), 516.

13. Monique Plaza, 'Our Damages and Their Compensation. Rape: The Will Not to Know of Michel Foucault', *Feminist Issues*, 1:3 (1981), 15.

14. MacKinnon, 'Feminism, Marxism', pp. 539, 538.

15. See John Berger, *Ways of Seeing* (London, 1972), pp. 46–7.

16. MacKinnon, 'Feminism, Theory, Marxism and the State, Toward Feminist Jurisprudence', *Signs: Journal of Women in Culture and Society* (1983), 8, 654. See Ellen Rooney's essay in *Rape and Representation* for a reading of MacKinnon's analysis of rape and law and its implications.

17. Plaza, 'Our Damages', p. 29.

18. MacKinnon, 'Jurisprudence', p. 651.

19. Foucault, *The History of Sexuality*, p. 94. See also *The Discourse on Language*, trans. Rupert Swyer (1971), in *The Archaeology of Knowledge*, pp. 215–37 (New York, 1972).

20. I am following here Kenneth Burke's designation of synecdoche in 'Four Master Tropes', *A Grammar of Motives* (New York, 1945), pp. 507, 509. In the sense that synecdoche in this novel works towards reduction, it tends towards Burke's definition of metonymy.

21. For an analysis of what it meant to be a 'White Man', see Edward Said, *Orientalism* (1978, reprint, New York, 1979), p. 227.

22. Ibid., p. 227.

23. Ibid., p. 229.

24. This is also the position of Hari Kumar in Paul Scott's *Raj Quartet: The Day of the Scorpion* (1968; reprint, New York, 1979).

25. Frantz Fanon, *Black Skin, White Masks*, trans. Charles Lam Markmann (New York, 1967), pp. 169–70, 166. For Fanon, the black man exists for whites as a synecdoche, a penis.

26. See Nellie McKay's essay in *Rape and Representation* for an analysis of this phenomenon in the United States. See also Jacqueline Dowd Hall, *Revolt Against Chivalry: Jessie Daniel Ames and the Women's Campaign Against Lynching* (New York, 1979). The patterns are similar, not the same; Mrs Turton's belief in the novel that Indian men 'ought to crawl from here to the caves on their hands and knees whenever an Englishwoman's in sight ...' (p. 216) not only reflects another of the negative effects of this 'chivalry' on white women, but alludes as well to the actual treatment of Indians during the Amritsar riots after a white woman was attacked.

27. See MacKinnon, 'Jurisprudence', p. 636; and Evelyn Fox Keller, *Reflections on Gender and Science* (New Haven Conn., 1985).

28. Susan Sontag, *On Photography*, cited in MacKinnon, 'Jurisprudence', p. 637.

29. Foucault, *The History of Sexuality*, p. 95. See also Teresa de Lauretis' use of Foucault's formulation in her discussion of male power and male resistance as playing by the same rules: *Alice Doesn't: Feminism, Semiotics, Cinema* (Bloomington, Ind., 1984), pp. 91–2. Her text is Nicolas Roeg's film *Bad Timing*, which has a rape as its central narrative impetus.

30. De Lauretis, *Alice Doesn't*, p. 93.

31. Said, *Orientalism*, p. 244.

32. Forster's '"No, not yet" ... "No, not there"' is echoed in Julia Kristeva's definition of 'women's practice as negative, in opposition to that which exists, to say that "this is not it" and "it is not yet"'. De Lauretis evokes this definition in her reading of the violated woman in *Bad Timing* who asks, 'What about my time' and 'what about now ...' (*Alice Doesn't*, pp. 95, 98–9).

33. Michael Ragussis, *The Subterfuge of Art: Language and the Romantic Tradition* (Baltimore, 1978), p. 156.

34. Gillian Beer; '"But Nothing in India is Identifiable": Negation and Identification in *A Passage to India*', in V. A Shahane (ed.), *Approaches to E.M. Forster: A Centenary Volume* (Atlantic Highlands, 1981), p. 18.

35. Barbara Johnson [see note 11] offers this speculation in her reading of the heroine's discovery of the power of voice in Zora Neal Hurston's *Their Eyes Were Watching God*: 'The reduction of discourse to oneness, identity – in Janie's case, the reduction of woman to mayor's wife – has as its necessary consequence aphasia, silence, the loss of the ability to speak' (p. 212). We might add ventriloquism to this list.

36. De Lauretis [see note 29] associates Kristeva's perception that 'women's practice can only be negative' with the concept of 'a radical and irreducible difference', and 'absolute negativity', that is not commensurate with the system that inscribes male power and resistance (p. 95). For de Lauretis, this difference is 'much more radical than the lack of something, be it phallus, being, language, or power ... an irreducible difference, of that which is elided, left out, not presented or representable' (p. 101).

37. Hartman, 'The Voice of the Shuttle', p. 352. For Ragussis [see note 33] in contrast to 'the word', which 'reports history', the recurring ellipses in the text '[pantomime] all that is outside history', establishing a space that can take on multiple meanings (p. 168). I would argue that when ellipsis becomes periphrasis, the space becomes a vacuum that denies those excluded by the elision their voice and their history.

38. Foucault, *The Discourse on Language*, p. 224.

11

A *Passage to India*: A Passage to the Patria?

PENELOPE PETHER

[This is the second part of Penelope Pether's essay on *A Passage to India*. The essay begins by suggesting that Forster constructs India as a 'national other' and that it therefore invests in a cultural construction of England. Egypt and India are seen by Forster, even as late as 1922–4, when he visited India, as among the territories of the 'enlightened Englishman's tradition'. It continues by discussing Forster's desire for the 'other' as belonging to a pastoral tradition, and then moves on to the sense of India as alien, by quoting from the early description of the Ganges. Ed.]

> So abased, so monotonous is everything that meets the eye, that when the Ganges comes down it might be expected to wash the excrescence back into the soil. Houses do fall, people are drowned and left rotting, but the general outline of the town persists, swelling here, sinking there, like some low but indestructible form of life.[1]

This fecund mutability, this habit of the Indian climate of breaking down both the organic and the work of human hands into a teeming, sprawling, mutating entity, signals the opposition of Forster's perception of India to what Stone called 'the geographical eternal moment',[2] a frequently recurring motif in Forster's work, and one which is an important marker of value. Its paradigm is perhaps the 'poetry ... [which] resides in objects Man *can't* touch – like England's grass network of lanes a hundred years ago'.[3] The Marabar Caves are the negative, the other, of the geographical eternal moment, as is signalled by Fielding's vision of the Marabar Hills at twilight from the verandah of the Club.

> It was the last moment of the light, and as he gazed at the Marabar Hills they seemed to move graciously towards him like a queen, and their charm became the sky's. At the moment they vanished they were everywhere, the cool benediction of the night descended, the stars sparkled, and the whole universe was a hill. Lovely, exquisite moment – but passing the Englishman with averted face and on swift wings. He experienced nothing himself; it was as if someone had told him there was such a moment and he was obliged to believe.
>
> (p. 187)

Sara Suleri[4] has identified this quality of the caves in proposing that they lack metaphoricity for the western imagination, and are indifferent to experiential time. Alien, they are unavailable to the memory which seeks to use place and history, conflated, to fashion a transcendent symbol which resists time, constructing 'out of the bones of the past something more real and more satisfactory than the chaos surrounding [it]'.[5]

The text identifies this quality of the caves with 'Indianness' when it describes Adela, at the 'Bridge Party':

> Miss Quested now had her desired opportunity; friendly Indians were before her, and she tried to make them talk, but she failed, she strove in vain against the echoing walls of their civility. Whatever she said produced a murmur of deprecation, varying into a murmured concern when she dropped her pocket-handkerchief. She tried doing nothing, to see what that produced, and they too did nothing.
>
> (p. 43)

Benita Parry's analysis[6] of Adela's experience in the Cave gives particularly helpful pointers towards the relation between Indian otherness, sexuality, and English experiences of nationality. She argues that rape in British Indian writing was typically constructed as the rape by Indian male of British female, and that the India constructed by Raj discourse became a figure of sexual menace, threatening to violate British values. I would suggest that the embodiment of this construction in *A Passage* indicates that the emphasis on the Caves as 'void' springs from an anxiety about the nature of 'Englishness', as against colonial 'Anglo-Indianness'. 'Englishness' in India marks a subject position threatened by the experience of its imagined other. It is not the Anglo-Indians but Adela Quested and Cyril Fielding –

for whom a Wordsworthian England is a touchstone of value – who find their senses of identity profoundly threatened by the India which the novel constructs. Ironically, of course, the threat to Adela, constructed as sexual, is presented as illusory. Her eroticised desire for connection with the other is both produced and frustrated by an ineradicable ignorance, as Forster suggests:

> Between people of distant climes there is always the possibility of romance, but the various branches of Indians know too much about each other to surmount the unknowable easily.
>
> (pp. 260–1)

The imperfect kiss between Fielding and Aziz at the novel's conclusion likewise describes nationality's defeat of a desire constructed as homoerotic.

Gillian Beer[7] has identified the text's ideology as manifested in space – 'the space between cultures, the space beyond the human, the space which can never be sufficiently filled by aspiration and encounter', and has identified in the opening section of the novel 'exclusion – which is extended as absence'. The absence, I would suggest, is the absence of Forster's construction of England, imagined as 'significant form' (p. 275). The opening chapter demonstrates this as it dramatises the perception of the geographical hierarchy of Chandrapore, and the resolutely sylvan – and thus to the English sensibility picturesque and scenic – way in which the inhabitants of the English 'rise' see, or rather do not see, Chandrapore.

Mrs Moore perceives that the 'snub-nosed worm' of envy released in her by the echo in the Caves is 'Before time ... before space also' (p. 203). Adela's perception of the 'meaning' of the experience in the Cave is that 'In space things touch, in time things part' (p. 189). The Cave is the paradigm of India: connection between Aziz and Fielding is resisted by time and place: it cannot happen yet; it cannot happen in India. Hamidullah, privileged by Forster in the novel because described as the only one of the company at Aziz's who 'had any comprehension of poetry' (p. 103), argues early in the novel that friendship between Indians and Englishmen is possible in England, while not in India. This claim is grounded in his own experience; he

> ... had been to that country long ago, before the big rush, and had received a cordial welcome at Cambridge.
>
> (p. 12)

The novel later acknowledges the soul's incapacity, 'in fear of losing the little she does understand', to extend sympathy beyond 'the permanent lines that habit or chance have dictated' (p. 240). It suggests the failure of Forster's proclaimed initial aim, to create in *A Passage* a bridge between East and West, to evoke the river of love which springs from the union of Ganges and Jumna. Only those who share a heritage can connect; place is productive of heritage. The reference to Cambridge here suggests that the novel's acknowledgment of limitation is authorial and not just narratorial.

[In a passage cut here, Pether discusses Forster's growing alienation from India, linking that to Forster's biography, to his relationship to Masood and to Mohammed-el-Adl, and to his own feeling for agricultural England. Ed.]

In 1922 Forster wrote to Goldsworthy Lowes Dickinson on the subject of the Krishna festival:

> I am anxious to see the celebrations, and shall take up my residence for part of the fortnight in the Old Palace, until the bugs and mosquitos expel me or all my socks are worn out, for in the Old Palace it is not permissible to wear boots. But how will the externals help me to the underlying fact? I only want to touch the fact intellectually, in order to understand with these folk and have done with them. I don't want the fact intellectually and emotionally, and there you are! Therefore, I shall never touch it, H. H. will say.[8]

This letter contains several references to source material for 'Temple'. Forster's incapacity to enter and render Indian mysticism is as precisely signposted as is the failure of connection – to other, and other country – which is the novel's *fons et origo* as well as its *telos*.

The text – and particularly its delineation of the connection between Godbole and Mrs Moore, and its construction of 'Hindu mysticism' – further confirms the essential Englishness of Forster's vision in *A Passage*. There is a pattern of association between Goldsworthy Lowes Dickinson and Mrs Moore, whose connection with Godbole – mediated through the wasp – has been frequently read as an exemplum of the communication between members of different races promised by the Krishna miracle. The bases of Mrs Moore's character are suggested in *Goldsworthy Lowes Dickinson*: they are Dickinson himself, and Mrs Moor and Mrs Webb, his 'two great women friends'. Dickinson accompanied Forster in his first visit to India, their responses to it differed widely,[9] and their dialogue on the 'Indian question' continued. A letter from Dickinson to Mrs Moor, written from India and quoted from by Forster in *Goldsworthy Lowes Dickinson*, suggests a possible source of the wasp motif.[10] Correspondence between Dickinson and Mrs Moor published in *Goldsworthy Lowes Dickinson* shows that the discussion of philosophical and religious questions formed the basis of their friendship. Mrs Webb, like Mrs Moore in *A Passage*, was a practising Anglican, and Dickinson's description[11] of Mrs Webb is strongly suggestive of the link between him, Mrs Webb, Mrs Moor, and Mrs Moore:

> ... all this leaves her as it were unsullied, uncomplaining, the most beautiful soul perhaps I have known or shall know, except, it may be, my sister Janet[12] and Mrs Moor. She also has a strong and sincere mind, which prevents swallowing any humbug. She is a member of the Church of England and the widow of a parson. But what she believes now I do not know, nor I think does she. But she has 'faith' in the sense of courage, love and hope. These are the last great qualities that abide when all other things go, and we can but wait our passage to annihilation or whatever else there may be.

While this pattern of connection is suggestive and not probative, other material points to the connection between Dickinson and Mrs Moore. Harold Bloom[13] has written that Mrs Moore is the true heroine of 'a narrative of Neo-Platonic spirituality'. He suggests that the 'spirituality' in question is a Plotinean version of Hinduism; Dickinson's fellowship dissertation sought to compare and harmonise the doctrines of Plato and Plotinus.

Forster could be describing Aziz's perception of Mrs Moore when he writes of Dickinson that

> His anxiety to learn, his great conversational powers, his intelligence and gentleness, his interest in religion, his readiness to enter into every point of view, made him popular with Indians of various types.[14]

As with Mrs Moore, however, the experience of India moved Dickinson – uncharacteristically – to cynicism and a querulous despair:

> For the hard worked and conscientious Anglo-Indians I met I felt a sympathy tinged with a kind of despair. For it seemed almost that the more conscientiously they did their work, the further they were from the native sympathy and mind. But that too may be illusion. I am, however, pretty sure that the irony that brought the English into contact with the Indians is only equalled by that which brought them into

contact with the Irish. The barrier, on both sides, of incomprehension is almost impossible. I feel this incomprehension very strongly myself. Indian art, Indian religion, Indian society is alien and unsympathetic to me. I have no sense of superiority about it, but one of estrangement. What indeed is there or can there be in common between the tradition of Greece and that of India; ...

There is no solution of the problem of governing India. Our presence is a curse both to them and to us. Our going will be worse. I believe that is the last word. And *why* can't the races meet? Simply because the Indians *bore* the English. *That* is the simple adamantine fact.[15]

Like Mrs Moore, India and Indians made Dickinson long 'vainly, to be alone'.[16]

The wasp, then, is a marker of difference which overrides sympathy, rather than a vector of oneness. The text identifies Mrs Moore's encounter with the wasp as confirming her 'otherness' in India. It is true that she has experienced a brief 'sense of unity, of kinship with the heavenly bodies' (p. 30) between the encounter with Aziz in the mosque and the sighting of the wasp. However the text emphasises the brevity of this epiphany, and its connection with the sky rather than with the Indian earth: she is 'caught in a shawl of night, together with earth and all the heavenly bodies'; the sense of kinship with the stars passes in and out of her 'like water through a tank, leaving a strange freshness behind' (p. 30). Her response to the wasp identifies its 'un-Englishness'; her expression of sympathy for it is banal and saccharine, and is productive of uneasiness, not harmony. Similarly, the encounter in the mosque emphasises the separation between her and Aziz, despite their sympathy for each other.

It is Aziz's 'Englishness', if you like, his conformity to the ways in which the English liberal middle classes behave, which makes him accessible and attractive to Mrs Moore and Adela, just as it is their determination to be guided by 'liking' which makes them assimilable into 'oriental' types by him. This attitude to Aziz is perhaps most suggestively sketched in the pattern of the encounter between Aziz and Mrs Moore at the mosque, where, until (English) conversation commences, each is the feared or hated, unidentifiable, unknown to the other, and the mosque is said (and here the narrator moves into Aziz's perspective) to ignite Aziz's pleasure and imagination because it is a mosque of Islam. It is Islam, rather than any place, which is Aziz's 'home'. The narrator has, just before this, described part of the mosque as creating the 'effect ... of an English parish church whose side has been taken out' (p. 20). At this moment the narrator may be speaking from Aziz's point of view: the description certainly comes in the middle of a group of sentences which describe Aziz's feelings and reactions; but the syntax and choice of words in this sentence suggest, somewhat ambiguously, that the narrator, for all his sympathies with Aziz, is fixing him, describing him, and calling on the English architectural vernacular to do so. This necessitates a withdrawal from the position of displaying Aziz's perspective. This separation of perception, it seems, is inevitable, and brings with it a failure of sympathy.

Godbole's envisioning of Mrs Moore and of the wasp is equally an indication of separation. His call to God to 'come' (p. 286) when he imagines himself in Mrs Moore's position, is answered by the '"No, not yet," and ... "No, not there,"'of the novel's conclusion. India and time resist connection, enforcing division, as is acknowledged when it is noted by the narrator that Godbole's sympathies are with internationality. Despite the fact that Godbole thinks that it makes no difference whether Mrs Moore, envisioned, 'was a trick of his memory or a telepathic appeal' (p. 286), he is undermined by the narrator's claims that:

> Not only from the unbeliever are mysteries hid, but the adept himself cannot retain them. He may think, if he chooses, that he has been with God, but as soon as he thinks it, it becomes history, and falls under the rules of time
>
> (p. 283)

under which rule, of course, 'things part'. Memory is, paradoxically, acknowledgement of loss, marker of separation.

[A third passage which has had to be excluded here makes links between Forster and Proust and discusses Forster's desire for a Hindu 'oneness'. Ed.]

If Mrs Moore is essentially Plotinean, and thus essentially English in the 'Cambridge' sense, so, too, is Forster's construction of Hinduism.[17] As John Drew has noted:

> From the time of Alexander the Great, India has been associated in the European mind with the philosophic life ... The philosophy the Greeks saw practised in India they likened to that of Pythagoras and Plato and the respectful attitude of the Neo-Platonists to India encouraged later European Orientalists to single out the mystical Vedanta as India's principal philosophical system and to discern an almost total identity between it and Neo-Platonism.[18]

Drew claims that 'shortly before publishing' *A Passage*, Forster 'subscribed quite consciously' to the idea of Neo-Platonism's identity with the mystical Vedanta. He notes that Forster had read a translation and summary of the *Enneads* of Plotinus while working on *Alexandria: A History and a Guide*, and that Dickinson was 'the only lucid English commentator on Plotinus' before the publication of MacKenna's five volume translation and commentary (1917–30). The philosophy of the 'Orient' then, is one imagined as identical to the philosophy which is the 'enlightened Englishman's tradition'. If the Marabar Cave is a metaphor for Plato's cave, ordinary, unenlightened individuals can only see in it and apprehend as real the shadows of themselves and their fellows; can only envisage the other as shadow of self, and can only suppose, if the wall of the cave reflects sound, that these echoes of their own voices are the voices of the shadows.[19] It is significant that in Plato's cave analogy, the illusions with which the occupants of the cave are beset include 'all works of poetry and art'.[20]

Finally, there is the significance of the joining and separating horsemen of the novel's closing scene. This is metonymically connected with the 'hit' of polo which Aziz and the subaltern have on the maidan. On that occasion, the comradeship of men in the physical pleasure of sport is celebrated; briefly, at least, the mood generated by such an encounter banishes nationality, separation. Later, at the club, the subaltern launches into a diatribe about the superiority of Indian troops in India. Drunken and confused, he is yet the articulator of the scene's irony, as his reference to 'Barabas Hill' warns. He is the foil for the beautiful, fecund, 'cow-like', intensely female Mrs Blakiston, who has become the sentimental focus of Anglo-Indian hysteria and has voiced it in her 'if only there were a few Tommies' (p. 181). In an intensely comic moment, the subaltern recalls his 'hit' of polo with Aziz, saying

> ... he was all right. Any native who plays polo is all right. What you've got to stamp on is these educated classes.
>
> (p. 181)

The subaltern probably owes his origins to the subaltern Kenneth Searight, whom Forster met en route to India in 1912. Well-read and romantic, he was what Lago and Furbank call a 'dedicated homosexual'.[21] Forster wrote to Florence Barger that Searight was 'very intimate with natives, and might show me a lot'.[22] Furbank records him 'astonishing' Forster 'with some of his 'minorite' [i.e. homosexual] anecdotes'. After lavish and boisterous hospitality was showered on Forster and his travelling companions Trevelyan and Dickinson by Searight's unit at Peshawar – including a dinner during which Searight made Forster dance with him – Forster wrote

> I feel compelled to alter my opinion of soldiers, these were so charming, and without the least side, and their hospitality passes anything I could have imagined ... In spite of their folly, many of them were sensible talkers and had even read a good deal.[23]

This material suggests the impulse for Forster's attempts – in 'Arctic Summer', *Maurice*, and *A Passage*, to reconcile the 'heroic' and the 'civilised' Englishman, whose opposition was represented by the Clesant/Martin dichotomy in 'Arctic Summer'. It also suggests why men's sporting contacts were used as a symbol of connection in *A Passage to India*.

The articulation of the association of the other with the homoerotic, and the significance of Forster's abandonment of the notion of the possibility of connection across 'national', or rather, 'ordinary' lines are evident, too, in biographical material which suggests the source of Forster's choice of the polo game as emblem of transor supra-national connection.[24] Forster's 'emblem' was associated both with friendship with a man of another nation, and with family, home, England, history, memory. In *Two Cheers for Democracy*, describing books bound by his aunt, Laura Forster, and left to him, Forster wrote:

> The most ambitious of all her bindings – the *Rubaiyat of Omar Khayyam* – I gave away after her death to an oriental friend. I still miss that lovely book and wish I possessed it. I still see the charming design with which she decorated its cover – polo players adapted from an ancient Persian miniature – a design for which the contemporary dust jacket is a poor substitute.
>
> However I am contemporary myself and I must get on to myself and not linger amongst ancestral influences any longer.[25]

Laura Forster died about a month before the publication of *A Passage*.[26] Furbank records her fetishising of tradition in place: rooms at her house, 'West Hackhurst', were named for loved places. She also planted a tulip tree at 'West Hackhurst' – which was built by Forster's father and which Forster inherited from her – because there had been one at 'Battersea Rise', the Thornton family house. Forster uses the tulip tree as the insignia of the continuity of English tradition, and a marker of the involvement of the writer in that tradition, in his 'Abinger Pageant'.

If Laura Forster's death marked a return to England in the life – prompted by the inheritance of what was in a curious sense Forster's 'father's house' – then so does the motif of horse and rider in *A Passage* signal a return in the works to the boundaries of the *patria*. The consciousness of retreat is signalled by the way in which the *patria's* other – the 'motherland' – is employed in the text. On both occasions it is associated with Aziz and with his conception of 'Oriental womanhood'. It is also specifically identified with nationalism. Pressed by Fielding to propose an alternative to English government of India, Aziz is forced to abandon his proposal that her rulers should be 'the Afghans. My own ancestors' (p. 316), entailing as it would the suppression of Indian divisions, and of the Hinduism which has become the novel's metaphor for internationalism. Finally

> he remembered that he had, or ought to have, a motherland. Then he shouted: 'India shall be a nation! No foreigners of any sort! Hindu and Moslem and Sikh and all shall be one! Hurrah! Hurrah for India! Hurrah! Hurrah!'
>
> (p. 317)

The narrator then speaks from Fielding's perspective:

> India a nation! What an apotheosis! Last comer to the drab nineteenth-century sisterhood! Waddling in at this hour of the world to take her seat! She, whose only peer was the Holy Roman Empire, she shall rank with Guatemala and Belgium perhaps! Fielding mocked again.
>
> (p. 317)

The antipathy of Fielding and the narrator to the idea of 'nation' – in the sense of nation-state – is clearly marked here. Earlier, the narrator – here not expressing a character's perception as if it was his own, and thus signally authoritative – says of Aziz's poems:

> they struck a true note: there cannot be a mother-land without new homes.
>
> (p. 289)

The text, though, signals the impossibility of new homes, the force of attachment to the old. And there is a further irony. The narrator notes that Aziz 'did not truly love' (p. 289) the motherland; his poems are all on the topic of 'Oriental womanhood' (p. 289) – an 'other' almost entirely absent from the novel – and Aziz's model project for Oriental womanhood is based on a version of feminism which suggests Adela. Sara Suleri has identified Adela's function as 'conduit or ... passageway for the aborted eroticism between the European Fielding and the Indian Aziz':[27] the motherland is a passage to the *patria*; the woman a passage to the man; the freedom of woman a passage to a reflection of Englishness.[28]

As Aziz's home is Islam,[29] so Fielding's is England's 'green and pleasant land', as his name suggests. The return to the knowable, the *patria*, articulated in Forster's 'Temple', is a return to the known as embodied in place. The nature of that place is twofold, and emphasised in the final chapters of 'Cave': the sacred sites of the 'enlightened Englishman's tradition', and an England of which Wordsworth is the inventor.[30] The inauguration of the 'spot of time' (prefigured in 'Tintern Abbey') marks the connection of time and space which is used by Wordsworth to invent England for pastoral purposes, which blots out evidence of recent industrialisation and of community breakdown, appropriating and suppressing their traces to reinstate the *heimlich*, erase the *unheimlich*.

In the novel, response to 'the lakes' is used as a symbol of the capacity to 'connect'. It is a point of connection for Mrs Moore and Adela on the trip to the Marabar; their exchange dramatises the forces which shape the English person's ways of seeing:

> '... I must admit that England has it as regards sunrise. Do you remember Grasmere?'
> ... Ah, dearest Grasmere!' Its little lakes and mountains were beloved by them all. Romantic yet manageable, it sprang from a kindlier planet. Here an untidy plain stretched to the knees of the Marabar.
>
> (pp. 136–7)

In an interval of 'decency', of generosity and ethical conduct, Ronny is described in this way"

> He might force his opinions down her throat, but did not press her to an 'engagement', because he believed, like herself, in the sanctity of personal relationships: it was this that had drawn them together at their first meeting, which had occurred amongst the grand scenery of the English lakes.
>
> (p. 82)

Later, condemned by Forster:

> Ronny's religion was of the sterilised Public School Brand ... he
> retained the spiritual outlook of the Fifth Form
>
> (p. 250)

he disparages Grasmere; he is tellingly placed by the tone of
rationalising self-pity in which his reflection in couched:

> She had killed his love, and it had never been very robust; they would
> never have achieved betrothal but for the accident to the Nawab
> Bahadur's car. She belonged to the callow academic period of his life which
> he had outgrown – Grasmere, serious talks and walks, that sort of thing.
>
> (p. 251)

The return to England is at first identified implicitly –

> Making sudden changes of gear, the heat accelerated its advance after
> Mrs Moore's departure until existence had to be endured and crime
> punished with the thermometer at a hundred and twelve. Electric fans
> hummed and spat, water splashed on to screens, ice clinked, and out-
> side these defences, between a greyish sky and a yellowish earth,
> clouds of dust moved hesitantly. In Europe life retreats out of the cold,
> and exquisite fireside myths have resulted – Balder, Persephone – but
> here the retreat is from the source of life, the treacherous sun, and no
> poetry adorns it because disillusionment cannot be beautiful. Men
> yearn for poetry though they may not confess it; they desire that joy
> shall be graceful and sorrow august and infinity have a form, and
> India fails to accommodate them. The annual helter-skelter of April,
> when irritability and lust spread like a canker is one of her comments
> on the orderly hopes of humanity. Fish manage better, fish, as the
> tanks dry, wriggle into the mud and wait for the rains to uncover
> them. But men try to be harmonious all the year round, and the
> results are occasionally disastrous. The triumphant machine of civili-
> sation may suddenly hitch and be immobilised into a car of stone, and
> at such moments the destiny of the English seems to resemble their
> predecessors', who also entered the country with intent to refashion it,
> but were in the end worked into its pattern and covered with dust
>
> (p. 206)

and then explicitly –

> Turning his back on it yet again, he took the train northward and ten-
> der romantic fancies that he thought were dead for ever flowered
> when he saw the buttercups and daises of June
>
> (pp. 275–6)

with a return to assurance of seasonal rebirth. The connection between the pastoral impulse and seasonality is suggested in the contrast between the Indian dry season and England:

> All over the city and all over much of India the same retreat on the part of humanity was beginning into cellars, up hills, under trees. April, herald of horrors, is at hand. The sun was turning to his kingdom with power but without beauty – that was the sinister feature. If only there had been beauty! This cruelty would have been tolerable then. Through excess of light, he failed to triumph, he also; in his yellowy-white overflow not only matter, but brightness itself lay damned. He was not the unattainable friend, either of men or birds or other suns, he was not the eternal promise, the never-withdrawn suggestion that haunts our consciousness; he was merely a creature, like the rest, and so debarred from glory.
>
> (pp. 111–12)

India's incapacity to provide renewal, and the desired other, is contrasted with a pastoral vision of desire attainable in England. The novel suggests this is because 'death interrupts' (p. 229) less in India than in England; death interrupting is identified as a characteristic of the modern world, suggesting the impetus for the development of the modernist *locus amoenus* as a function of memory, anchored in familiar, circumscribed space and past time. The English mind cannot 'take hold of such a country' (p. 135) as India; it has not the apparatus for describing her.

The gender specificity of the pastoral return to England is signalled by its being Fielding's passage, not Adela's. She thinks that 'we ought all to go back into the desert for centuries and try and get good' (p. 193). Unsurprisingly, Fielding re-embarks for Europe from Alexandria and proceeds through Greece and Italy.[31] Mrs Moore's ghost – female – fails to enter the Mediterranean, lacking, perhaps, the 'enlightened Englishman's tradition'. Having abandoned the idea of love, of connection with the friend, she is portentously cast off at Egypt.[32] Given her association with the Plotinean, the casting off of the (albeit Anglocentric) fantasy of oneness between Europe and the Orient is thus signified.

Fielding finds in the natural and monumental Alexandria, in Greece and in Italy, the sources of his civilisation's tradition of beauty of form, identified as foreign to India and Indians. In celebrating 'the harmony between the works of man and the earth that upholds them, the civilisation that has escaped muddle, the spirit in reasonable form with flesh and blood subsisting' (p. 275) the narrator proposes – employing highly self-conscious rhetoric to do so – that for an Englishman of Fielding's – and the narrator's – class, educated as he has been, there is no choice as to the places that he will have imaginative access to, and will value. The suggestion is that the knowledge of and the way of seeing the 'native place' are the forces which generate these patterns of understanding and valuing:

> Writing picture post-cards to his Indian friends, he felt that all of them would miss the joys he experienced now, the joys of form, and that this constituted a serious barrier. They would see the sumptuousness of Venice, not its shape, and though Venice was not Europe, it was part of the human norm.
>
> (p. 275)

By contrast, Aziz sees India as shaped by 'the architecture of Question and Answer' (p. 69), but this perception is intermittent and – characteristic of the novel's construction of the 'Oriental' – it lacks conviction. What follows the quotation above, in its change in tense, in its absoluteness, signals its significance:

> The Mediterranean is the human norm. When men leave that exquisite lake, whether through the Bosphorous or the Pillars of Hercules, they approach the monstrous and extraordinary, and the southern exit leads to the strangest experience of all.
>
> (p. 275)

The passage through Suez to India[33] is to the strangest of these 'monstrous and extraordinary' destinations – the uncanny, the *unheimlich*. England – a destination for which Fielding entrains from, rather than exits from the Mediterranean, is, then, perceived of as one with it.

The process of Fielding's abandonment of a hope, a belief that he can be intimate with Indians, is sketched in the chapter's final sentence:

> Turning his back on it yet again, he took the train northward, and tender romantic fancies that he thought were dead for ever flowered when he saw the buttercups and daises of June.
>
> (pp. 275–6)

The opening participle enacts the reluctance and inevitability of this movement in its form and meaning respectively. The reluctance to admit failure is held in the opposition between the rejection inherent in 'turning his back' and the sense of (past) possibilities of 'yet again'.

At the beginning, so at the end. Like Aziz and Fielding in the closing chapter, the civil station of the opening chapter 'shares nothing with the city except the overarching sky' (p. 10); place, 'something racial' (p. 254) separate them like the colour of their skins: 'coffee-colour versus pinko-grey' (p. 254). To a non-Indian, because he is a non-Indian, 'nothing in India is identifiable' (pp. 83–4). 'Nothing embraces the whole of India' (p. 143) for a mind which England, not India, 'bore, shaped, made aware',[34] because India is itself divided it is constructed as the place for the revelation of division. Sara Suleri has claimed that *A Passage* 'most clearly delineates the desire to convert unreadability into unreality, and difference into an image of the writing mind's perception of its own ineffability'.[35] The frequent shifts of the narratorial voice into characters' subject positions, though, subverts any possibility of ineffability and dramatises how local are any claims to it. For all its transcendental politics – perhaps because of them – the novel can only write England's narrative: re-tell 'Tintern Abbey', not the *Vedanta*. It displays what John Beer[36] has called 'the tendency of the mind that has become aware of an uninterpretable void to concentrate on finding a firm point of organisation, if possible in terms of space and time': in short, the *Temple*, the 'sacred space', and the 'ritualisation of memory', which the closing chapter of 'Caves', and 'Temple', explicitly and then implicitly describe.

The evidence set out above of Forster's responses to the death of el-Adl and the relationship with 'Kanaya' demonstrate that these embodiments of the other had been 'unknowable' and had led him to the loss of his conception of himself for which the encounter in the Marabar was a metaphor. This negative 'pastoral of desire', *A Passage to India*, describes its negative *locus amoenus* as the shadow of its ideal, an England both signified by and signifier of the 'greenwood' imagined in *Maurice*.

From *Sydney Studies in English*, 17 (1991), 88–120.

NOTES

[This essay reads Forster biographically, but focuses on an argument that *A Passage to India* fails to imagine the 'other' and endorses a myth of England as pastoral and not touched by modernism. The name 'Fielding' for the hero is suggestive here because of the very 'English' nature of the author of *Tom*

Jones who is recalled by it; so are the references to the Lake District ('Grasmere'), the home of Wordsworth and Coleridge, essentially a romantic spot. Further, Pether accuses Forster of being unable to enter and render Indian mysticism. In proposing that *A Passage to India* affirms the importance of the native place and of the individual's attachment to it, Pether finds Forster, along with other English modernists, reactionary. As a concomitant to the sense that the empire is coming to a close there is a celebration of the nation-state, and a sense that it cannot die. The argument that finds Forster buying into an ideology of Englishness has implications for all of his fiction, and has bearings on a discussion of the films which further negotiate a nostalgic sense of England. Ed.]

1. *A Passage to India* (Harmondsworth, 1961) p. 9. All further references are given in the text.

2. W. Stone, *The Cave and the Mountain: A Study of E. M. Forster* (Stanford, Cal.; London, 1966), p. 195.

3. E. M. Forster, 'The Last of Abinger' in *Two Cheers for Democracy* (London, 1972), p. 369. The image was first recorded in Forster's Commonplace Book in 1928.

4. Sara Suleri, 'The Geography of *A Passage to India*' in *E. M. Forster*, ed. Harold Bloom (New York, 1987), p. 173.

5. E. M. Forster, 'English Prose between 1918 and 1939' in *Two Cheers for Democracy*, p. 288.

6. Benita Parry, 'The Politics of Representation in *A Passage to India*', in *A Passage to India: Essays in Interpretation*, ed. John Beer (London, 1985), p. 154.

7. Gillian Beer, 'Negation in *A Passage to India*' in *A Passage to India: Essays in Interpretation* (London, 1985), p. 46.

8. E. M. Forster, *Selected Letters, Volume Two, 1921–1970* (Cambridge, Mass., 1983), p. 10.

9. See E. M. Forster, *Goldsworthy Lowes Dickinson* (1934, London, 1973), pp. 112–17; P. N. Furbank, *E. M. Forster. A Life*, II (New York, 1977–8), 124, 126.

10. In a letter written to Mrs Moor from India Dickinson wrote 'A wasp has been depositing paralysed spiders in a hole in one of the tables, laid her eggs, and carefully sealed it up with wax. What a thing nature is! How do the spiders feel? Let's hope they're unconscious! In the face of these things, most religious talk seems "tosh". If there's a God, or gods, they're beyond my ken. I think perhaps, after all, the Hindus took in more of the facts in their religion than most people have done.' (Cited in *Goldsworthy Lowes Dickinson*, p. 116.) It is not clear when Forster became aware of the letter's substance.

11. Cited in *Goldsworthy Lowes Dickinson*, p. 48.

12. Janet was an early name for Adela (Oliver Stallybrass, introduction, *The Manuscripts of a Passage to India* (London, 1978]).

13. Harold Bloom, introduction to *E. M. Forster's A Passage to India*, ed. Harold Bloom (New York, 1987), p. 5.

14. *Goldsworthy Lowes Dickinson*, p. 114.

15. Cited in *Goldsworthy Lowes Dickinson*, pp. 114, 117.

16. *Goldsworthy Lowes Dickinson*, p. 114.

17. Trilling wrote that '... the Indian gods are not [Forster's] gods, they are not genial and comprehensible. So far as the old Mediterranean deities of wise impulse and loving intelligence can go in India, Forster is at home; he thinks they can go far but not all the way, and a certain retraction of the intimacy of his style reflects his uncertainty. The acts of imagination by which Forster conveys the sense of the Indian gods are truly wonderful; they are, nevertheless, the acts of imagination not of a master of the truth, but of an intelligent neophyte, still baffled.' (Lionel Trilling, *E. M. Forster* [London, 1962], pp. 124–5. See also P. N. Furbank, *A Life*, I, 217).

18. John Drew, 'The Spirit behind the frieze?' in *A Passage to India: Essays in Interpretation* (London, 1985), p. 81.

19. See Plato, *The Republic*, tr. H. D. P. Lee (Harmondsworth, 1955), p. 279.

20. Plato, p. 275, p. 370.

21. E. M. Forster, *Selected Letters, Volume One, 1879–1920*, p. 141.

22. E. M. Forster, *Selected Letters, Volume One, 1879–1920*, p. 140.

23. E. M. Forster, *Selected Letters, Volume One, 1879–1920*, p. 155.

24. P. N. Furbank (*A Life*, I, 248–9, 252–4) reports incidents which suggest other sources for the choice of the concluding image of separation of Englishman and Indian on horseback; the second of these, and another encounter described by Forster in a 21 November 1912 letter to his mother (*Selected Letters, Volume One, 1879–1920*, p. 159) suggest additional bases for the association of the erotic and of masculine connection, respectively, with riding.

25. *Two Cheers for Democracy*, p. 310.

26. Forster had, however, frequented her house in his childhood and adolescence.

27. Sara Suleri, 'The Geography', p. 174.

28. Aziz is said to envy 'the easy intercourse [of the English] that is only possible in a nation whose women are free'.

29. Aziz is described as being 'rooted in society and Islam. He belonged to a tradition which bound him ... Though he lived so vaguely in this flimsy bungalow, nevertheless he was placed, placed.'

30. See Marjorie Levinson, 'Insight and oversight: reading "Tintern Abbey"' in *Wordsworth's great period poems: Four essays* (Cambridge, 1986), pp. 14–56. Forster admitted that 'Wordsworth is in the background ... in the reference to Grasmere' (James McConkey, *The Novels of E. M. Forster* [Ilthaca, NY, 1957] p. 83).

31. Forster had long associated Italy with the homoerotic, calling it that 'beautiful country where they say "yes"' (see P. N. Furbank, *A Life*, I, 90–1, 96).

32. Forster's embarkation point at the end of his last visit to el-Adl (en route from India) was Port Said.

33. Whitman's 'Passage to India' was, of course, written to celebrate the opening of the Suez Canal.

34. Rupert Brooke, 'The Soldier'.

35. Sara Suleri, 'The Geography', p. 171.

36. John Beer, '*A Passage to India*, the French New Novel and English Romanticism' in *E. M. Forster: Centenary Revaluations* (London, 1982), p. 128.

12

A Disconnected View: Foster, Modernity and Film

PETER J. HUTCHINGS

Since 1984, five of Forster's six novels have been adapted for the screen – *A Passage to India* (dir. David Lean, 1984), *A Room with a View* (dir. James Ivory, 1986), *Maurice* (dir. James Ivory, 1987), *Where Angels Fear to Tread* (dir. Charles Sturridge, 1991), and *Howards End* (dir. James Ivory, 1992) – leaving only *The Longest Journey* as yet unfilmed. These adaptations have been generally acclaimed as exemplary in their literary qualities and evocation of a period, and have come to represent the cultural values that a British film industry seems to stand for. 'Solidly' scripted, in the sense that dialogue is considered important, well-acted, featuring lavish and meticulous production design and costume, the films embody various forms of nostalgia: for their Edwardian period, but also for an idea of art and culture threatened by the codes of mass and avant-garde culture. They have been successful in Britain and in the USA, winning BAFTAs and Oscars (see appendix), and screening in multiplex cinemas alongside Hollywood's latest action blockbuster. *A Room with a View* has earned US$20 million, an extraordinary amount for a 'quality' film.

Yet the films have also been criticised for much the same reasons as they have been celebrated. The appeal to the past in subject matter and modes of presentation offers a conservative, selectively backward-looking view of the issues that are so contemporaneously fraught in the novels. In the era of Thatcher and Reagan, the films have happily met with an audience who conceive of the present as 'worth living only if it guarantees to be "just like the past"',[1] a desire which makes both present and past into decorous species of kitsch. As Cairns Craig has put it,

> The audience is invited to understand the plot of the film as though we are *contemporary* with the characters, while at the same time indulging our pleasure in a world which is visually compelling precisely because of its *pastness*.[2]

The invitation to a contemporary understanding of the plot produces some telling anachronisms. In Sturridge's *Where Angels Fear to Tread* Mrs Herriton's (Barbara Jefford) pretentious '*an* hotel' compared to the novel's correct 'a hotel', either betrays the film's straining after gentility, or works as a neat marker of the Herritons' otherwise unmarked suburban *arrivisme*. Forster's readership might have been of the same class as the Herritons, but they knew they'd only just got into society; perhaps, like the Honeychurchs, owing their position to a house a few years older than the others in the district.

But such distinctions are largely absent from the film versions, so that in the celebration of the literary and cultural values of the films there is an implied model of the literary and the cultural which elides these issues of history, class and gender. Given the industrial and technological nature of cinema, this may hardly be surprising: cinema is the art most dependent upon the elision of its processes and conditions of production, leading Walter Benjamin to remark that 'the equipment-free aspect of reality here has become the height of artifice'.[3] Here, the aesthetic values and cultural functions of two kinds of texts – Edwardian novels and contemporary films – are disparate in suggestive ways: the novels' troubled negotiations of connection compared to the films' comfortable presentations of bourgeois Englishness.

Regarded more critically, however, the films' popularity and success provide an occasion for a reappraisal of the issues addressed in the novels – issues that are more evident because of differences in media and cultural context.

CONNECTIONS AND VIEWS

Only connect![4]

The problem of connection features throughout Forster's fiction. Written out of a moment of crisis both for English bourgeois society and for a sexually and culturally confused subject – the moment of modernity as Foster experienced it – the text's project of forging connection is called up by the deeply imbricated experiences of modernity and tourism.[5] For such a project, the role of perspective is crucial: the clear-sighted, ironic perspective of the realist narrator meets the culturally informed, sophisticated perspective of the ideal tourist. Forster's fiction struggles toward the production of an all-encompassing viewpoint, from which the essence of a country or a culture may be figured and recognised.

Tourism is at once a product of modernity and its technologies of transport and, more significantly, an archetypically modern activity in the sense of Martin Heidegger's analysis of the world picture, of 'the world conceived and grasped as picture',[6] whereby tourism is thought of as a practice of bringing things nearer, a form of connection.[7] A large proportion of the problematics of the novels – and, in some cases, the films – are involved with these questions of world picture, visualisation and subjectivity. Indeed, it is paradoxically crucial to the very project of realist fiction. Despite Forster's refusal to allow film versions of his novels, his fiction is intensely concerned with vision, and with the Wordsworthian consolations afforded by the surveying gaze, consolations which the films certainly offer more extensively. In that concern with vision, Foster is at his most modern in terms of Heidegger's conception of modernity.

The fictional practice through which this view is figured involves activities of condensation and displacement, making real topoi over to the novel's designs rather than being restricted by their actuality, as is evident in Forster's predilection for inventing a fictional place – e.g. Monteriano or Chandrapore – out of modified versions of actual places. We are asked to recognise such places as typical – a requirement linked to a tourist practice based upon the typical, such that the 'typical tourist' is one who seeks the typical or archetypical in their experience of 'otherness' – and thus these places form part of universal, ahistorical patterns even as their specificity is one of their seductive qualities.[8] The use of locations in cinema – even if, as in *Where Angels Fear to Tread* it happens to be San Gimignano, Foster's model for the fictional Monteriano – often practises a similar making over of the actual into the typical. A desire for the typical has its own imperialist aspect, as noted by Salman Rushdie in David Lean's ill-advised comments on his reasons for making *A Passage to India*: 'as far as I'm aware, nobody has yet succeeded in putting India on the screen'.[9] Lean's imperious dismissal of the Indian film industry might also be related to Forster's attempts in that novel to describe India through its views, an attempt which Lean seems keen to emulate cinematically. Equally, the limitations of Lean's 'screening' of India indicate his ignoring of Foster's awareness of the limited nature of any understanding of India which was conceived solely in terms of the visible and knowable, as depicted in the nothingness of the Marabar Caves (the troubling limit of Foster's aesthetic).

For Forster, then, having a room with a view assumes the same significance as having a room of one's own does for Virginia Woolf. It is the place from which the writer can resolve the tensions – of modernity and desire – that would otherwise lead to disconnection, disintegration. One of the paradoxes of Forster's fiction is its attempt to deal with modernity through this most modern of tropes, continuing the project of a realist narrative predicated upon a controlling vision – precisely the project called into question by modernity and in artistic modernism.[10]

In the novels connection is found through the acquiescence in a certain kind of bourgeois culture and world view, after a firstly estranging and finally enriching detour through the exotic. Bourgeois complacencies are ironised but finally accepted, albeit with some deformation. A classically English, liberal middle ground is espied. *Howards End* best demonstrates this, especially with its central concern with its eponymous place, which also represents a comforting pastness. There, Forster's tourist gaze is tellingly evident: the anxieties about modernity – embodied in the Wilcoxes – are juxtaposed with the values of Place, as understood and expressed by Margaret Schlegel. Formally, the tense, personal engagements with modernity are contrasted with the panoramic considerations of a non-industrial, Home Counties English countryside, while in Ivory's film everything becomes picturesque, a comforting pastness restaged for the present.

NOSTALGIA: THE TOURIST CONNECTION

> One knew that she [Mrs Wilcox] worshipped the past, and that the instinctive wisdom the past alone can bestow had descended upon her – that wisdom to which we give the clumsy name of aristocracy.
>
> (*Howards End*, ch. 3, p. 19)

> If the past is a foreign country, nostalgia has made it 'the foreign country with the healthiest tourist trade of all'.[11]

National heritage is the backward glance which is taken from the edge of a vividly imagined abyss, and it accompanies a sense that history is foreclosed.[12]

What is true of Howards End is more extensively true of all the places with their associated evocations of times past in the films: the different times and places of the films offer a comforting antidote to contemporary disconnections. And so what can be true only of a particular place reached at the conclusion of a drama of disconnection and connection in one novel, becomes true of the film adaptations as a whole, from beginnings to ends.

This phenomenon – seeking a particular place which embodies the past, as a retreat from the present – figures a deformation in the tourist experience, which now presents travel across time, reminding us of the early modern relation between nostalgia as homesickness and travel.[13] Nostalgia may now be relieved – rather than occasioned – by tourism.

Conversely, the appeal of these nostalgic cinematic recreations of an Edwardian world lies in their presentation of a near-idyllic past for present pleasure. Where the novels could offer a contemporary readership an experience of cultural, and even class, tourism, the films provide their audiences with the possibility of travelling across time, culture and class. In this respect, American-born James Ivory, Indian producer Ismail Merchant, and their frequent screenwriter Ruth Prawer Jhabvala, have constituted something of a heritage tours industry, taking on adaptations of Henry James' *The Europeans* (1979) and *The Bostonians* (1984), before going on to their Forster films. Their film-making career, which began with treatments of contemporary Indian situations, has increasingly turned toward treatments of past periods and foreign cultures, and is now the ironic site of the construction of an Englishness that never was. Where the novels are involved with a modern constellation of technology, tourism and desire, the films inflect the last of these with nostalgia.

But it is hardly a general nostalgia: it is specifically rooted in contemporary, Anglo-American history, and, as Bryan Turner suggests:

We might also assume nostalgic periods to be associated with the loss of colonies, or at least with the memory of such a loss. In contemporary Britain, there is a strong mood of post-colonial nostalgia, represented powerfully in Paul Scott's *The Raj Quartet* (1987) and in the recent plethora of films and television documentaries on the loss of imperial power and world influence.[14]

Among these, we could include *The Jewel in the Crown* (dir. Jim O'Brien and Christopher Morahan, 1984, based on Paul Scott's *Raj Quartet*), *The Far Pavilions* (dir. Peter John Duffell, 1984), and *Heat and Dust* (dir. James Ivory, 1983), as well as *A Passage to India*, as specific responses to a sense of the decline of both Great and White Britain.[15] As Salman Rushdie puts it, 'the rise of Raj revisionism ... is the artistic counterpart of the rise of conservative ideologies in modern Britain'.[16] In this context, the Forster films function as exhibits in an Edwardian theme park, providing a vision of a period in which none of the conflicts felt in that period – and felt, albeit differently, today – need to be noticed, or in which the present is the tragedy awaiting that world. The vision of these films often presents an historical husk, a static, untroubled past only disturbed by the banal negotiations of romantic love.

A Passage to India places all of the subsequent film adaptations in the context of post-colonial, post-imperial nostalgia – that same nostalgia exploited and satisfied in the 1982 Falklands War, and in Margaret Thatcher's 'redeclaration of the Second World War'[17] (that definitive moment in the termination of the British Empire) on behalf of a lost bourgeois *imperium* – and thus serves to explicate the nostalgic strains of the Forster film adaptations from their inception. Beginning with Lean's revisionist view of the British in India, which considers the novel to be excessively 'anti-English, anti-Raj and so on',[18] the films that follow are tainted by a taste for supposedly simpler times, free from anxieties about race and class.

Lean's film opens and closes in rainy England, in contrast to the novel's Indian beginning and ending, and it 'straightens' out Forster's narrative by focusing on Adela rather than on Aziz and Fielding. As the film's central character. Adela is positioned as a hysterical female subject, especially through the additional scene involving erotic temple carvings and lewd monkeys (monkeys which later appear as Indians just before the court case, in case the implicit racist equation has escaped our notice), and her subjection, through flashback, to quasi-psychoanalytic scrutiny by taking her back to the 'primal scene' of the Marabar Caves. Lean's ending shows his lack of interest in the Aziz–Fielding relationship and, more tellingly, the novel's presentation of the fictional Indian Native State of Mau, a place and a culture which the novel's preceding parts have attempted to prepare its readers to understand, thus effecting a double displacement and censorship of the novel's interrelated discourses on sexuality and imperialism.[19] By contrast, the scenes involving Aziz and Fielding in 'Temple' are the climax of the novel's attempt to think a connection between East and West, between Indian and English.

An equally telling change involves a production anecdote concerning the Barabar Caves (Forster's models for the Marabar Caves). Lean was so unimpressed with the caves that he decided not to use them for the film, using dynamite to excavate a more appropriate set, choosing a group of sacred, and supposedly protected, rocks. This act of imperialist vandalism – all-too-characteristic of the activities of the foreign film crews in India – offers an extreme example of the desire for a controlling, typifying vision in realism and tourism, as well as confirming Lean's incomprehension of Forster's more challenging realisation of the invisible, unknowable aspects of India. It is comparable with Lean's realist, anti-Indian indiscretion in framing Aziz at the mouth of the caves (to show that he really was there, and that it wasn't just Adela's hysterical imagination), and with the casting of a brown-faced Alec Guinness as the Brahmin Professor Godbole (Colonial Hearts and Coronets?), which would be inconceivable in a Merchant–Ivory film. Where the novel presents troubling uncertainty, the film presents prosaic evidence of the kind appropriate to an imperial vision.

Such a vision turns both from the issues of the novels, and from the contemporary contexts in which these films are made. And in so far as audiences have, in viewing these films, similarly disconnected their views from their own circumstances, we might begin to account for the films' popularity, and to see something of their social function. It is a species of disconnection which Forster was drawn to comment upon in the case of the American success of *A Passage to India*:

> A few years ago I wrote a book which dealt in part with the difficulties of the English in India. Feeling that they would have no difficulties in India themselves, the Americans read the book freely. The more they read it the better it made them feel, and a cheque to the author was the result.[20]

Exactly the same failure of cognitive connection, the same species of cultural and historical tourism, can be seen in the popularity of these films.

THE DISCOMFORTS OF STRANGERS: CASTING

There is a certain incestuousness in these films ... The same cast in the same period costumes gives the feel almost of a repertory production, with actors who know well each others' strengths and limitations and directors who know perhaps too well their audience's expectations.[21]

So far, these film adaptations might seem to have little to recommend them either as adaptations, or as films. Yet, read against the cosiness of a repertory company, the vicissitudes and vagaries of casting offer a reading of character identity and repetition (in the sense of repeated types) in both novels and films. Apart from the common direction involved in three of the films, the cross-casting enables us to make other kinds of connection between these and other texts.

Helena Bonham Carter emerges as a Forsterian first lady, featuring in four out of five films: going from Lucy Honeychurch via a 'lady at cricket match' in *Maurice* to Caroline Abbott on the way to Helen Schlegel. Crispin Bonham Carter appears as Colonel Fussell in *Howards End*. Rupert Graves begins with Freddy Honeychurch, graduating to Alec Scudder before taking refuge in Philip Herriton. Judy Davis is 'transformed' from Adela Quested to Harriet Herriton, and James Wilby suffers a no less telling transformation from homosexual Maurice Hall to homicidal Charles Wilcox. Denholm Elliot begins with dottily liberal Mr Emerson and ends in the repressive Dr Barry, while Simon Callow goes from Rev. Arthur Beebe to Mr Ducie, with an uncredited appearance as a don in *Howards End*.

Thus far, the details bear out Cairns Craig's critique cited above, but there is more to it than this. In one respect the casting strategies (of a variety of casting and film directors) seem to give these films a sense of homogeneity and homeostasis: an audience knows what it is in for, and so it goes. Such casting also suggests that the characters are much the same *types* – further figuring a desire for the typical – at the expense of attentions to the details of Forster's character descriptions. For instance, in *Where Angels Fear to Tread* both Philip and Caroline are described as tall, an important marker of their class positions and aspirations, whereas both Bonham Carter and Graves are burgerishly short.

In another respect, casting is one of the cultural claims of these films, one way in which their Englishness-as-Culture is proclaimed.

Hence the use of 'character actors' (often Royal Shakespeare and Royal National Theatre actors) such as Elliott, Rosemary Leach (*A Room with a View*, but also *The Jewel in the Crown*), Joan Henley and Maggie Smith (*A Room with a View*), in an appeal to a British cinematic and, more importantly, *theatrical* heritage. Philip Strick claimed that 'the performances are so dominantly satisfying as to refute ... the recurring urge to damn British cinema for its reliance on theatrical skills', while also commenting that, as the Misses Alan 'Fabia Drake and Joan Henley revive memories of Dame May Whitty with just a touch of Hinge and Brackett'.[22] The choice of a theatrical Dame such as Peggy Ashcroft, a stage actress who had limited her film appearances (but had just appeared in *The Jewel in the Crown* and who happily resembled the former Empress of India), as Mrs Moore for *A Passage to India*, or of Vanessa Redgrave as Mrs Wilcox for *Howards End* involves a valorisation of these actresses as national treasures, as embodiments of the values of the films presuppose, posit, and address in other ways.

But there are at least three jokers in this pack. What about Antony Hopkins – now indelibly associated with his Oscar-winning performances in the role of Dr Hannibal 'The Cannibal' Lecter in *Silence of the Lambs* (dir. Jonathan Demme, 1991) – as Henry Wilcox, the avatar of colonialist capitalism? Equally resonant are the echoes in *A Room with a View* of Daniel Day-Lewis's performance in *My Beautiful Laundrette* (dir. Stephen Frears, 1985) – a paradigm of an alternate, non-nostalgic British cinema – and Simon Callow's 'out' status.[23] (Indeed, *My Beautiful Laundrette*'s deft, commercially successful combination of sexuality, race and imperialism reflects upon the deficiencies of both Lean's *A Passage to India* and Ivory's *Maurice*.) These elements complicate the sexual and cultural politics of these films, particularly of *A Room with a View*, the most generally-lauded of the films.

STRAIGHTENED VIEWS AND STRANGERS ON TRAINS: THE ITALIAN FILMS

A Room with a View opens with an elegant period touch combining Edwardiana and opera, using the song 'Oh! mio babbino caro' (taken from Puccini's *Gianni Schicchi*), which happens to contain the essence of the film's plot rendered ironically through its Italian cultural detour:

Oh! mio babbino caro,
mi piace, e bello, bello,
vo'andare in Porta Rossa
a comperar l'anello!
Si, si, ci voglio andare!
E se l'ammassi indarno,
andre sul Ponte Vecchio,
ma per buttarmi in Arno!
Mi struggo e mi tormento!
Dio, vorrei morir!
Babbo, pieta, pieta ...

Oh, dear daddy,
he pleases me, he's so handsome,
I want to go to Porta Rossa
to buy the ring!
Yes, yes, I do want to go!
and if I were to love him in vain,
I'd go to the Ponte Vecchio,
and throw myself in the Arno!
I fret and suffer torments!
Oh, God I wish I could die!
Daddy, have pity, have pity!

No matter that Lucy doesn't have a father, and that the only things thrown in the Arno are her bloodied postcards: the song lets us know what to expect. Even if an audience doesn't recognise or understand the song, it opens the film in a musically and emotionally climactic mood, in an eradication of narrative tension that is of a part with what has been termed the film's 'evacuation of history'.[24]

While the film is able to use a song as a signpost toward certain issues, it has greater difficulty in indicating or approximating the manners and class distinctions which are germane to the crucial opening scene. What it does do is characterise the Socialist ex-journalist Mr Emerson (Denholm Elliott) as some sort of uncouth buffoon, and give him a large amount of extra dialogue to bridge the gap between the manners the book hardly need do more than signal, and those the film cannot assume an understanding of. This characterisation, without any reference to socialism, is of a piece with the presentation of the only other character who reads: Cecil Vyse (Daniel Day-Lewis). Even in 'literary' films, those who read are either trying to attain to a culture outside their class designation, or they are decadent and effete.

Forster's concern with sexuality as the site of negotiation of class and cultural values is all but obscured in the film's concentration on heterosexual romance, abetted by the observation of textbook screenplay niceties, such as distributing the action around the cast so that Miss Lavish gets lost with Charlotte and not (as in the novel) Lucy. This after having rearranged the novel's sequence of church–piano to piano–church, in order to make a clearer connection between Lucy's potential romantic power (as signified by the way she plays Beethoven) and her relationship with George (Julian Sands). When, in the novel, Lucy rejects Mr Emerson's appeal for her to understand

George, Forster suggests that she misunderstands her own affirmative spirit as displayed through her piano-playing.

All of this is but a prelude to the moment of Lucy's violent introduction to male physicality and intimacy in the piazza murder scene. Director Ivory renders her sightseeing experience through a menacing montage of statues in aggressive and martial postures preceding the brawl and murder. Here, the threat of Italy to bourgeois proprieties and sublimations actually makes it onto the screen, only to vanish as quickly as the fallen Italian and we are back in romance mode. Shock isn't really something that can be accommodated within the film's limpid aesthetic, it seems a species of bad taste. Similarly, the pastoral love scene is without any sudden turn or realisation which – for Forster – is the necessary precondition for erotic connection. The loss of the violets, and Lucy's visual shock as she suddenly comes upon them, is significant here. Forster's Lucy doesn't know where she's going, or why; but, due to Ivory's taste for panoramas, Bonham Carter (and everyone else) can see exactly where George is.

Once we see Cecil, we see why George is the young man for Lucy. As the foppish Cecil Vyse, Daniel Day-Lewis is immediately identifiable as an 1890s-inspired version of his contemporary gay role in *My Beautiful Laundrette*, and the film plays upon an opposition between Cecil's effeminacy and George's more forthright, exuberantly physical heterosexuality. On this level, the film 'outs' aspects of the novel, exposing homosexual undercurrents, as is evident in both George's scene with Lucy, and Lucy's scene with Cecil. After George has told Lucy that Cecil is 'the sort who can't know anyone intimately, least of all a woman. He doesn't know what a woman is', going on to implore Miss Bartlett not to 'stop us this time', there is a cut to the view through a window (from Miss Bartlett's point of view) of Cecil outside, frantically fighting off an insect and spilling his tea, effectively underlining Cecil's effeteness. At the end of the scene, Lucy goes outside with her tennis racket and is framed alongside Cecil as he reads from Eleanor Lavish's book: reiterating a contrast between physical exuberance and intellectual prissiness. In case the point hasn't been made, in the scene entitled 'Lying to Cecil' Bonham Carter repeats the novel's line 'you're the sort who can't know anyone intimately', but adds the phrase 'least of all a woman'. Cut to a reaction shot of Day-Lewis enacting the novel's 'A horrified look came into his eyes'.

If the film is quite clear about these implications, it doesn't seem so clear about those associated with Simon Callow's Rev. Beebe.

While his presence obviously draws out the implicit homoeroticism of the pond scene, his more interesting contribution is to draw attention to a charting of a sexual geography in discussion of travel to Greece and Constantinople. Asking Cecil if he'd ever met the Miss Alans, Beebe goes on to say 'Ah, well then, you're not in a position to appreciate the romance of this *Greek* visit'. The novel's word 'wonder' has been replaced by 'romance', and the emphasis on '*Greek*' seems entirely Callow's. Similarly, his:

> Constantinople, isn't it delightful? I really believe they shall end by going around the world

plays off contemporary sexual slang in a way that reminds us of Forster's sexual geography: Italy, for heterosexual romance, Greece for homosexual love, Constantinople as a gateway to polymorphous perversity.

Although readable, these implications don't seem to have any definite function in the film, even if they denote an awkwardness about the novel's sexuality which runs through all of the films, even *Maurice*. In the film, the troubled conflict between Clive's homoerotic and Maurice's homosexual desire is treated through the inserted episode of Risley's arrest, prosecution and conviction on indecency charges, and Clive's trip to Greece which seems to show him that he doesn't want all that Greek love allows. As Finch and Kwietniowski have argued,[25] *Maurice* is a remarkably 'straight' film, as are all the adaptations, notably (and to its detriment) *Where Angels Fear to Tread*, the other Italian novel, which had already been linked to *A Room with a View* by giving Dench's Miss Lavish the story to repeat as a piece of gossip.

While *A Room with a View* begins and ends in Florence, *Where Angels Fear to Tread* begins and ends on railway platforms. This kind of symmetry is a feature of the novels, but it is inflected with quite different meanings in these films, especially in the case of this displacement of the novel's final scene from a train leaving Italy to a suburban, English railway platform, a displacement in keeping with the film's peculiar avoidance of homoeroticism (given that Sturridge and Granger had directed and produced *Brideshead Revisited*, 1981).

Where Angels Fear to Tread offers cogent examples of Forster's use of scenes and moments of travel to dramatise conflicts of values and understanding. The joke about 'only connect' as an advice to